NIGEL ROEBUCK ▪ JOHN TOWNSEND
Editor: BARRY NAISMITH

GS Publications

Published by:	Garry Sparke & Associates P.O. Box 360, Glen Waverley, Victoria. 3150
Designed by:	Rob Alston
First Published:	January, 1988 © Garry Sparke & Associates
Printed by:	Owen King Pty. Ltd.
Colour Separations:	Scanagraphix Pty. Ltd.
Bound by:	M&M Binders
Typesetting by:	G.S. Typesetting
Photographer:	John Townsend
Writers:	Nigel Roebuck, Alan Henry.

Overseas Distributors:
Golden Press, 717 Rosebank Road, Avondale, Auckland, New Zealand.
Motorbooks International, 729 Prospect Avenue, Osceola, Wisconsin 54020.
Motor Racing Publications Ltd., Unit 6, The Pilton Estate, 46 Pitlake, Croydon CR0 3RY, England.

National Library Cataloguing-in-Publication Data:
Grand Prix ISBN 0 908081 27 8

ACKNOWLEDGEMENT
The Publisher gratefully acknowledges the assistance of AUTOSPORT (U.K.) in the production
of this publication.

CONTENTS

NOT QUITE GREAT

When the man who deserved the title ran too close to the edge once too often, the rival who had tasted the championship twice before, joined the exclusive ranks of Brabham, Stewart and Lauda.

At 1.21 on the afternoon of October 30, 1987, at Suzuka in Japan, Nelson Piquet became world champion a fortnight before the world championship was scheduled to end in Australia. At the time, the Brazlian was in his Williams-Honda, but this was Friday, and the engine was shut down.

Half a mile away Nigel Mansell had crashed. It was a big accident, and the Englishman was hurt — not seriously in the absolute sense, but very much so in terms of his championship aspirations. He would miss the Japanese Grand Prix, and that alone was sufficient to confirm his team-mate as world champion.

Rough luck on Mansell — for the second season in succession. Well, yes and no. On the one hand, you could point this time to a driver error, where his tyre failure at Adelaide in 1986 was very definitely not that. You could say, too, that in the previous season he had the title as good as locked away when he arrived in Australia: third place would do the job, no matter what happened to his rivals. This time —despite twice as many race victories as anyone else — he was the one doing the chasing. Piquet's quite fantastic finishing record had seen to that.

Equally, you could argue — and the man himself would agree — that Nigel's driving was better in 1987, that he seemed to have a virtual monopoly on such reliability problems as the Williams-Hondas had. And you could say, too — and again Mansell would concur — that in the previous season the title did at least go, finally, to the best driver on earth. In 1987 such was assuredly not the case.

This is not wholly to detract from Piquet's achievements. This was his third world championship (and achieved in seven seasons), which bracketed him, statistically, with such as Brabham, Stewart and Lauda.

Nelson devoted his season to the scoring of points, and many consider this an admirable way of going about the business of grand prix racing. For Piquet, championships and records come before winning races: that was seen at Kyalami, the final race of the '83 season. When he knew that third place would clinch the title, he simply slipped back from a dominant lead — to third place. Not glorious, but effective.

And we can't deny that future generations, consulting their Formula One history books, will note Piquet's myriad titles, wonder how there was so much fuss about Moss, Peterson or Villeneuve.

True, he won three races in 1987, more than many a world champion of the past. But none was clearcut, dominant, incisive. Hockenheim he inherited from Alain Prost during the last five laps; at the Hungaroring he led the last six after Mansell had lost a wheel; and Monza — his best race of the season — he won when Ayrton Senna's leading Lotus slid off the road, with seven laps left.

He was always there or thereabouts, rarely pushing hard. And very often the softly-softly approach means title. If not legends.

So this was not a great world championship. Worthy, yes, perhaps, but not scintillating. It said more about reliability than magnificent driving. On pace, Nelson was invariably overshadowed by Mansell; on aggression he was no match for Senna; on class, he did not approach Prost.

The season began reasonably for him, with a second in Rio, but during qualifying at Imola he crashed massively when a tyre failed. All his raging and cajoling failed to move Professor Watkins: you have had severe concussion, grand prix racing's surgeon said, and you will not race. His judgement was clearly sound, too, for Nelson claims never to have felt absolutely 'right' since.

On the Sunday, while Piquet commentated for Italian TV, team-mate Mansell took a virtually unopposed victory. A fortnight later, at Spa, the Englishman did his celebrated two-step with Senna

IN THE RIGHT CORNER
'And very often the softly-softly approach means a title. If not legends'

on the first lap, and Nelson then led for a while —until a turbo failed.

From then on it became hard to remember the sight of Piquet in the pits. That was race three: the Brazilian would not retire again until Suzuka, race fifteen, six months later. And everywhere he scored.

Undoubtedly, Nelson had Honda in his corner. Since he moved from Brabham to Williams, the Japanese paid the bulk of his US$3.3m annual retainer, and consequently they regarded him as their man. When Mansell beat Piquet, Honda did not like it. More remarkably, it attached no blame to the Brazilian; rather, blamed the Williams management for not exerting control over the 'number two' driver. It was this, largely, which led to its decision to drop Williams for 1988 — despite the team's domination of 1987.

In this, it must be said, Williams had considerable help from its main rivals. We might have expected that the main threat to Mansell and Piquet would come from world champion Alain Prost and the McLaren-TAG, and Ayrton Senna's Lotus, now with Honda power. And strictly that was right; but in neither case was the degree of competition as strong as anticipated.

In brief, Lotus, campaigning their 'active' suspension in earnest, never gave Ayrton a car worthy of him; and McLaren reliability — a paragon in earlier years — fell away drastically. Often Prost was in a good position to win, and then some trifling problems would put him out.

For both men, then, 1987 was frustrating. For the third season running, Senna was pegged on a couple of victories, and Prost, given a more trouble-free time of it, could certainly have won six. Their problems made life unexpectedly straightforward for the Williams-Honda men.

Above: If spectator support counted for anything, Piquet drank of national pride wherever he went. This is in Germany.
Left: Piquet — rare sight in the pits.
Below: The season began on course for Piquet with a second place at Rio.

Mansell you had to admire for his totally committed approach, for the fact that he ran constantly at or near the limit. As a racer, he outclassed Piquet, several times overtaking the Brazilian for the lead — as at Paul Ricard, Silverstone, Zeltweg, and so on. It never happened the other way round.

All season long, though, there were those who said Nigel had to drop sooner or later, that he couldn't continue to run so close to the edge so much of the time. And, sadly, when the accident came, during practice in Suzuka, they were quick to say they had told us so.

Mansell made a mistake in Japan, no question. It was his misfortune that it came at a corner with insufficient run-off area. Quite often a driver has an accident like that, and walks back to the pits. But the Williams-Honda hit a tyre barrier very hard, bounced high into the air, came down hard. And Nigel's season — and championship hopes — were over. It was not less than tragic: this was a title he deserved.

Prior to the accident we had wondered about Honda's dilemma. A few weeks earlier the Japanese had shaken Formula One by confirming the rumours that, yes, they would be parting from Williams at the end of 1987 — a year earlier than the contract stipulated. At the Monza announcement there was a lot of old toffee about a "mutual decision to part." Together, the announcement said, Williams and Honda had scaled the heights: now was the appropriate time to split. It fooled no one. The bare facts were that Honda was dropping a team which has come to dominate Formula One. Its two teams in

THEY TOLD US SO
'He ran constantly at or near the limit'

1988 would be McLaren and Lotus. Piquet would remain a Honda man and Mansell — staying with Williams — would not.

As Keke Rosberg, a man with considerable Williams-Honda experience, pointed out: "There's no way Honda can allow Mansell to win the title. They just want a world champion who's going to be with them again next year . . ."

And so the rumours and accusations started: Honda wanted the title for Piquet — indeed it would ensure he got it. In absolute terms, this would take a bit of working out, for Nelson was quite clearly unable to beat Nigel in a straight fight on the track.

The media criticism — indeed, condemnation — of its decision to drop Williams, perhaps to favour Piquet over Mansell, appeared to have shaken the Japanese. When Mansell won in both Spain and Mexico, his shot at the title although a long shot, was very much on. To keep his hopes realistically alive, he had to win in Japan. And in Japan, Honda wished to see its World Champion — Nelson Piquet — crowned.

In the end, it worked out for Honda. After Mansell's accident, Piquet was able to stage his world championship press conference. But it was otherwise a dreadful weekend for Honda: in front of its own people it was trounced by Ferrari.

Above: Mansell occupies his usual place in the season's ranking. This was the closest they got to him in most races.

Left: Mansell — the Honda cap soon disappeared.

THEY WERE SMILING AGAIN

'... the red cars — in particular Berger's — were a match for anything'

Left: Alboreto looks for a glimmer of hope. The revolution in approach and personnel at Ferrari took a while to be translated into competitive times.

Right: Berger was ill at ease during the slow transformation of the F187. Once it showed speed, he took off.

And, indeed, it was the Italian team which made progress through the second half of the year. At Rio, the opening race, Michele Alboreto and Gerhard Berger were four seconds off the pace in qualifying; in the late stages of the season, the red cars — in particular, Gerhard's — were a match for anything.

A combination of factors was involved here. In 1987 Ferrari had a new 90-degree V6 turbo engine, and intensive mid-season development work considerably increased both power and driveability. Unfortunately, though, reliability — usually a Maranello watchword — remained poor.

And Harvey Postlethwaite, easily overlooked in the razzmatazz surrounding John Barnard's arrival at Ferrari, began to achieve great things in the team's new, highly sophisticated, wind-tunnel. "He's incredible," Alboreto said. "Before we arrive at a track, he has the set-up all worked out, and when we get there, all we have to change are details. Basically, the settings are right from the start."

Postlethwaite began attending all the races, while Bernard — whose autocratic ways had not gone down well with the Italians — stayed in England, designing future Ferraris. John's absence, it must be said, played a significant part in the lifting of the mechanics' morale: suddenly they were smiling again, enjoying their motor racing — particularly as the cars moved steadily up the grid with every passing race.

Until the F187 was brought up to speed, Berger was something of a disappointment, seldom as quick as expected, often crashing. But as the car became competitive, so also did Gerhard. He threw away Estoril with a late spin, retired from the lead in Mexico. But in Japan No. 28 led all the way, and Formula One — most of it, anyway — rejoiced that Ferrari was back, after the longest victory drought in its history.

KEPT FROM THE CHALLENGE

'... he remained the best driver on earth'

Left: The big problem for McLaren was reliability. Prost was hobbled in his bid to defend his title.

Below: Prost — the situation was hopeless but he never cruised. Win No. 28 remained his only realistic objective.

Berger's lapse in Portugal came after sustained pressure from Prost, who duly came in for the 28th grand prix victory of his career, thus becoming the most successful F1 driver in history. Trivial reliability problems kept Alain from a sustained challenge to the Hondas through the year, but we saw enough of the little man's genius to have no doubts about his status: the world championship may have gone, but he remained the best driver on earth.

He won at Rio, at Spa, at Estoril. But the drive which tells most about the man came at Suzuka — a race he positively knew he was going to win. Fastest in the warm-up, he tailed Berger around the opening lap, then got a puncture at the start of the second. An agonisingly slow drag back to the pits, a wheel change, and back out. Already he was more than a lap back, and the situation was plainly hopeless. In these circumstances, most men would cruise for the afternoon. Not Prost. In a display of consummate brilliance, he drove flat out all the way, and by the

end was up to seventh. His fastest lap was 1:43.8; no one else beat 1:45. And he took back almost a full lap from the victorious Berger. It was a mesmeric demonstration.

It was Stefan Johansson's great misfortune that he should join his dream team — McLaren — just as its star began, comparatively, to fade. The Swede is a splendid racer, achieved some good results. If he has a serious fault, it appeared to be in qualifying: often he started from back on the grid, giving himself unnecessary work in the race.

It was ludicrous that by season's end, he was without a drive. Stefan knew when he signed that his stay at McLaren would be a temporary one. In Ron Dennis's sights for 1988 was Ayrton Senna, who had another 'not quite' season with Lotus.

Below: Johansson laments the joining of McLaren on the team's downside. He achieved some good results despite this.

PAUL CROSS

COPING WITH BUMPS

'The active suspension... proved something of a double-edged sword'

The Brazilian once again had to be content with just a couple of victories. It was a trying season for him. By the end of it, he was describing the 99T as nothing more that a 98T with a Honda engine, and this was valid. By comparison with most its rivals, the car was big and bulky.

It also had 'active' suspension, controlled by an on-board computer. The system did away with conventional bits and pieces, such as spring/damper units and anti-roll bars. The potential advantages, acknowledged by all, were massive. For one thing it enabled the car to run at its ideal ride height, whatever the fuel load, which allowed optimum handling throughout a race. Throughout the year Williams, too, developed a system, albeit a far less complex one. The 'active' Williams made its first appearance at Monza, and won.

The Lotus displayed a tremedous ability to cope with bumps, and it is no coincidence that Senna's victories were both scored at street circuits, Monte Carlo and Detroit.

At the same time, though, the active system, at this stage of its development, proved something of a double-edged sword. To be able to maintain optimum handling for the whole race was great — so long as you can find it in the first place. And usually, in 1987, Lotus could not. As the season progressed, the frustrated Ayrton grew more discontent, although his driving was never less than superb.

Part of Honda's Formula One grand plan was to have a Japanese driver in the game somewhere, and in 1987 Satoru Nakajima arrived, No. 2 at Lotus. A nice fellow, and a brave one, he didn't find Formula One easy. On merit, he would not be in the sport at this level.

Left: Senna's commitment and talent remained intact. But he grew frustrated that Lotus could still not supply a car worthy of him, even with Honda power and 'active' suspension.
Below: The Lotus was big and bulky and very complex. The suspension coped well with bumpy circuits but was difficult to set-up elsewhere.

PAUL CROSS

EXCEPT FOR RELIABILITY

'The Belgian showed himself to be a truly aggressive racer, cowed by no-one'

Williams, McLaren, Lotus, Ferrari . . . and Benetton: these were the competitive teams in 1987. Using the Ford V6 engine, Benetton was there for most of the season. Rory Byrne came up with another first-class chassis, and Cosworth made big strides with the motor.

In its first season it lacked horsepower, but over the European winter more of that was found — at the expense of throttle response. By mid-season that, too, had been rectified, and now the engine was pretty well a match for anything. Except in reliability . . .

For a time, at mid-season, Cosworth ran their engines at unrealistically low boost, in the interests of reliability. That they certainly got, but it was sad and pathetic to watch a driver of Boutsen's class drifting round Silverstone in 10th place.

In later races the wick was turned up, and of course that hurt the Ford's lasting qualities. But at least it was now a front runner, and from Thierry Boutsen — at last in a car worthy of him — we had a string of fine performances. The Belgain showed himself to be a truly aggressive racer, cowed by no one, and in Mexico he led until the car failed.

Teo Fabi was far less impressive than his team-mate, and it appeared that his Formula One career was coming to an end.

Benetton, then, consistently threatened, never delivered. Too many times, one felt, preparation was not to the highest standards. And in Formula One nothing less will do the job.

Above: When the boost was turned up the Benetton-Ford turned into a front runner, but not a finisher.

Left: Boutsen was the wild card of the season with a string of fine drives.

11

THE MID FIELD

'As the season progressed, Warwick and Cheever found their competitiveness waning'

At the beginning of the year there were signs that Arrows, after so many years in midfield, were set to make a quantum leap up the grid. There was a new designer, Ross Brawn (late of the Haas Lola team), and he came up with a nice, neat, car for the two new drivers, Derek Warwick and Eddie Cheever.

Sponsorship, from USF & G, was considerably up on previous seasons, and a subsidiary of the company, Megatron, bought up all the 'upright' four-cylinder engines from BMW, and stuck their own name on the cam covers. No one ever doubted the sheer horsepower of this engine — but its reliability was never good, its throttle response even less so. In 1987 those problems remained, and the BMW's strongest card — its ability to accept a lot of boost — was negated by FISA's new four bar limit, controlled by means of the controversial 'pop-off' valve.

As the season progressed, Warwick and Cheever found their cars' competitiveness waning. For most of the time, indeed, they found themselves in midfield again, where Arrows had always been. These were both fine drivers, capable of excellent performance. What seemed to be lacking in 1987 was development.

'De Cesaris financed his way . . .'

At Brabham, meanwhile, the 'laydown' BMW engine was retained for a final season. Riccardo Patrese stayed on as team leader, and the unpredictable Andrea de Cesaris financed his way into the second car.

The BT56, a strikingly attractive design by something close to a consortium, often featured quite strongly, but engine reliability was simply lamentable. Patrese took a fine third in Mexico, de Cesaris a similar place at Spa, but that was effectively it. Sad to see.

'Arnoux and Piercarlo Ghinzani had a wasted season'

Ligier had an appalling season. Originally the up-and-down French team was due to run the new Alfa Romeo four-cylinder engine, but after Rene Arnoux publicly compared it unfavourably with used food, Fiat (which had bought Alfa, and didn't, in any case, want the company in Formula One) had a perfect excuse to end the contract. Guy Ligier's only short-term alternative was to reach a swift accommodation with Megatron for the balance of the season. It was a disaster. The cars were heavy and unbalanced, the engines low on staying power. Arnoux and Piercarlo Ghinzani had a wasted season.

'The small German team . . . did not make the progress anticipated'

The same was true of Martin Brundle, who moved from Tyrrell to Zakpeed for 1987. The small German team, which manufactured its own four-cylinder turbo engines, did not make the progress anticipated. Martin and Christian Danner habitually found themselves short of both horsepower and grip.

Trying to run two cars, the team seemed to overreach itself; there was too little testing, too little development.

'Alessandro Nannini . . . consolidated his reputation'

Alessandro Nannini, outstanding his first Formula One season in 1986, continued with Minardi and consolidated his reputation. The man is a natural grand prix driver, with an easy, flowing style. Adrian Campos, by contrast, was out of his depth at this level, and did not impress.

Osella, financially precarious as ever, continued, running a single car for Alex Caffi, another of the promising young Italians. The team ran somehow, on a well of enthusiasm, which seemed never to dry up. There were, of course, no results worth the name, but Caffi has still the opportunity to show his talent.

'Palmer was consistently excellent'

And, of course, normally-aspirated cars were back in 1987, notably from Ken Tyrrell, who reverted to his first love: the Cosworth V8. The overrated Philippe Streiff was retained, and Jonathan Palmer took over Brundle's place, Martin having taken his at Zakspeed! To no one's surprise, the team had very much the best of it in the 'non-turbo' class, and Palmer was consistently excellent. By the end of the year, there was little doubt that he had had very much the better of the swap with Brundle . . .

Gerard Larrousse, former team manager at Renault and Ligier, formed his own team for 1987, running a Lola-Cosworth for the quick, but erratic, Philippe Alliot. The car, designed by Ralph Bellamy, was often quicker than the Tyrrells, and the same was true of Ivan Capelli's March, but neither had a distinguished finishing record. AGS, by contrast, were usually there at the end with their massive and unwieldy creation — primarily because Pascal Fabre never drove it fast enough to hurt it. The Frenchman was simply not ready for grand prix racing, and neither was his team.

At the end of it all, you could look back on a season in which Mansell won the most races, in which Berger emerged as a major star, in which Prost consolidated his reputation as the outstanding grand prix driver of the generation. But in which Piquet, deposit account building with points, took the world championship. It was also the season in which Williams-Honda dominated, then broke up, in which Lotus's 'active' suspension was usually a little too active for Senna's tastes, in which McLaren reliability took a dive, in which Ferrari came back from nowhere. A good season. But not a great one.

Above left: Arrows failed to make the hoped for leap up the grid due to the boost restriction.

Above: Ligier simply played out the season with a stopgap engine.

Right: Brabham continued to produce a pretty car without competitive substance.

Below: Tyrrell turned back the clock by re-marrying with Ford Cosworth. It allowed Palmer to shine, a star on his own little stage.

DOING IT HIS WAY

**The scene's enduring enigma stuck shrewdly, some would say deviously, to his grafting approach to winning the championship.
Finally he was vindicated.**

Nelson Piquet is an enigma. Some days his driving can put him in a class of his own although not so often in '87. But his tactical approach to the business of gathering championship points is something that leaves enthusiasts cold and unimpressed.

He is the antithesis of the romantic image of the never-say-die racing driver who wants to win races at all costs. Championships are what Nelson is after and, as he says, his softly-softly approach works. With his third world championship and 20 grand prix victories under his belt, it's difficult to argue with his place in the Formula One record book.

Nelson has changed a great deal in the past three years. From 1979 through until the end of 1985, he was the Brabham team's baby. He numbered the mechanics amongst his closest friends and they simply adored him. Practical jokes were his stock in trade. He was light-hearted and didn't seem to have a care in the world. But he was also underpaid by the standards of the Prosts, Laudas and Rosbergs of the day. It was contract renewal time and he put a figure to Bernie Ecclestone which grand prix racing's czar simply baulked at.

Shortly afterwards, the Brazilian did the big buck deal with Frank Williams for 1986 and '87. He was signed up as number one, nobody even giving his partner in the team a second thought. It was Nigel Mansell. You know, good old, hard-trying 'Noige'... At best, a solid number two, but already on the receiving end of too much F1 bad luck. Still, you never know, he might luck into an occasional win. If Piquet retired...

That's where it all went wrong for Nelson. He might have had a good old laugh at Rio where 'Noige' speared off the track after a first-lap lunge inside Ayrton Senna, but the lugubrious Englishman soon stopped being the joke he clearly was in Piquet's mind. He'd already won two races at the end of 1985. Now he was out to get Piquet. And Nelson didn't like it.

By the end of '86, it was clear that Piquet's position as number one was under threat. He won only four races to Mansell's five — and lost the championship. Nelson was an extremely angry boy when he left Adelaide at the end of '86, having failed to prise the title from Alain Prost's vice-like grip. "If Williams had kept to their contract and given me all the support I was promised, we wouldn't have ended the season like this," he said with feeling.

At the start of 1987, some people within the Williams team thought they detected a subtle change in Piquet's approach. They thought that Nelson would go out with the idea of beating Mansell fair and square, rather than continuously complaining about his lot. However, much of the wind was knocked out of the Brazilian's sails in an enormous accident at Imola during San Marino Grand Prix qualifying.

The shunt was almost certainly caused by a tyre failure. Briefly unconscious, Nelson was forbidden by FISA medical supremo Professor Watkins from taking part in the race. By his own admission, the shunt took a great deal out of him, perhaps accentuating his inclination towards driving tactically for the rest of the season. Yet he steadfastly refuted any suggestion that he was lucky to win the World Championship.

"I finished a lot of races and scored a lot of points," he said, "and, to me, that's the whole purpose of the exercise. Score points — win championships. With Nigel it was always all or nothing. That wasn't my way. I always thought he was risking a lot by running so hard, so near the limit, so much of the time."

Yet if Nelson's approach to the title chase was a tactical one, there were times when it looked just plain lucky. It was all very well for the Brazilian to complain that Williams would not slow Mansell down, but how would such a policy have helped things in the opening stages at Monaco? Or Hungaroring?

At Monaco, Mansell was running away with the race ahead of Senna, with Nelson trailing a poor third. He never looked as though he would be able to get on terms with the Lotus 99T, let alone get a sniff of his number two. And at Budapest he trailed Michele Alboreto for many miles before taking second place. Basically, forcing Mansell to play second fiddle to Piquet would have meant seriously jeopardising the team's chances of victory in several races. The fact remained that Nelson was not as quick as Mansell in 1987.

Not that Nigel played things perfectly, either. His first lap pirouette at Spa, where he and Senna had their famous tangle, could have been tailor-made to benefit Piquet. But the young Brazilian's engine blew, so Nelson failed to finish.

Thereafter, every Mansell retirement handed Nelson a bonus. Unquestionably, he was lucky in that respect. All other things being equal, Nelson's failure to finish at both Suzuka and Adelaide could have handed Nigel the championship. But Nigel wasn't there; he was in hospital, having flown off the road in Japan trying to beat Piquet's time in first qualifying. At that point it was all over. Nelson had done the job, realised his ambition.

By this time the Williams team was totally ambivolent to Piquet. He had repaid what he saw as their lack of interest in his point of view by signing for Lotus just before the Hungarian Grand Prix. "It was a master stroke," said one Williams team member with a mixture of admiration and bitterness, "In one move, he's screwed Williams, he's screwed Mansell, he's screwed Senna — and kept Honda!"

No question about it, Nelson's decision to switch to the Hethel team was a master stroke. After two season's aggravation and confrontation, he opted for a situation which would put the clock back to the halcyon days at Brabham. Days when he was indisputed number one, with only a makeweight partner in the second car. All resources would be focussed on Nelson Piquet. History had repeated itself.

Privately, Nelson is just that a private person. He can't be doing with all the bullshit. He does the bare minimum of personal appearances, sponsor's promotions, yet, by some strange paradox, is excellent when he does turn his hand to the PR side of the business.

Off-track, most of the time he's happy with the material trappings of his success. The Learjet, the new ocean going yacht which he is having built, his Hughes helicopter. He seems ideally cast in the role of the millionaire beachcomber...

Where does he go from here? "I plan to race until I'm 40. I don't need to do it for the money now; I can just enjoy the way it goes. I want to win more races and, perhaps, some more championships. I reckon I've got the best chance of doing that, my way, if I go to Lotus."

You may disagree with his methods, but you can't argue with his results. His Way has worked...

Above: The mechanicals of Piquet's Williams-Honda proved uncannily reliable in Piquet's experienced hands. He ensured he made maximum use of that feature of the car by finishing where winning would have required taking risks.

Right: For all the prickles in the Piquet personality, he still had a legion of adoring fans. The fan club was out in force at Estoril, Portugal.

Far right: There were three wins in 1987, through a large element of luck. Mostly Nelson Piquet was one or two steps down the rostrum and in the shadow of his team-mate.

BACK IN THE RED

There had been heart-rending slumps before in the fortunes of Ferrari, but none that required such major surgery, created so much pain in putting the Italian institution on the right track again.

By mid 1986 it was clear that Ferrari had tragically lost its way. In 1985 Michele Alboreto and the 156/85 had battled with Alain Prost for championship honours but this car's successor was just not up to scratch. the F186 had a smaller frontal area than its immediate predecessor, but it suffered badly from lack of wind tunnel testing. Alboreto and team-mate Stefan Johansson were most definitely consigned to the role of also-rans.

In the European summer of 1986, Ferrari decided it was time to regroup and start again from as near scratch as possible. At about the same time, McLaren International chief designer, John Barnard, was feeling increasingly frustrated with his role. With his superb MP4-TAG design heading towards its third straight world championship, he clearly needed a fresh challenge. He admitted that he was even considering dropping out of F1 altogether. He had been approached by BMW to design the Munich firm's own F1 chassis before a change of strategy on the part of the German manufacturer ended that prospect.

Then came the offer, through an intermediary, of a job in charge of design for a major European-based team. Having crossed Peugeot off his mental list as the only other possible candidate, Barnard quickly realised that the offer was from Maranello, although the preliminary talks carried on a little longer before Ferrari drew aside its cloak of anonymity.

Basically, Ferrari wanted Barnard to take charge of the overall F1 design process and produce a winner, keeping his mind's eye firmly focussed on the new 3.5-litre F1 which was due to come on stream in 1988/89. Barnard, however, was rather reticent about the whole business. Yes, he liked the sound of the offer but, no; he didn't want to work in Europe under any conditions. He wanted to stay in England.

Thus, after due consideration, Ferrari agreed to an unheard of concession. John would be allowed to established an independent design studio in the U.K., working virtually independently of the main Maranello factory, but interlocking with it inasmuch

as everybody was working towards the same end result. At least, that was the intention.

The most immediate task for Barnard was the finalisation of the 1987 turbocharged F1 car. Gustav Brunner had already started work on this project, so the basic monocoque shape was finalised by the time Barnard took over. John later admitted that, had he started from scratch, he would have produced a slightly different shape, but there was nothing he could do to change the basic configuration, so he busied himself finalising the suspension geometry, added the distinctive waisted rear end which had become his trademark at McLaren and fitted the sculptured aerodynamic ramps either side of the gearbox.

Barnard stipulated that a longitudinal gearbox should replace the transverse unit which had featured on the car ever since the advent of the 120-degree V6 turbo, and before that on the flat-12 three-litre cars. The result was a thin, six-speed box lying along the central axis of the F187, mated to the new 90-degree V6 engine which now replaced the original Ferrari turbo.

The trouble was, of course, that Ferrari was under pressure, although he would never admit it. Barnard was perceived as the great saviour, rushing over on his white charger from the rival McLaren set-up with the ability to transform things overnight. It was a quaint concept, but had little to do with reality. By the time John had set up his design studio at Shalford, near Guildford, it was almost too late for him to have as much influence over the F187 as he would have liked.

The other problem was one of personal chemistry. Barnard wanted to change the team's *modus operandi* in a fundamental way. He re-structured the way in which the mechanics worked, a process which, incidentally, cut out their lambrusco at lunch during mid-winter tests. This may seem a minor point to the uninitiated. It may not be the lifeblood of the team, but to a worker from Maranello, it comes pretty close . . .

At the start of the year it seemed as though the team was in danger of polarising into two camps. One had the easy-going Gerhard Berger at its head, and was aligned with Barnard. The other was almost symbolically led by Michele Alboreto, lined up behind Harvey Postlethwaite, the English engineer who had been at Ferrari since the end of 1981 when he had joined the team in order to set up its new composites department. Harvey had taken his wife and family to live in Italy, unlike Barnard, and was accepted as one of the locals. Put simply, Barnard's new approach grated.

However, it would be wrong not to see John's viewpoint. Here he was, entrusted with the task of recovering Ferrari's F1 form, working for what has traditionally proved itself to be the most idiosyncratic team of all. Anybody who was naive enough to expect instant results was being unrealistic and, as things turned out, sorely disappointed.

After attending the first few races of the year, pressure was building up for Barnard to get on with the development of the naturally aspirated 1988 car. No matter how good the F187 might turn out to be and no matter how long it might be kept in service through 1988, under the new 2.5-bar turbo boost regulation, there was no doubt that the new chassis to accommodate the 65-degree 3.5-litre V12 was the long-term priority. Yet media and pseudo political pressures from Italy exerted their own unseen influence. Somehow it seemed necessary that Barnard had to be at the race. Eventually, after Hockenheim, he put his foot down and stayed home working on the new car.

Now Postlethwaite resumed his previous role in charge of the cars in the field. Earlier in the season the team completed an exhaustive programme of aerodynamic development in the Maranello wind tunnel which had come into operation, full-time, in the European autumn of 1986. Relying on data thus gathered, the team let the factory-based computer work out optimum chassis set-ups for individual circuits. The first time such a set-up was tried was on Alboreto's F187 at Spa. He ran ahead of Prost's McLaren in the race, albeit quite briefly. And from that moment on this was the way in which the car were set up, never deviating from what the computer had told them. However much the driver may have been tempted to experiment, the computer tended to be right. "We just set them up — and leave them for the entire weekend," explained Harvey with a grin.

It was also particularly interesting to watch the way in which Berger and Alboreto got to terms with the cars. Earlier in 1987, when the team was still struggling, Michele seemed to come to grip with the problems with greater ease than Gerhard. In fact, after the Austrian had made a pig's ear of the British Grand Prix, where he spun into the barrier at Abbey Curve early in the race, and then went on to suffer a front suspension breakage at Hockenheim (not his fault) during practice for the German Grand Prix, he might have been forgiven for thinking that he ought to have accepted the McLaren number two seat alongside Prost after all.

However, once the F187 started to come right, Berger's talent flowered impressively. He put the F187 onto the front row for the Hungarian Grand Prix at Budapest and thereafter remained a force to be reckoned with right through to the end of the season when he bagged those superb triumphs in Japan and Australia.

Interestingly, Gerhard displayed much maturity by assessing the significance of that Suzuka win with crystal clear accuracy. Yes, it's a satisfying win. But Mansell was out after that qualifying shunt, Piquet didn't have to try and Prost was delayed by a puncture. It was the same honesty which endeared him to the entire team at Estoril after he spun the lead away under pressure from Prost. "I just spent too much time watching my mirrors — and not enough watching the road!"

As for Alboreto, his status in the grand prix community can be measured from Prost's words. "If that had been Michele in front of me at Estoril, I don't think I would have pressed him into a mistake." Michele just grinned when he heard of Alain's remark. "Let's just hope he thinks that if we ever get into that situation again!" he responded.

For fans all over the world, Ferrari's return to the winning circle provided them with a long overdue bonus with which to round off a season which had begun on such a frustrating note. But with Barnard, Postlethwaite, the drivers and technicians now all pulling in the same direction as they enter the non-turbo era again, the sky could once again be the limit for the Prancing Horse . . .

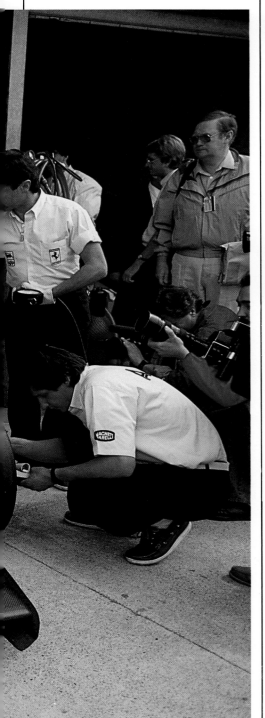

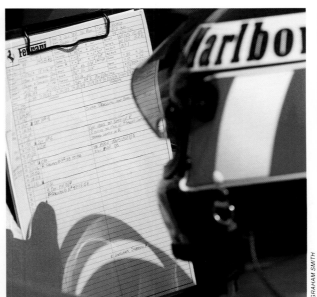

Above left: After two seasons of stumbling, the famous horse was prancing again. But it took a revolution and some outside help to do it.

Far left: The Ferrari F187 was gradually evolved in 1987. New suspension geometry, aerodynamic modifications to the Brunner-designed bodywork, a longitudinal gearbox and new engine began to work in unison after mid-season.

Left: Hmmm. That looks better. Gerhard Berger begins to see some light at the end of the tunnel as the team gradually finds more speed.

GRAHAM SMITH

THE BEST IN THE WORLD

In Formula One there is the elite within the elite. They regularly dominate the podium at the end of each grand prix and set the pattern of a season. They are few enough to count on your fingers.

End of term photo: back row (left to right), new boy Modena, Alboreto, Johansson, Prost, Cheever; Palmer, Dalmas, Warwick, Nakajima, Boutsen, Campos, Capelli, Patrese, and a message for Mansell; front row, Danner, de Cesaris, Berger, Ghinzani, Alliot, Streiff, Piquet, Brundle, Arnoux, Senna, Fabi, Nannini and Moreno.

1 *Alain Prost*

Age: 32
Born: France
Debut: 1980 with McLaren
GPs contested to 1987: 105
Wins to 1987: 25
World champion 1985, 1987

What have Spa, 1986, and Suzuka, 1987 got in common? Answer — they were both scenes of two storming drives by Alain Prost when he had nothing but his self-respect on the line. He finished sixth and seventh respectively in those races, but as an index of his true stature as the brightest star in today's grand prix firmament, they were performances every bit as impressive as any of his victories. Many top liners either give up, or over-drive into trouble, following first lap delays, but those outings proved that, wherever he is running, Prost is a factor for his rivals to fear. His effort is total, his commitment to perfection unremitting.

I not only rate Prost as the best of his era, but also as the best of all time. Now I agree that's a sweeping statement which may tremble slightly under the objective analysis of other enthusiasts. But my reasoning is based on not simply what Alain has achieved, which is enough in itself, but takes into account the calibre of the opposition he has had to defeat. It's all very well to talk about Stirling Moss and Jim Clark as the greatest, but when did either of them have to race highly competitive team-mates in equal cars as Prost had to do at Renault in 1981-82 (Rene Arnoux) and McLaren in 1984-85 (Niki Lauda) and 1986 (Keke Rosberg)? Also, it should be borne in mind that Prost only had cars which were in the class of the field in 1984. Since 1985 he has waged a lonely struggle against the might of the Williams-Honda line-up. And that hasn't always been easy.

Out of the cockpit, Prost's steady temperament gives you another pointer to his true quality. Self-assured, but never cocky; confident, but with no trace of arrogance. It's difficult to fault any facet of his make-up. On the circuit he handles his McLaren with a fluid artistry so far unmatched by his peers. If he has a weak point, who knows what it is?

2 *Ayrton Senna*

Age: **27**
Born: **Brazil**
Debut: **1984 with Toleman**
GPs contested to 1987: **46**
Wins to 1987: **4**

I agonised long and hard before placing Senna ahead of Nigel Mansell. The last two seasons have seen the English driver rocket to the forefront of attention, yet still he proves himself vulnerable to mistakes. Not that Senna is free from that criticism; he crashed heavily during practice at Mexico City as he wrestled with his unwieldy Lotus-Honda on a weekend which saw his title hopes finally fading away. Yet the equipment he used in 1987 always ensured that he was something of an outsider. That he carried the battle so far is a testimony to his extraordinary talent.

Senna has always been chillingly serious about his motor racing. Over grand prix weekends there is no time for banter or lightheartedness. His concentration and feel have become something of a legend within the Team Lotus ranks. Who needs telemetry when you've got a talent as sensitive as Senna's on hand?

Yet, paradoxically, this gifted Brazilian still has to make his mark. No longer a newcomer, he is now at the end of his fourth season in F1 and has only six grand prix wins to his credit. His talent says that he should have achieved more. That's why he is switching to McLaren in 1988, hoping that at last he will be in a team where he doesn't have to worry. All he will have to do is drive.

Yet Senna's quest for perfection could conceivably prevent him from realising his enormous potential. Toleman could not provide what he wanted, neither could Lotus. Not even with Honda power. His reputation goes on the line in 1988 when he shapes up to Alain Prost in identical cars. In Ayrton's mind there is no question that he can come out on top. If he doesn't, it will be no disgrace. But don't expect Senna to see it that way . . .

Nigel Mansell

Age: **34**
Born: **England**
Debut: **1980 with Lotus**
GPs contested to 1987: **90**
Wins to 1987: **7**

A man who attracts nothing but admiration from his adoring fans, of whom there are many. If he drove brilliantly in 1986, his performances were even more remarkable in 1987. Dauntless, courageous beyond belief, his willingness to run flat-out, right on the limit, has earned him enormous respect from all quarters. And some splendid race wins. Think of either Silverstone or Osterreichring and the image is of Williams-Honda teetering absolutely on the limit of adhesion. On the two fastest tracks in the F1 business, the Englishman was in a class of his own, on both occasions displacing team-mate Nelson Piquet from the lead in breathtakingly audacious manoeuvres. Time and again he dealt out winning performances, yet he was not always correspondingly rewarded.

There were some cruel disappointments. At Monaco he had destroyed the opposition before a fractured exhaust pipe put paid to his hopes. In just the same commanding style, he dominated the Hungarian Grand Prix at Budapest before a wheel retaining nut worked loose — and then flew off. It all seemed so bitterly unfair.

Yet Mansell was not without fault. That willingness to run flat-out all the time, admirable in most circumstances, worked against him at Spa and Suzuka. In the Belgian race he got tangled up with Senna on the opening lap of a race he was on course to win by a mile. Similarly, in the Japanese Grand Prix practice he overdid things battling with Piquet for fastest time in Friday qualifying. His critics would say there was no point in running so hard so soon. Mansell would reply that he is a racing driver and that's what racing drivers should do . . .

4 *Nelson Piquet*

Age: **35**
Born: **Brazil**
Debut: **1979 with Ensign**
GPs contested to 1987: **126**
Wins to 1987: **17**
World champion 1981, 1983

Was Nelson Piquet's stealthy, tactical and extremely lucky path to the 1987 World Championship any less edifying than Niki Lauda's success in 1977 with Ferrari? Or even Keke Rosberg's championship in 1982, when he won only a single race? Those are conundrums which have been bothering me ever since the Brazilian driver backed into his third world championship at Suzuka.

On balance, I don't think Nelson emerges with a great deal of credit. Agreed, he won the title and now has 20 grand prix victories under his belt. But there can be few championship challenges which were conducted with such outward lethargy, even allowing for the fact that he was quite badly knocked about in that Imola practice shunt. He fought shy of getting too closely involved with Mansell in wheel-to-wheel dicing and spent far too much time complaining to the Williams team that he was not being treated fairly, in accordance with his interpretation of the 'number one' stipulation in his contract.

He drove well enough at Monza and Silverstone, but you would be hard pressed to describe any of his 1987 races as classic victories in the real sense of the word. There is no doubting that Nelson is shrewd and calculating, roundly condemning Mansell for his 'flat-out at all times' driving style. But he was lucky to win the 1987 title and to try and attribute his success to some sort of calculated strategy has little credibility. In that respect, Piquet is trying to be wise after the event.

27

 *Gerhard Berger*

5

Age: **28**
Born: **Austria**
Debut: **1984 with ATS**
GPs contested to 1987: **36**
Wins to 1987: **1**

When Gerhard Berger turned down the No. 2 McLaren seat in favour of a Ferrari contract, there were many people who thought he had made a major tactical error. In fact, the F187 was so average for the first half of the season that the lanky Austrian must have had some moments when he doubted the wisdom of his move. But it all turned out alright on the night and Berger ended the Maranello drought with a fine victory from the front, in the Japanse Grand Prix at Suzuka and maintained the momentum in Adelaide.

Berger's driving style reflects his personality. Enthusiastic, extrovert and slightly over-anxious. Yet he has matured considerably during his first season with Ferrari. He seems to have relaxed slightly and, from the time that his F187 first made the front row of the grid at Budapest, has been a consistent force with which to reckon. It looked as though he might first win for Ferrari at Estoril, but cracked under relentless pressure from Alain Prost. Berger spun back to second place, later admitting candidly: "I spent too much of my time watching my mirrors for Alain." No excuses, no complaints.

Come Suzuka, and again Gerhard admitted he was slightly fortunate. "There was no Mansell to worry about, so Piquet wasn't under any great pressure and Prost had trouble. It was easy for me." Such a well balanced and honest approach to his rivals and racing make Berger an even more capable world championship contender. As the man who put Ferrari back on top after its longest ever spell away from the winner's circle, he is obviously highly regarded by the Maranello management. A man with a world championship beckoning.

 *Thierry Boutsen*

Age: 30
Born: Belgium
Debut: 1983 with Arrows
GPs contested to 1987: **57**

The key to Thierry Boutsen's potential is his temperament. Many drivers are quick, but few as as cool, calm and collected as this Belgian whose talent came into very public view in 1987 at the wheel of the promising, yet very unreliable, Benetton-Ford B187.

For three seasons Boutsen struggled with a generally uncompetitive Arrows, but still managed to demonstrate an underlying strand of competitiveness and commitment. His driving style is immaculate, controlled and stylish. In many ways he reminds the onlooker of Prost. Out of the car a placid nature conceals immense determination and will to succeed.

That Boutsen is a world class driver first became crystal clear at the Osterreichring. In the early stages of the Austrian Grand Prix he nailed his Benetton to the gearbox of Nelson Piquet's Williams-Honda and refused to be shaken off by the Brazilian. It seemed as though the fine-handling Benetton might at last be able to challenge the Williams-Hondas in a straight fight but, as had occurred all too frequently through 1987, Boutsen was delayed with mechanical troubles and could only finish fourth.

From then on, Thierry became a force to be reckoned with. At Monza he ran second for a long way and in Mexico the Belgian surged into the lead of a grand prix for the first time, only to be sidelined by a minor electrical problem.

It is a pretty open secret that Williams would have liked Boutsen on their team strength in 1988 to replace Nelson Piquet, but he had another season of his Benetton contract to run.

GAVIN HATFIELD

7 *Michele Alboreto*

Age: **31**
Born: **Italy**
Debut: **1981 with Tyrrell**
GPs contested to 1987: **89**
Wins to 1987: **5**

Michele occupies one of the least enviable positions in Formula One today. The first Italian at Ferrari for more than a decade, on the face of it he has found his position usurped by Berger's success at the end of the 1987 championship. In 1987 precious little went right for the popular Michele, but there were several occasions when his abundance of natural flair went on very public display.

His climb through the field at both Osterreichring and Suzuka, after encountering early problems, put Michele's true talent on show and went some way to compensate for an otherwise bitterly disappointing season. At Ferrari now for four seasons there are signs that Maranello's love affair with the former Tyrrell ace may be cooling, but, in honesty, this pleasant Italian has battled against a succession of indifferent cars for the last couple of seasons. He is acutely aware of the spotlight of critical attention

from his own country, yet remains philosophical about the fact that Berger made it to the winner's rostrum before he did. "We needed to win — Ferrari needed to win — for so many reasons," conceded Michele, "and that was the important thing . . ."

Out on the circuit, Alboreto is not a man to be trifled with. Uncompromising and unyielding, he is firm in his likes and dislikes. He brands Prost "the best" without a second's hesitation and has been extremely critical of Senna's tactics on several occasions, chastising the Brazilian for weaving on the straights at Hockenheim. "And the shame is that he is such a good driver he doesn't need to do that . . ."

8 *Stefan Johansson*

Age: **31**
Born: **Sweden**
Debut: **1983 with Spirit**
GPs contested to 1987: **41**

Anybody going into Alain Prost's team faces a problem. That was Keke Rosberg's view after spending the final season of his F1 career vainly trying to get to the bottom of Prost's seemingly magical touch with the TAG-engined cars. In 1987 that role fell to the genial and talented Stefan Johansson.

Stefan has been unlucky over the past couple of seasons, particularly during qualifying sessions. But he is a good, strong, instinctive racer, as he underlined as Spa (where he trailed Prost home to complete a McLaren 1-2) and Suzuka, where only the TAG turbo's fuel consumption prevented him from finishing second to Berger's Ferrari. In my estimation if you accept that drivers are either 'naturals' or 'workers', Stefan falls into the former category. Immensely popular and promotable, he still has plenty of competitive life left in him.

9 *Riccardo Patrese*

GRAHAM SMITH

Age: **33**
Born: **Italy**
Debut: **1977 with Shadow**
GPs contested to 1987: **144**
Wins to 1987: **2**

It seems only yesterday tht we regarded Riccardo as the wild man of F1, a precocious kid with an irritatingly self-confident smirk on his face. I will recall his weaving on the straight at Anderstorp rendering the late Ronnie Peterson absolutely speechless with fury after the 1978 Swedish Grand Prix. But those impetuous early days are now submerged in the mists of racing history. At 33 years old, Patrese is the most experienced man in the business. He is also a consistently undervalued performer.

These last couple of seasons he has been wrestling with under-financed, under-powered Brabham-BMWs. Yet his team is amazed just how much determination, commitment and enthusiasm he brings to bear on his profession. He is still quick, has an abundance of experience which now generally keeps him out of trouble.

10 *Jonathan Palmer*

GEOFF MORROW

Age: **33**
Born: **England**
Debut: **1983 Williams**
GPs contested to 1987: **39**

Jonathan Palmer had run out of time with the Zakspeed team, after two seasons of driving for the tiny German outfit. Disappointed he was not signed as Prost's No. 2 at McLaren, 'the Doc' was thrown together with Ken Tyrrell a matter of a week or so prior to the first race of the season. It was fortunate for both of them.

Palmer has matured into a shrewd, tactical and extremely fast driver who no longer deserves to be passed over for a top team position. On a personal level he has matured considerably and now has sufficient experience to acquit himself respectably in whatever team he finds himself. Another driver with the right temperament for the job . . .

PYE AUDIO

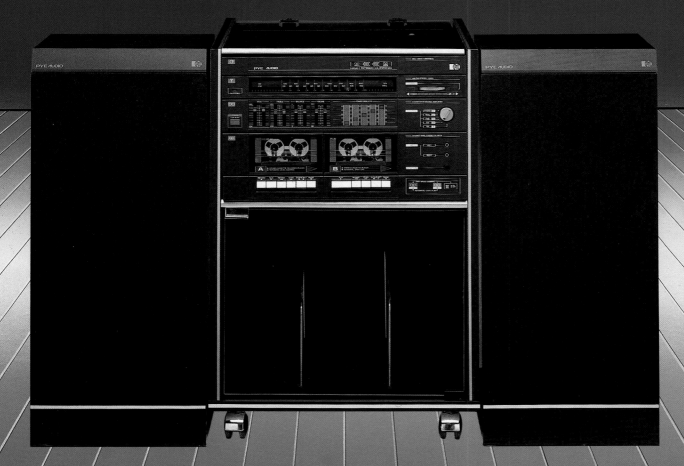

SH2964 — 3 in 1 Furniture Stereo Music System featuring High Speed Dubbing.

Features:—

- Two-speed semi-automatic turntable, FM Stereo/AM radio with FM stereo indicator.

- Dual cassette decks which feature slow-eject door mechanisms, high speed dubbing and continuous play functions. Has one touch recording facility on Tape 'A', Stop/Eject Rewind, Fast Forward, Play and Pause.

- Sliding bass and treble, volume and balance controls with LED power indicators.

- Vented bass reflex speaker enclosures for optimum sound reproduction and multi-purpose storage cabinet with castors and is fitted with glass door and is covered by 12 months parts and 3 months labour warranty.

You can rely on Pye

NSW & HEAD OFFICE (02) 742 8411 VIC (03) 542 3348 QLD (07) 844 2222 TOWNSVILLE (077) 75 6299 SA (08) 348 2533 WA (09) 277 4199

 **Brazil**

ROUND ONE: April 12, 1987

THE MORE THINGS CHANGE . . .

Dramatic changes in the scene during the off-season only served to give the defending world champion the buzz of a new challenge.

Some of the cars were different, some of the driver line-ups new, but in the twenty-four weeks that had passed since Alain Prost's triumph against the odds in Adelaide, nothing had really changed in substance.

Sure the Lotuses had turned yellow in deference to a new sponsor, grown Honda engines like the Williams and had embraced the controversial computerised suspension system in a bid to gain technical superiority. The Benettons had new engines too and normally aspirated, three-litre cars were back, as part of the phasing out of the super-powered turbo cars. Even the McLarens looked different.

But for all the changes, the championship-winning car of the previous three seasons was much the same under the skin, still a winning proposition when it mattered — on race day. So was Alain Prost, defending resolutely again and in the same winning frame of mind he had been in for Adelaide.

In the lead up to the season opener, Prost had not been happy with the revisions of the McLaren. It would take time to sort out, he felt, but already with a stronger version of the TAG engine and greater downforce from the chassis alterations, it was a quicker machine than in 1986.

With other new factors to consider — like the effects of the new 'pop-off' valve and control tyres from Goodyear — Prost played his usual waiting game after the start, then loomed as the heat of the day and the abrasion of the Rio circuit took its toll on his opposition. The Williams-Hondas had been the sound and fury of qualifying, as expected, but reigning world champion Prost was about to have another day that was close to perfection.

It was the usual Rio story: oppressive humidity, watch your pockets and Alain Prost looking good. He had won before in Rio — 1982, 1984 and 1985 and now, as the first man to successfully defend the world championship since Jack Brabham, the illustrious little Frenchman was out to do it again — win at Rio and then onto another championship.

After an encouraging winter working on the heavily revised McLaren TAG and all that Rio testing, Alain's weekend started to really come good into the half hour warm-up session, as had been so often the case with the Prost-McLaren combination in previous seasons. It told so much more about what had been speculated about during a European winter behind workshop doors and the two days of 1987 qualifying which had gone before the first race.

For a short while though Prost, and every other top driver, had been diverted by the new superlicence payment row, which actually threatened the running of the event. The row was resolved the day before qualifying began. And in the end the drivers paid up, this confirmed in a sanctimonious statement from FISA the following day, its tone that the little boys had been brought to heel.

Throughout the days preceding Rio, many of the drivers — notably Alain Prost and Nelson Piquet —

1.

were adamant that they would not pay the controversial new licence fee (which varied from driver to driver, according to the number of points scored in 1986 — the more points, the more you pay). Nelson spoke of a race boycott, while Alain said he would be happy to race, but would *not* pay the requested fee.

For these two — and for Nigel Mansell — the figure in question was more than $US12,000, as opposed to the basic fee of $825 (this paid by all new drivers, and all those who scored no points in 1986. It wasn't the money, Prost and others argued, but the principle: a licence was a licence; they didn't object to paying a fee, but felt it should be the same for everyone.

Members of the governing body, including its new marketing chief, Brabham's Bernie Ecclestone, held the view that those best fixed financially should fork out more: "Who do they think pays for safety and so on in this business?" Bernie demanded. To which Prost replied: "Safety? What safety? Three days we tested here last week — and there was no rescue helicopter in the place . . ."

However, by Friday morning all 23 drivers in Rio had paid up, and were in their cars ready to go. And FISA chose to crow about it: "The FIA rejected any compromise," its statement read, "and the regulations retained their force. The International Sporting Authority confirmed to drivers the decisions of the Executive Committee of December 1986, namely that over the next four years the Superlicence fee would only be increased in line with the cost-of-living index."

There was some small concession there. One of the drivers' primary concerns had been FISA's future plans for the licence fee: who knew what it might be in years to come? Now they knew it would be increased only by inflation. At the same time the statement confirmed one of the primary reasons for their discontent: why, if these decisions were taken in December, were the drivers informed of them three months later, a mere fortnight before the opening race?

In purely financial terms, it was difficult to lose any sleep for the drivers. In Nelson Piquet's case, the fee was around $12,200, which his Williams-Honda retainer pays him every 32 hours or so. But the *principle* was a different matter, and although the drivers — or, in some cases, their teams — paid up, the row may well recur in the future. One consequence was that the Grand Prix Drivers Association, moribund for many years, was reformed with Prost in charge. The world champion handled himself superbly through the events in Rio, using a blend of diplomacy and firmness.

When the dispute blew over, Prost qualified fifth in the new McLaren-TAG MP4/3, and spoken highly of its potential: "More downforce than the old car, for sure, and the latest engine is *much* stronger. But the car is new, you know, and we lost a lot of testing time with the rain last week. We don't know it yet, it's that simple, and so setting it up takes longer than usual. But I think . . . two or three races, and we should be in good shape. At the moment I'm not very happy with the set-up."

Alain on row three found it difficult to see beyond the Williams for the race, for Nigel Mansell and Nelson Piquet were simply untouchable in qualifying, each day a clear second ahead of anyone else.

On Friday, Piquet and Mansell were in the 27s, and Ayrton Senna's Lotus was a scratch over 1:29. There was no one in the 28s, although Ayrton and the impressive Benetton of Teo Fabi made it down there on Saturday. Whereupon the Williams-Hondas — Mansell ahead now — moved into the 26s. Without qualifying tyres, and with pop-off valve, Nigel was within six-tenths of Senna's 1986 pole time.

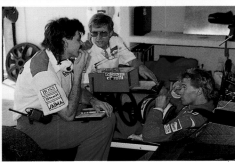

1: In the stifling heat of Rio the world champion starts to make his move forward. New car, revised engine, new rules, it made no difference to Alain Prost.
2: Air intakes at the side and sleeker styling were the most outward signs of a changed McLaren for the defence of the championship.
3: Ferrari's celebrated new boy, Gerhard Berger, is readied for his debut with new team Ferrari.
4: Looking for tenths: McLaren's new engineering boss, Gordon Murray, left, engineer Tim Wright, and Prost's new team-mate Stefan Johansson confer during qualifying.

Previous page: The new season blasts off under the hot Rio sun. The boys from Brazil exploited pole man Mansell's excess of wheelspin.

Mansell on the pole, then, in Brazil, despite the best efforts of that country's two favourite racing sons — and its national airline. Nigel was one of many racing folk to check in for the Wednesday night flight to Rio, only to be told that the DC10, a tardy aircraft at the best of times, would be a little late getting away. Until some time, Thursday, in fact. A first class ticket and a famous name helped with alternative arrangements, but even so, Mansell did not arrive until late Thursday evening.

A water pump leak on his race car put Nigel temporarily into the spare FW11B on Friday morning, but otherwise his practice days were as good as troublefree. Or almost. There was, he admitted, a good dose of anger in his pole position lap. A fracas late in the final session, between team-mate Piquet and Alessandro Nannini's Minardi meant that Mansell, on his hot lap, had to back off and start again. In the old days of qualifying tyres, there would have been no such option, but the Goodyear 'control' rubber allowed him another run, and this was the lap which reduced the Brazilian crowd to sullen silence.

The absence of Q-tyres made little difference to

reverted to the programme used in testing. Still far from perfect, it was beaten only by the Williams pair, and afterwards Ayrton, far from depressed, reaffirmed his faith in it. And the real test of the system, everyone agreed, would be race day, when the system's ability to maintain an ideal ride height throughout the race — full tanks or empty — should be seen to best advantage.

If you had any doubts about the potential of the system you had only to stand at the last corner and watch Senna power away down the bumpy pit straight. Where the other cars — even the Williams and McLarens — bucked and hopped, the Lotus flowed, as if the rug had been pulled straight. None got off the corner, though, like the Williams, both drivers confirming that suspension geometry changes over the winter had considerably improved traction. Mansell and Piquet came onto the pit straight like slingshots, and Honda-powered cars were constantly fastest through the speed laps. Indeed rivals muttered darkly that Oriental cunning had found a way round the pop-off valve: ultra-fast turbochargers forcing through so much boost that the valve literally couldn't cope with it.

1.

2.

the pattern of qualifying, merely stretched it a little. "Even with race tyres," Nigel said, "you're still only talking about a maximum of three really quick laps. The difference is that you can get quite a few reasonably quick laps out of them." You certainly can. His second set was past its best when he got the pole.

Throughout testing, other teams had suggested that Lotus, with their 'active' suspension system, just might be sand-bagging. Senna had been among the quick times wherever he had tested. When it came to it, they suggested, Ayrton and the Honda-powered 99T might paralyse everyone. As it was, the Brazilian was third fastest in both timed sessions, but this was clearly driver rather than car.

Having reached something of a performance plateau in testing, Lotus decided to send home Peter Wright, the engineer most closely involved with the active system, for some re-programming work. "It would probably have been OK for the Safari Rally," team manager Peter Warr remarked, "but not too good here." Senna confirmed that the car felt terrible on the opening day, and for Saturday Lotus

Actually, there were few 'pop off' complaints from the Williams drivers, and none at all from McLaren. The explanation for this, Alain Prost explained, was that problems with the valve — cutting in at progressively lower boost — seemed to occur only when the valve was actually *used*, which tended to weaken it. The McLaren plan, therefore, was to set boost at 3.6 bar (well below the four bar limit), so that the valve on the TAG V6 engine would never be pressed into service — and therefore not be weakened. And the plan seemed to work well enough. Worrying for the other teams, though, was that if Prost truly was running only 3.6, his lap time in the new MP4/3 was highly impressive.

Alain admitted that grand prix racing suddenly seemed like a new game. For the first time since 1984 he was working with something unfamiliar, a car he couldn't set up in his sleep. But with its stronger engine and improved downforce, on straightline speed Prost was giving little away: Piquet, Senna and newcomer Satoru Nakajima all topped 193 mph through the trap on the main straight, and then we had Mansell. And Prost at 3.6 bar!

1: Senna turns completely yellow. He fully endorsed the decision to use the controversial 'active' suspension exclusively from the first race in a bid to gain some advantage.

2: Piquet had the upper hand on team-mate Mansell in the first event as the rivalry continued for the second season. Mansell finished a lap down after being delayed by a puncture.

3: A Honda engine materialises in the back of Senna's Lotus. But would it work as well in the Lotus chassis?

4: Senna was less than happy with the 'active' suspension in the debut for the Lotus-powered Honda, but it was good enough to get him into the lead early. Then the other new part — the engine — let him down.

5: Former race leader Piquet powers back up the field after a premature stop to clear litter out of the radiator intakes.

FIA decals proudly emblazoned the controversial new valves, drawing attention, as someone said, to the only piece of crude engineering on the modern Formula One car. Problems were expected, and duly materialised. "Don't talk to me about bleeding pop-off valves," growled Derek Warwick after the first session. "Most of the time mine was cutting in at 3.5 or thereabouts, and some of the time it was at 2.6! The whole thing's a joke . . ."

Other drivers told similar stores. "One turbo was cutting at 3.7, and the other at 2.7," Thierry Boutsen reported after trying first qualifying session. And Peter Collins reckoned that was a loss of around 200 horsepower (as a rule of thumb, the loss of 0.1 bar equates to a loss of about 20bhp).

In their distaste for the things, however, all seemed united, and there were moves afoot to have them removed for the race, where there was no chance of anyone *daring* to run close to four bar, anyway. but FISA came up with its favourite word: *non* . . . Better to risk a cock-up than be seen to back down. "It's quite reassuring in a way," said one team manager. "Seeing that nothing changes, I mean, if they started being sensible after all these years, it'd be a bit unsettling. And, of course, they'd lose their stickers on the cars, wouldn't they?"

Of the others, Benetton was best, but the Ford Cosworth turbo-powered cars did not quite live up to their testing promise when Fabi was fastest of all, but Teo qualified a solid fourth, and would probably have edged Senna out of third had not his best lap on Saturday been inadvertently spoiled by Mansell: "I can't complain," he admitted, "because I did the same to him yesterday." Fourth and sixth, Fabi and Thierry Boutsen sandwiched Prost on the grid, and the Belgian, despite encountering frequent pop-off valve problems, was delighted with his car.

So testing, it seemed, had not deceived, Williams, Lotus (Senna's car, anyway), McLaren and Benetton were about where expected. Ferrari, new car and engine and ex-McLaren team manager, John Barnard and all, were not impressive, apparently very short of downforce, and Arrows were higher than for many a year.

In the race morning warm-up, Alain found his car working much better than before, and for the race he worked out a simple plan of campaign; run as little wing as realistically possible, to save fuel, concentrate on absolute smoothness through the turns, to save the tyres. The last was crucial, he reckoned, for the word was that Williams were planning three tyre stops. Two, he thought, would do the job for him.

The other drivers spoke in awe of the TAG-Porsche's fantastic "race day horsepower". It wasn't that at all — simply that Prost and new team-mate Stefan Johansson had virtually as much as in practice. In the late evening Alain reported that, yes, he felt quite good about the race.

As in 1986, he began quietly, leaving the thrashing to others. While Piquet charged into an early lead — nearly three seconds up on Senna after only two laps — Prost ran sixth, on the tail of Thierry Boutsen's Benetton-Ford, which he picked off on lap three, then moved into the mirrors of Fabi's sister car.

Mansell, at this point, was making more obvious progress. Too much wheelspin had meant a slow getaway, but he went from fifth to fourth to third in succeeding laps, quickly moving up to threaten Senna. As early as this, though, he knew he was in strife: "The temperatures were starting to go off the clock — after only a handful of laps the water was up to 120 when it should have been around 105 . . ."

Piquet, too, was in temperature trouble, but at this early stage there was a more obvious cause: on lap seven he was into the pits to have waste paper — always a hazard at a race in Brazil — removed from his radiators. At the same time, naturally, he was given new tyres, and rejoined 12th.

That left us with Senna leading in the 'active suspension' Lotus 99T. As in practice he was less than thrilled with the car's behaviour, but in this, its first race, it was good enough to run at the front. And Ayrton's commitment to it is total: "Gerard Ducarouge believes it is the way to go," he commented. "Look at the regulations now — we have a limit on horsepower, a limit on weight, and a limit on tyres in that we all use the same Goodyears. So this

3.

4.

5.

was maybe the one area where some advantage could be gained. We decided two weeks ago that we would run only 'active' throughout this season, and I agree completely. In fact, I don't want to drive a car with normal suspension again. Yes, the system has a weight penalty" (said to be around 25 kg), "but when it works well, it's incredible . . ."

But so new at Rio, the car was never quite on the pace, and one felt throughout the weekend that Senna's talent was flattering it. "We just haven't got the programming right here," Peter Warr admitted, "and we knew that going wholeheartedly with the programme from the first race was a risk. But we think we'll make better and quicker progress that way."

By as early as lap 11, tyre changes were beginning: Mansell was first in, and two laps later Senna came in, at the same time surrendering the lead to the looming Prost. And it was now that the pattern of the race was set. Open to question only was the

reliability of new car and substantially revised engine. Alain's part in the proceedings you could take for granted. "I was surprised how easily everything went in the race," he grinned afterwards. "So many things have changed, you know. We came here with a new car three years ago, and won, but this time I really doubted we were in a position to compete. I am still a worrier, and I like to have everything under control. But we had so little testing . . ."

Out on the track, there was no sign that very much was awry. Inch-perfect of line, as always, Prost pulled out a 10 secs lead over Boutsen, Piquet (climbing dramatically after his early stop), Mansell (ditto) and Derek Warwick's Arrows. Senna, on fresh tyres, was seventh.

The first of Prost's planned tyre stops came on lap 16, and he rejoined in fifth place, confident now that two sets would do the job, and absolutely certain that the Williams duo would need three. At least.

The field was thinning out now. Ivan Capelli's

normally aspirated March had not so much as made the grid, having blown its sole remaining Cosworth DFZ during the warm-up, and the Minardi of debutant Adrian Campos had been disqualified immediately for a reason which can only be described as novel. Very late in the day the Spaniard realised he had forgotten to put in his earplugs; by the time these had been inserted, the field was away on its parade lap, and as he caught up, Campos — his inexperience showing — carved through to his original place, rather than starting from the back.

There were more significant retirements, too. Fabi, who looked really strong in third place during the opening laps, lasted only nine laps before a turbo failed. Boutsen's sister Benetton, though, gave a lift to Ford hearts all afternoon, and delighted its driver. The first tyre stop, at 20 secs, was way too long, however, and soon afterwards, on lap 27, Thierry was back for more — his right rear punctured and disintegrating. This dropped him from serious contention, of course, but he ran strongly to the finish, and in the points.

Which was more than could be said for the luckless Warwick, rejuvenated now at the whiff of a competitive car. Through practice all the Arrows problems had come Eddie Cheever's way, but in the race Derek was out after only 20 laps. "We had a sixth gear which was too low," he said, "and all along the main straight I was banging up against the rev limiter . . ." A piston failed.

On reliability and horsepower, if not on handling, the Ferraris looked assured of a reasonable result, new partners Michele Alboreto and Gerhard Berger running in tandem for much of the way. But the cars were very short of grip, the drivers very obviously working. By the end of the race Gerhard was completely spent, half stumbling as he climbed from the car.

At the end of lap 37 came that frantic scream from the main grandstand which indicates either that a Brazilian has just passed somebody, or that somebody is in trouble, which could be to a Brazilian's advantage! Prost was heading down pit lane, but really it didn't matter. He had said he would be in on lap 37, confirmed it by radio (an innovation for McLaren, this), and he had a lead of better than half a minute. A few seconds later they groaned as the red and white car rejoined, still leading Piquet's Williams.

A lap later Nelson was in, needing three sets to Alain's two, and the last semi-realistic threat to the world champion was gone. Prost now had 24 secs over Senna, and then came Johansson, making a very strong impression on his McLaren debut, Piquet, Mansell and Berger.

Nigel's wretched day took a further drive on lap 46, when his left rear Goodyear punctured, which meant more than half a lap on three wheels, and dropped him from fifth to ninth. "I can't remember a more miserable race," he said. "All that for a single point. The whole afternoon was a complete joke. Because of overheating I was having to lap five seconds off the bloody pace. In fact," he concluded, moodily, "I reckon I could have got by with only one tyre stop — if it hadn't been for the puncture . . ."

Senna, who pulled off with 11 laps to go, while running fourth, deserved better after a wonderful drive in a difficult car. "The engine was going to seize. I knew it, I felt it a couple of times. No point in going on."

Such excitement as there was during the late stages came from Piquet's efforts to separate Johansson from third place, which succeeded finally on lap 44. Interesting, too, was Berger's pursuit of team-mate Alboreto, whom he had headed until making a third tyre stop on lap 48. Exhausted he may have been, but the Austrian really charged at this point, unlapping himself on Prost, and swiftly closing on Michele. With four laps left the Ferraris were right together — and the consequences were nearly disastrous.

On the main straight the rear underbody of Michele's car suddenly collapsed, and there was a frightening flurry of sparks. Gerhard, right on his team-mate's gearbox, managed to jink out and past without contact, but it was fortunate for both that Alboreto had the presence of mind not to lift off instantly when he felt something give.

In its revised state, the Italian's car oversteered wildly, and a lap later he spun off into retirement, while Berger hurtled on to fourth place — and, perhaps, first claim on the T-car for the rest of the season. This race, the Italians said, was to decide that privilege.

As the McLaren drivers, first and third, stepped from their cars, Johansson, seriously troubled by cockpit heat through the afternoon, was ready for as much liquid as he could force down. Prost, by contrast, accepted a single sip, and looked like a man who had taken a brief jog. His stamina is a match for any of the other qualities which make the world's best race driver.

"Today's race was really amazing for me," he beamed. "I mean, how perfect everything was. Different car, different engine, and also a different race engineer, Neil Oatley, who is working with me this year. You know, I can expect that my car will be much, much better at Imola in three weeks . . ."

Far left: The venerable Cosworth V8 reappears in F1. Jonathan Palmer's Tyrrell was the first of the Cosworth-powered cars home, but three laps behind the winning turbo car.

Below left: Just a few laps into the new season, Piquet dashes away from his team-mate, Senna and the new Ford turbo engined Benetton of Boutsen. Then came Prost, already looming ominously.

Left: Two championships on the trot and now a win first up in the new season for Prost.

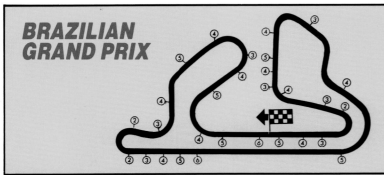

BRAZILIAN GRAND PRIX

Round 1: April 12, 1987
Circuit: Jacarepagua, Rio

Race data:	61 laps of 3.127 mile (5.00 km) circuit
Weather:	Very hot, dry
Fastest lap:	Piquet, Williams FW11B, 1:33.861, 119.926mph
Existing record:	Piquet, Williams FW11, 1:33.546, 120.308mph

ENTRIES

No	Driver (Nat)	Car/Chassis	Engine
1	Alain Prost (F)	McLaren MP4/3-3	TAG V6 Turbo
2	Stefan Johansson (S)	McLaren MP4/3-2	TAG V6 Turbo
3	Jonathan Palmer (GB)	Tyrrell DG/016-2	Ford Cosworth V8
4	Philippe Streiff (F)	Tyrrell DG/016-1	Ford Cosworth V8
5	Nigel Mansell (GB)	Williams FW11 B/3	Honda V6 Turbo
6	Nelson Piquet (BR)	Williams FW11 B/2	Honda V6 Turbo
7	Riccardo Patrese (I)	Brabham BT56/3	BMW S4 Turbo
8	Andrea de Cesaris (I)	Brabham BT56/2	BMW S4 Turbo
9	Martin Brundle (GB)	Zakspeed 861/2	Zakspeed S4 Turbo
10	Christian Danner (D)	Zakspeed 861/3	Zakspeed S4 Turbo
11	Satoru Nakajima (J)	Lotus 99T/1	Honda V6 Turbo
12	Ayrton Senna (BR)	Lotus 99T/4	Honda V6 Turbo
14	Pascal Fabre (F)	AGS JH22/02-032	Ford Cosworth V8
16	Ivan Capelli (I)	March RT 879/01	Ford Cosworth V8
17	Derek Warwick (GB)	Arrows A10/1	Megatron S4 Turbo
18	Eddie Cheever (USA)	Arrows A10/2	Megatron S4 Turbo
19	Teo Fabi (I)	Benetton B187-04	Ford V6 Turbo
20	Thierry Boutsen (B)	Benetton B187-03	Ford V6 Turbo
21	Alex Caffi (I)	Osella FA11	Alfa Romeo V8 Turbo
23	Adrian Campos (E)	Minardi M186-002	Moderni V6 Turbo
24	Alessandro Nannini (I)	Mindardi M186-003	Moderni V6 Turbo
27	Michele Alboreto (I)	Ferrari F187-096	Ferrari V6 Turbo
28	Gerhard Berger (A)	Ferrari F187-097	Ferrari V6 Turbo
28	Gerhard Berger (A)	Ferrari F187-095*	Ferrari V6 Turbo

* Race car

QUALIFYING

FRIDAY: Hot, dry Driver		SATURDAY: Hot, dry Driver	
Piquet	1:27.822	Mansell	1:26.128
Mansell	1:27.901	Piquet	1:26.567
Senna	1:29.002	Senna	1:28.408
Prost	1:29.522	Fabi	1:28.417
Boutsen	1:30.166	Prost	1:29.175
Fabi	1:30.439	Boutsen	1:29.450
Alboreto	1:31.218	Berger	1:30.357
Johansson	1:31.343	Warwick	1:30.467
Berger	1:31.444	Alboreto	1:30.468
Patrese	1:32.001	Johansson	1:30.476
De Cesaris	1:32.402	Patrese	1:31.179
Warwick	1:32.531	Nakajima	1:32.276
Cheever	1:33.084	Cheever	1:32.769
Nannini	1:33.980	Nannini	1:33.729
Nakajima	1:34.445	Campos	1:33.825
Campos	1:34.832	De Cesaris	1:34.115
Danner	1:36.178	Danner	1:35.212
Brundle	1:37.235	Palmer	1:36.091
Palmer	1:37.488	Brundle	1:36.160
Streiff	1:38.822	Streiff	1:36.274
Caffi	1:39.931	Caffi	1:38.770
Capelli	1:43.580	Fabre	1:39.816
Fabre	1:44.126	Capelli	2:02.966

STARTING GRID

No	Driver	Time
5	Mansell	1:26.128
6	Piquet	1:26.567
12	Senna	1:28.408
19	Fabi	1:28.417
1	Prost	1:29.175
20	Boutsen	1:29.450
28	Berger	1:30.357
17	Warwick	1:30.467
27	Alboreto	1:30.468
2	Johansson	1:30.476
7	Patrese	1:31.179
11	Nakajima	1:32.276
8	De Cesaris	1:32.402
18	Cheever	1:32.769
24	Nannini	1:33.729
23	Campos	1:33.825
10	Danner	1:35.212
3	Palmer	1:36.091
9	Brundle	1:36.160
4	Streiff	1:36.274
21	Caffi	1:38.770
14	Fabre	1:39.816
16	Capelli	1:43.580

RESULTS

Pos	No	Driver	Car	Laps	Time/Retirement
1	1	Prost	McLaren-TAG	61	1-39:45.141
2	6	Piquet	Williams-Honda	61	1-40:25.688
3	2	Johansson	McLaren-TAG	61	1-40:41.899
4	28	Berger	Ferrari	61	1-41:24.376
5	20	Boutsen	Benetton-Ford	60	
6	5	Mansell	Williams-Honda	60	
7	11	Nakajima	Lotus-Honda	59	
8	27	Alboreto	Ferrari	58	
9	10	Danner	Zakspeed	58	
10	3	Palmer	Tyrrell-Cosworth	58	
11	4	Streiff	Tyrrell-Cosworth	57	
12	14	Fabre	AGS-Cosworth	55	
R	18	Cheever	Arrows-Megatron	52	Engine
R	12	Senna	Lotus-Honda	50	Engine
R	7	Patrese	Brabham-BMW	48	Loose battery
R	8	De Cesaris	Brabham-BMW	21	Gearbox
R	17	Warwick	Arrows-Megatron	20	Engine
R	21	Caffi	Osella-Alfa Romeo	20	Engine
R	24	Nannini	Minardi-Moderni	17	Rear suspension
R	9	Brundle	Zakspeed	15	Turbo
R	19	Fabi	Benetton-Ford	9	Turbo
R	23	Campos	Minardi-Moderni	3	Disqualified

FASTEST LAP

Driver	
Piquet	1:33.861
Cheever	1:33.978
Mansell	1:34.602
Johansson	1:35.299
Senna	1:35.312
Boutsen	1:35.737
Berger	1:35.769
Alboreto	1:35.773
Prost	1:35.811
Fabi	1:36.511
Warwick	1:36.553
Patrese	1:36.846
De Cesaris	1:38.194
Nakajima	1:38.482
Nannini	1:38.108
Danner	1:40.112
Brundle	1:40.683
Campos	1:40.714
Palmer	1:41.495
Streiff	1:43.049
Fabre	1:43.129
Caffi	1:44.130

CHAMPIONSHIP POSITIONS

DRIVERS
1	Prost	9
2	Piquet	6
3	Johansson	4
4	Berger	4
5	Boutsen	2
6	Mansell	1

CONSTRUCTORS
1	McLaren-TAG	13
2	Williams-Honda	7
3	Ferrari	4
4	Benetton-Ford	2

JIM CLARK CUP
1	Palmer	9
2	Streiff	6
3	Fabre	4

COLIN CHAPMAN CUP
1	Tyrrell-Cosworth	15
2	AGS-Cosworth	4

San Marino

ROUND TWO: May 3, 1987

ALONE AT THE TOP

Behind there was nobody to stop him taking the championship lead. No team-mate, no world champion and no concern about the pole-winning yellow car.

There were three serious race contenders when the transporters were unloaded at thirsty Imola. One was ruled out in the violent shunt on Friday that sent the Williams camp into a huddle and Goodyear technicians into a flurry over the cause. Another quit 14 laps into the grand prix when first the tacho, then the whole electrics failed in the familiar red and white machine.

That left Nigel Mansell on his own. And there he finished, the new world championship leader after one of the simplest wins of his career. The Williams had never missed a bit. An earlier than expected pit stop, due to a wheel balance flinging off, was not a concern and neither was some intermittent brake lock that sent him gardening for a few furious seconds, but without anyone around to contribute to having a more serious moment.

For perhaps 30 secs at the start, Ayrton Senna might have been viewed with concern. On pole, the first time for an 'active' suspension car, the Lotus system showed that it was a long way from perfection by taking Senna on a temperamental ride for the latter stages of the race.

It brought the Brazilian under attack from the Italians. Buoyed by the local support, it was first Michele Alboreto who dealt with the fickle Lotus, then a surprise, a vintage Riccardo Patrese in the revised Brabham. However, neither the Ferrari nor Brabham saw out the race in good health, loss of boost the Ferrari problem of the day and alternator for the resurgent Brabham.

Watching it all through glass darkly was Nelson Piquet, forbidden by doctors from taking part in the event. Hired to commentate for Italian TV for the day, he didn't find it an edifying experience, given the on-going rivalry within the Williams empire.

Nigel Mansell will rarely have a more straight-forward win. Ayrton Senna may have started from the pole, but even Ayrton doubted his ability to run with Williams and McLaren on race day. The 'active' Lotus-Honda was getting there, but it was not there yet. Nigel voiced fears about the car after qualifying — "If it's really working well tomorrow, Senna might walk it" — but in reality he knew his opposition was in the singular: Alain Prost.

The world champion went through unusually troubled qualifying days, but towards the end of the final session everything was coming right: "If I have no problems with the car, I think I will win," Alain smiled.

The opening day of practice, of course, was dominated by Nelson Piquet's mammoth accident. Has a greater impact been survived with less hurt? You saw the TV coverage of the shunt on Friday evening, then bumped into Nelson in the paddock the next morning. Was this really the fellow who had been in *that* less than 24 hours earlier? It would be an overstatement to suggest he was his usual smiling gypsy self, but he could at least reflect on the good fortune of having a Patrick Head car about him when he crashed. Mansell, not surprisingly, took a close look at the FW11D when they brought it back. To find the cockpit and footwell intact after an 180 mph

impact with a concrete wall can only do good things for your confidence.

Piquet had been fastest at the time of the shunt, and indeed the time remained unbeaten for the balance of the session. Perhaps no one truly liked stepping into what Eddie Cheever calls "the red area" that afternoon. "I passed the scene very soon after Nelson crashed," Senna muttered quietly, "and it looked to me like he was very badly injured."

But he wasn't. And there was great relief at that. The following day it was business as usual, but with one contender for pole position not taking part — pleading to be allowed to run, but bowing eventually to wiser counsel from those who know about the possible after-effects of severe concussion. Before the race, however, he was allowed to appease his countless Italian fans by riding a slow lap of honour on his new Ducati.

It was about 20 mins into the first time session when it happened. The red flag was out and the last few cars past the pits had throttled sharply back after powering through the first corner, Tamburello, a long loping left-hander taken absolutely flat out. Under qualifying conditions the faster cars are close to 170 mph as they cross the start-finish line, and all through Tamburello and down towards the Curva Villeneuve the speed builds. It is emphatically not a place to go off.

But someone clearly had. And soon word came that it was Nelson. At the scene was Teo Fabi, who had realised the enormity of the accident, and pulled off. Using his on-board cockpit radio Teo communicated with Benetton team manager Peter Collins, who immediately took himself down to the Williams pit, there to keep Frank Williams and Patrick Head and everyone in instant touch with what was happening. It looked very bad. Piquet, Fabi said, was out of the car and lying beside it. Get the doctors down here, for Christ's sake!

And then hopeful words started to filter in. There was some talk of arm and rib injuries, but it seemed there was no threat to Nelson's life. Some sense of normality began to seep back into the proceedings, Frank saying they would not being going out again until satisfied that Piquet's car had not failed. Mansell sought and found a motorbike, rode off down to the scene.

Nelson was speedily removed to the track's medical centre (one of the best in Formula One use), and not long afterwards F1 doctor, Professor Watkins emerged with heartening news: "He's all right — concussed and badly shaken up, but nothing seems to be broken." Thereafter Piquet was taken to the Bellaria Hospital in Bologna for a brain scan. This revealed nothing untoward, but as a matter of course they kept him in for the night for observation. The following morning he was released.

In the meantime the details of the shunt — and the full extent of Nelson's extraordinary escape — had become clear. From the start of the session he had been fast, and at the time of the accident had set the best time. At the beginning of his eighth lap he overtook Adrian Campos's Minardi on the outside at Tamburello, and the Spaniard later reported that the Williams was on a normal line when suddenly it snapped out of control, spinning twice before hurtling off the road backwards, across the narrow verge and into the wall. The speed of impact was colossal, yet when the car finally came to rest, Piquet was able to get himself out of the cockpit, then immediately collapsing next to the car.

Once the state of Nelson's health had been established, thoughts turned to the cause of the accident. Tyre failure? Had something broken? Could it have been driver error? This last could be disregarded, Campos reckoned. Loss of control — the car flicking sideways — had been too sudden for that.

Inspection of the car gave Patrick Head little to go on. There had been the suggestion that something — tyre or suspension — had failed in the left rear corner of the Williams (despite the fact that, on a left-hander, it would have been the right hand side which was under most load), but this was wiped off in the impact with the wall. "I can't believe it was driver error," Patrick said, "so it looks as if it was a component failure of one sort or another.

At the same time Head was as confident as he

Previous page: The Kevlar armoured skins of the warriors' steeds intimidate before the contest. The new colours for some took a little getting used to.

Far left: Mansell carves up the field on the way to an untroubled win. There was nobody left to challenge him once he asserted himself.

Left: Before he took up the Williams-Honda cause by himself, Mansell made sure Piquet's colossal accident in practice hadn't been caused by a car failure. It gave him confidence.

Below: Zakspeed had a new car on hand for Imola. Brundle's version ran out of brakes in the race, but he managed to nurse it home for the German team's first world championship points.

reasonably could be that the suspension had not failed: "I could be wrong, of course, but this configuration is essentially the same as we put on FW10B in late 1985, and we've done an awful lot of running with it since. It's true that we're looking for more downforce all the time, and you have to allow for that as time goes by. But I'd be surprised, I must say, if it proved to have been car failure here."

Tyre failure, indeed, looked like the most logical explanation. The rubber Goodyear brought to Imola was different from that on which the teams had tested a week earlier, and many reported severe blistering through the day. Goodyear however took the bull by the horns after the first practice day and collected up all the tyres issued to the teams for the Imola weekend.

What followed was a remarkable operation which started with chartering an aircraft to bring out 400 tyres from the company's base at Wolverhampton. These arrived in Italy at 3 am on Saturday, and by the start of practice had been mounted up, ready to go.

Additionally, a truck was dispatched to nearby Maranello to pick up nine sets in residence at the Ferrari factory, and another 20 tyres were already at the track, leftovers from testing a week earlier.

These 'substitute' tyres were, in fact, the type used

— and found satisfactory in every way — throughout the test days. Why, therefore, were they not brought to Imola in the first place? The short answer would seem to be that there were insufficient quantities to supply every car with its quota. This was the month of May, and Akron's attention was necessarily focussed on Indianapolis and the month-long 500 build-up. For Saturday and Sunday at Imola, every car was restricted to four and a half sets apiece.

Compliments, nevertheless, to Goodyear. To decide on the overnight change was to make public admission of a mistake, and that takes corporate courage. Inevitably there were those who saw the move as instant response to Piquet's accident, and perhaps this did, indeed, tip the scale. But through the morning complaints of serious blistering persisted and plainly a basic problem existed.

What was the difference between the 'Friday' tyres and those which replaced them? In construction they were not quite the same, but mainly, one engineer said, the second type was, "rather more heavy duty." In feel, the drivers reported that there was little to choose. You were talking slight variations in balance, nothing more. It was not inconceivable Goodyear's Lee Gaug suggested, that one set could go the distance, and indeed the normally-aspirated

teams (who found the second type much better suited to their cars) proposed to try.

For the turbos, though, it was a different matter. Could Prost contemplate the whole race on one set? No way, he said, but there would only be one stop.

On Saturday morning Patrick Head closely inspected the scene of Piquet's accident. "All I can tell you from the marks on the road," he said, "is that the left rear tyre was deflated before the car went off."

Patrick is not a man to seek excuses, and nor was he trying to point the finger at Goodyear. Everyone involved in grand prix racing was in Goodyear's debt (for without the American company how could there have been any Formula One in 1987), but no one could reasonably expect infallibility. Better by far to establish the true cause of Piquet's accident, to accept that there is an inevitability that these things will happen occasionally in Formula One, to try to eliminate repetition of them.

Nelson, meantime, was out of hospital and back at the circuit, insisting he wanted to drive. Stiff and store and limping, he said he felt fine, but the doctors wanted none of that, thank you. After behaving like a sulky child, the Brazilian finally accepted that maybe they did have his best interests at heart. And perhaps he later reflected that he had been remarkably fortunate to have had this accident in the late eighties, such are the wonders of carbon fibre. Not too many years ago the consequences of a shunt as fearful as this would almost certainly have

been fatal. As it was, Nelson came out of it with a headache and a sore foot. Facts such as these must be gratifying for an engineer. And for those of Patrick Head's calibre, in the design of a grand prix car, safety is *always* the first priority.

Once it became clear Piquet had suffered no serious injury everyone relaxed and began to concentrate again on the matter of qualifying.

We were left with a three-way fight for the pole —Mansell, Senna or Prost. During testing the previous week the world champion had been fastest, and that in itself was worrying for the rest. "My God," Eddie Cheever muttered, "usually he's only quickest on Sundays . . ."

Right enough. We have grown accustomed to the sudden emergence of McLaren when race set-up is what counts, but before there was a limit on turbo-boost Prost was rarely an outright contender for pole position, for Porsche were never asked to build an out-and-out qualifying engine for TAG.

In recent days, though, Alain had stressed his admiration for the advances in power and fuel efficiency which Porsche have made over the winter. "We have never run a lot of boost in qualifying," he says, "and now, of course, some of the others are having to run a lot less than they did." With the regulations as they are (together with Porsche's own improvements), the latest TAG V6 was immensely potent.

A glance at the startline speed trap figures on Friday afternoon, for example, revealed that car No. 1 was at the very top, at 166.392 mph, fractionally faster than the Hondas. Then you looked at the lap times for the session, however, and found Prost down in ninth place, just a shade faster than Satoru Nakajima.

It had been a frustrating afternoon, Alain said. Apart from anything else, there had been tyre problems. He didn't find the car so well balanced as in testing — when Goodyear had supplied different tyres, of course. More to the point, the engine in his car had blown up. Then he had gone out in the spare MP4/3: same story. And the TAG V6 in Johansson's car had also expired.

"Annoying, yes, but not really worrying," Prost said. "It shouldn't happen tomorrow." The engines had been running too lean. It was a matter of the wrong 'chip', and is a phenomenon of modern Formula One which we had seen before, notably with Honda. Engines fly apart, and a whole day is lost.

On Saturday morning Prost had a third engine failure, and was late coming out for the final session. A lot of time had been lost, one way and another, and he did some work on the handling balance before going for a time in the closing minutes. As two o'clock approached he was down to 1:26.1, but then the chequered flag was out, and that was that. He was fourth fastest overall, and with Piquet's enforced absence that meant third on the grid. Quite content.

Mansell, though, was decidedly unhappy with second place, for the pole had seemed his for the taking. On Friday he had been second quickest to Piquet at the time of Nelson's accident, and before the session restarted, Frank Williams suggested they should devote the balance of it to race testing on full tanks, that it wouldn't be appropriate to go for Piquet's time when he was unable to defend it.

Nigel concurred, and on Saturday knew for sure he was the only Williams driver for the rest of the weekend. His opening run in the final session set a new mark, but he wasn't happy with it: "I had Cheever on my tail, and didn't want to let him past and lose my clear road. So I brought the tyres up to temperature too quickly, and they weren't at their best. It was a pole lap at the time, but it wasn't a good lap. Then the team made a bad decision . . ."

At that point no one was close to Nigel's time. The team erroneously believed pole position was safe so reverted to a practice which used to drive Alan Jones crazy in days of yore: race testing in a timed session. Mansell was sent out in the spare FW11B, running a lot of fuel. And then, from nowhere, the name of Ayrton Senna appeared at the top of the times.

"I know the race is what it's all about . . . but at the same time I knew we could have gone a lot quicker," Nigel muttered. "Senna went and beat our time, and

Above: Another fresh addition to the GP circus at Imola was the Gerard Larrousse-run Lola for Frenchman Philippe Alliot. Using Cosworth power it at least finished at its debut, but next to last.

Left: Alboreto got the better of Senna to take secod in a truly ruthless passing move. But soon the Ferrari would lose boost and fall back to third.

Inset: New darling of the Ferrari worshippers, Gerhard Berger holds court for the Italian media at his first race for Ferrari on the team's home ground.

Below: March returns to F1 at Imola. The gaudy new car, piloted by Ivan Capelli, ran Cosworth power in the contest for the first Colin Chapman Cup.

with 15 mins to go I got back in the race car for another go."

He paused, "The engine just didn't bloody work. It had been perfect earlier on, but now it misfired and popped and banged, and there was no power. For some reason best known to themselves, the Honda people had changed the chip . . . I came in, and they went back to the original chip, and it still didn't work properly, don't ask me why. That was it, the end of the session, and I just never got the chance to get the pole back. I reckon we could have gone nearly a second quicker."

Senna on the pole, then, in the 'active' Lotus-Honda 99T. This was the dramatic Senna, darty and two-wheeling over the kerbs at the chicanes, Senna in Villeneuve mode. "I did a 26.4 on my first set, I think, but only got one clear lap. Traffic was a big problem, I came in, changed the car a bit, went out. More traffic, then a clear road, I did 25.8, and that was it. I didn't want to try to go quicker than that, and preferred to concentrate on improving the spare car, which had given a lot of trouble on the first day."

The suspension was obviously working more efficiently than in Rio? "Yes, yes, but it's very complex, you know. We have so much to learn about it. The car is really not handling that well at all — even if we are on pole position. I'm *surprised* to be on pole, and I don't think it means a lot. I think we have some way to go to be competitive with McLaren and Williams in a race."

In with a shout were the Benetton-Fords (Fabi fourth, Boutsen a troubled 11th), but the cars rarely ran well for long during practice, and Teo spoke of too much understeer, too much throttle lag. Berger and Alboreto pleased the locals with fifth and sixth, but the places came only after a lot of engine and gearbox problems. And sweat. "We seem OK on economy," said Michele, eyes streaming from hay fever. "We should have enough *fuel* to get to the finish, but how long will the engine need the fuel?"

After that the serious business. They did their final parade lap, came back to the grid, and suddenly arms were being waved out of cockpits. Cheever had stalled. And Boutsen. And Brundle. Wisely the new grand prix starter decided against pressing the green button, and engines were shut down. Twelve minutes later they tried again: there was another formation lap, and to allow for it the race distance was reduced from 60 to 59 laps.

"That was a relief," Mansell said. "This place is *so* marginal on fuel that one less racing lap might make all the difference."

At the green Prost tried to cut between Senna and Mansell, but was firmly pincered out. Down through Tamburello the yellow Lotus was ahead, but Mansell simply pulled out and drove past as they approached the left-hander at Villeneuve. He was quickly asserting himself, no doubt of that.

Meanwhile Alain knew he could run with anyone. At least that. For two or three laps he was held up behind Senna, but as Mansell started lap six he saw the familiar red-and-white nosecone in his mirrors. Next time round it was a little bigger.

On lap 15, thought, it suddenly wasn't there any more, and Alain was pulling off on the grass, parking, to roars of Latin approval. Typically, he was sanguine about it. "I can't ever remember a car that felt better, in every way. Brakes, handling, power, everything. I was running minimum boost, and there was absolutely no problem with the fuel. Everything was *perfect*. Easy to say, but it was true. Then the rev counter stopped working, but for half a lap everything else was normal. Then the red light came on in the cockpit, and I called them up on the radio. The engine cut out, and they told me from the pits that the generator had failed. That was it."

Thereafter, something of a procession. Mansell was left with a 10 secs lead over Alboreto, who had recently displaced Senna. After his despondency in qualifying, Michele was pleased with the Ferrari in race conditions. It was not truly competitive, but better than he had expected. Behind him ran Patrese — any race in Italy is worth a second a lap to Riccardo — Berger and Johansson.

A great wailing at the end of lap 15 indicated that something bad had befallen a Ferrari, and in came Berger. Quicker than his team-mate in practice, he

had been unexpectedly subdued from the start, and now the reason became clear: "The engine was down on power all the way. I was just losing more boost all the time." No. 28 was pushed sorrowfully into its pit, and the grandstand focused solely on Alberto.

Fabi, too, had been less fleet than expected. Fourth on the grid and fastest for much of the morning warm-up, he had been languishing down in eighth, and after 18 laps was in for a long stop. "The start was very quick — red light, then green immediately after. I wasn't ready for it, and made a slow start . . ." As the Benetton struggled away from the grid, it was clipped by Cheever's Arrows, and the end plate of its right front wing was damaged. Result: understeer. After a new plate had been fitted Teo

really got the hammer down, but he was doing it from way back, in 12th place.

Mansell was in for tyres on lap 22, which seemed like a bit early, and was, "I'd lost a wheel balance weight," he said, "and that meant a big vibration through the tyres, which I found very worrying. After the stop, though, I had no problems, apart form the rear brakes locking occasionally. One one lap, in fact, I went over the grass at the Acque Minerali chicane."

As Prost has always said, it is nice to be without pressure at Imola, for there are too many other things to worry about. It is a compromise, this circuit. You need the right blend of downforce and economy — and the two do not belong together. During practice Mansell had agreed: "For optimum lap times — and a good feeling of security — you need to run more wing than we are doing. People are saying how quick we are in a straight line, and I don't deny it. But that's because we're running as little wing as we can get away with — for the sake of going easy on the fuel."

As it was, Nigel was able to run a conservative race, drive the car well within its limits. After his tyre stop he dropped temporarily to fifth, but pit stops by those ahead had him back in front by lap 28, and there he always looked like staying, despite the relatively close attention of . . . Patrese!

The Italian was indisputably having one of his 'on' days, and was only a couple of seconds back of the Williams for several laps. He had, however, yet to make his tyre stop, and when he came in — on lap 37 — the final semblance of a threat to Mansell was gone.

After the race a disappointed Johansson said he believed he could have finished second for Mclaren, had he not needed a second stop, on lap 43, to replace a front wing end plate which had simply fluttered away. Prior to this, he had been into a heady set-to with Patrese for fourth place. And ahead was a similar dispute over second between Senna and Alboreto, Michele pulling a beautifully ruthless move on Ayrton at Acque Minerali on lap 43. Simply, he got the Ferrari alongside the Lotus, and kept the nose pointing straight at the chicane. Senna was

presented with a simple choice: give away or have an accident.

Ayrton wisely yielded, and soon afterwards was also passed by the remarkable Patrese, now storming along on new tyres. In no time at all the Brabham was also by the Ferrari, and into second place once more! We hadn't seen a Brabham move like this since Nelson left.

It couldn't last, and didn't. At the end of lap 50, with nine to go, the blue and white car was late, and when it appeared it was stumbling. The alternator had broken, and wasn't giving enough juice. Riccardo slipped sadly down to a ninth place finish.

Senna, in the meantime, was back into second place, having passed Alboreto through Tamburello in a manner which seemed a little too effortless.

Michele was in trouble, his Ferrari losing boost, as had Berger's earlier in the afternoon. But the car was at least to see him through to the flag.

There were hard luck stories aplenty behind. After its early delay, Fabi had driven a beautiful race in the Benetton, setting fastest race lap along the way, but on lap 52 he was into the pits, unhesitatingly flicking off his belts. A turbo had failed, just three laps after Boutsen's sister car had lost fifth place with a blown engine.

No fortune for Benetton, then, and none either for Arrows. Cheever's car eventually blew up, after misfiring from the start, but Warwick put in a great performance at Imola, and was always in the picture. Until four laps from the end when he pulled off, tank dry, fifth place gone.

This was to the benefit of Brundle, whose new Zakspeed had been all but brakeless for most of the race. "I nearly came in several times," Martin said, "but decided to stay out, pump the pedal." Erich Zakowski was very glad he did, for his new driver collected two points, the first for the little German team.

And sixth, to the delight of Peter Warr and the countless Japanese who now people Formula One, was Satoru Nakajima. He had started dead last from pit lane, driving Senna's spare Lotus-Honda which was hastily adapted to his diminutive statue. A battery short circuit on his car had meant no power for the 'active' suspension computer, which meant no suspension. Since the battery is awkwardly located, replacing it would have taken time Lotus didn't have. Nakajima did a fine job for Lotus, and was afterwards almost overcome at the realisation that he had scored a world championship point, the first Japanese to do so.

Not a memorable race, this, by any means. Afterwards Senna diplomatically said that the active suspension had been "temperamental" for part of the race, but he was delighted that it had finished, managed a full race distance. At present, as he said the car was not truly a rival for Williams and McLaren.

Neither was anything else.

Far left: *The proliferation of under three litre cars produced a race within a race. Tyrrell duo Palmer and Streiff clear an incident involving Alliot's Lola and Fabre's AGS.*

Left: *Senna, Mansell and Alboreto take to the champers. Only Mansell had any reason to be pleased with the day.*

SAN MARINO GRAND PRIX

Round 2: May 3, 1987
Circuit: Imola

Race data:	59 laps of 3.132 mile (5.04 km) circuit
Weather:	Warm, dry
Fastest lap:	Fabi, Benetton B187, 1:29.246, 126.338mph
Existing record:	Piquet, Williams FW11, 1:28.667, 127.151mph

ENTRIES

No	Driver (Nat)	Car/Chassis	Engine
1	Alain Prost (F)	McLaren MP4/3-3	TAG V6 Turbo
2	Stefan Johansson (S)	McLaren MP4/3-2	TAG V6 Turbo
3	Jonathan Palmer (GB)	Tyrrell DG/016-2	Ford Cosworth V8
4	Philippe Streiff (F)	Tyrrell DG/016-1	Ford Cosworth V8
5	Nigel Mansell (GB)	Williams FW11 B/3	Honda V6 Turbo
6	Nelson Piquet (BR)	Williams FW11 B/2	Honda V6 Turbo
7	Riccardo Patrese (I)	Brabham BT56/3	BMW S4 Turbo
8	Andrea de Cesaris (I)	Brabham BT56/2	BMW S4 Turbo
9	Martin Brundle (GB)	Zakspeed 871/2	Zakspeed S4 Turbo
10	Christian Danner (D)	Zakspeed 861/3	Zakspeed S4 Turbo
11	Satoru Nakajima (J)	Lotus 99T/3	Honda V6 Turbo
12	Ayrton Senna (BR)	Lotus 99T/4	Honda V6 Turbo
14	Pascal Fabre (F)	AGS JH22/02-032	Ford Cosworth V8
16	Ivan Capelli (I)	March RT 871/01	Ford Cosworth V8
17	Derek Warwick (GB)	Arrows A10/1	Megatron S4 Turbo
18	Eddie Cheever (USA)	Arrows A10/2	Megatron S4 Turbo
19	Teo Fabi (I)	Benetton B187-04	Ford V6 Turbo
20	Thierry Boutsen (B)	Benetton B187-03	Ford V6 Turbo
21	Alex Caffi (I)	Osella FA1H/01/87	Alfa Romeo V8 Turbo
22	Gabriele Tarquini (I)	Osella FA1G/85/02	Alfa Romeo V8 Turbo
23	Adrian Campos (E)	Minardi M186-05	Moderni V6 Turbo
24	Alessandro Nannini (I)	Minardi M186-03	Moderni V6 Turbo
25	Rene Arnoux (F)	Ligier JS29B/2	Megatron S4 Turbo
26	Piercarlo Ghinzani (I)	Ligier JS29B/3	Megatron S4 Turbo
26	Piercarlo Ghinzani (I)	Ligier JS29B/3*	Megatron S4 Turbo
27	Michele Alboreto (I)	Ferrari F187-096	Ferrari V6 Turbo
28	Gerhard Berger (A)	Ferrari F187-095T	Ferrari V6 Turbo
30	Philippe Alliot (F)	Lola LC87/01	Ford Cosworth V8

* Race car

QUALIFYING

FRIDAY: Warm, dry Driver		SATURDAY: Warm, dry Driver	
Piquet	1:25.997	Senna	1:25.826
Mansell	1:26.204	Mansell	1:25.946
Senna	1:27.543	Prost	1:26.135
Fabi	1:27.801	Fabi	1:27.270
Berger	1:28.229	Berger	1:27.280
Patrese	1:28.447	Alboreto	1:28.074
Warwick	1:28.887	Patrese	1:28.421
Boutsen	1:28.929	Johansson	1:28.708
Prost	1:29.317	Cheever	1:28.848
Nakajima	1:29.579	Boutsen	1:28.908
Alboreto	1:29.653	Warwick	1:29.236
Cheever	1:30.379	Arnoux	1:29.861
Johansson	1:30.416	De Cesaris	1:30.382
De Cesaris	1:30.627	Nakajima	1:30.545
Arnoux	1:31.078	Brundle	1:31.094
Nannini	1:31.789	Campos	1:31.818
Brundle	1:31.931	Danner	1:31.903
Caffi	1:32.308	Ghinzani	1:32.248
Ghinzani	1:32.873	Streiff	1:33.155
Danner	1:32.977	Caffi	1:33.298
Alliot	1:34.458	Alliot	1:33.846
Palmer	1:34.632	Capelli	1:33.872
Streiff	1:35.001	Palmer	1:36.127
Capelli	1:37.463	Fabre	1:36.159
Fabre	1:39.747		
Campos	1:41.520		
Tarquini	1:43.446		

STARTING GRID

No	Driver	Time
12	Senna	1:25.826
5	Mansell	1:25.946
1	Prost	1:26.135
19	Fabi	1:27.270
28	Berger	1:27.280
27	Alboreto	1:28.074
7	Patrese	1:28.421
2	Johansson	1:28.708
18	Cheever	1:28.848
17	Warwick	1:28.908
20	Boutsen	1:28.908
11	Nakajima	1:29.579
8	De Cesaris	1:30.382
9	Brundle	1:31.094
24	Nannini	1:31.789
23	Campos	1:31.818
10	Danner	1:31.903
26	Ghinzani	1:32.248
21	Caffi	1:32.308
4	Streiff	1:33.155
30	Alliot	1:33.846
16	Capelli	1:33.872
3	Palmer	1:34.632
14	Fabre	1:36.159
22	Tarquini	1:43.446

RESULTS

Pos	No	Driver	Car	Laps	Time/Retirement
1	5	Mansell	Williams-Honda	59	1-31:24.076
2	12	Senna	Lotus-Honda	59	1-31:51.621
3	27	Alboreto	Ferrari	59	1-32:03.220
4	2	Johansson	McLaren-TAG	59	1-32:24.664
5	9	Brundle	Zakspeed	57	
6	11	Nakajima	Lotus-Honda	57	
7	10	Danner	Zakspeed	57	
8	4	Streiff	Tyrrell-Cosworth	57	
9	7	Patrese	Brabham-BMW	57	
10	30	Alliot	LC-Cosworth	56	Out of fuel
R	17	Warwick	Arrows-Megatron	55	Out of fuel
R	21	Caffi	Osella-Alfa Romeo	54	
13	14	Fabre	AGS-Cosworth	53	
R	19	Fabi	Benetton-Ford	51	Turbo
R	20	Boutsen	Benetton-Ford	48	Engine
R	18	Cheever	Arrows-Megatron	48	Engine
R	3	Palmer	Tyrrell-Cosworth	48	Clutch
R	8	De Cesaris	Brabham-BMW	39	Spun off
R	23	Campos	Minardi-Moderni	30	Gearbox
R	22	Tarquini	Osella-Alfa Romeo	26	Gearbox
R	24	Nannini	Minardi-Moderni	25	Engine
R	16	Capelli	March-Cosworth	18	Electrics
R	28	Berger	Ferrari	16	Turbo
R	2	Prost	McLaren-TAG	14	Alternator
R	26	Ghinzani	Ligier-Megatron	7	Handling

FASTEST LAP

Driver	
Fabi	1:29.246
Johansson	1:29.543
Mansell	1:30.711
Senna	1:30.851
Alboreto	1:31.054
De Cesaris	1:31.160
Prost	1:31.409
Patrese	1:31.564
Warwick	1:31.582
Boutsen	1:31.586
Nakajima	1:31.891
Cheever	1:32.262
Berger	1:32.929
Alliot	1:33.668
Nannini	1:34.036
Caffi	1:34.506
Brundle	1:34.573
Campos	1:34.709
Ghinzani	1:34.817
Danner	1:34.996
Streiff	1:35.406
Palmer	1:36.182
Capelli	1:37.839
Fabre	1:38.543
Tarquini	1:40.126

CHAMPIONSHIP POSITIONS

DRIVERS

1	Mansell	10
2	Prost	9
3	Johansson	7
4	Piquet	6
	Senna	6
6	Alboreto	4
7	Berger	3
8	Boutsen	2
	Brundle	2
10	Nakajima	1

CONSTRUCTORS

1	McLaren-TAG	16
	Williams-Honda	16
3	Ferrari	7
	Lotus-Honda	7
5	Benetton-Ford	2
	Zakspeed	2

JIM CLARK CUP

1	Streiff	15
2	Palmer	9
3	Fabre	8
4	Alliot	6

COLIN CHAPMAN CUP

1	Tyrrell-Cosworth	24
2	AGS-Cosworth	8
3	Lola-Cosworth	6

49

Belgium
ROUND THREE: May 17, 1987

DOING HIS USUAL THING

He realised that caution and patience were called for in the beginning. Oh, how right he was, his opposition taking care of themselves, firstly two at a time, then one by one.

Alain Prost did his usual race-day thing. Sixth on the grid after two days of chaotic weather for qualifying, he set fastest time in the warm-up, won another grand prix, moved back into the championship lead, approached the point of grand prix canonisation.

This second win of the season was his 27th, equalling Jackie Stewart's long-standing record for the most number of grand prix victories, but those who watched Prost have a quiet winning afternoon at Spa, not having to pass anybody, staying in the lead through his pit stop, were probably loath to concede that Prost's record-equalling feat was any less worthy.

Prost's opposition took care of itself this time, but the McLaren driver had to be there, make the finish to win. He made sure he would be, was wary at the start, miles away from the almost inevitable opening lap carnage and bumping at Spa that took out six cars before the red flag came out.

At the re-start he was just as circumspect, in fifth early and then in third as he rushed by the site of Ayrton Senna's Lotus and Nigel Mansell's Williams, comprehensively and controversially sandpitted. Shortly afterwards Prost was aware of Gerhard Berger's Ferrari belching clouds that rivalled the bringers of rain swirling threateningly above the circuit.

There was just Nelson Piquet and Michele Alboreto to worry about. In an instant Piquet crawled pitwards with the engine electronics having gone beserk and Alboreto slowly ground his way to the grass, a wheel bearing having given up.

That just left the clouds, which controlled their temper in deference to a demonstration run by the world champion.

Alain Prost admitted he was worried before the race. His worries were two fold; that the region's wild weather would hold, and that he would get through the first corner — the hairpin at La Source — in one piece. Otherwise, he felt he had everything under control.

"When I made it through La Source," he smiled, "I thought, OK, now I can win this race. It seemed like the rain would hold off, and everything was fine. Then I saw the red flags when the race was stopped, and realised that meant another start! Merde! That second time I was very careful to keep out of the way . . ."

So, too, he was. As the McLaren came down to the hairpin that time, two wheels were over the white line, in the dirt. It was not to happen again for the rest of the day.

Alain's victory was straightforward in the manner of Nigel Mansell's at Imola. This time there was no need to fight, even to overtake anyone. His opposition took care of itself, some of it in highly controversial style.

Practice had meant less than usual, thanks to the rain. Sunday as Michele Alboreto put it would bring "a lotteria". In the meantime, the elements in the region of the Ardennes where Spa is sculptured, were living up to their reputation for being startlingly capricious. Highly localised rain storms continue to

1.

2.

be a matter of day-to-day life here. Literally it could be dry at one corner, awash at the next. Such was indeed the case.

At 4.3 miles, the shortened, modern track is plenty long enough to suffer from the local climate. "It's amazing," Gerhard Berger said, "to have some corners wet, and others dry. And when it's like that, it's never exactly the same from one lap to the next."

The Austrian, second fastest for Benetton during qualifying the season before, set the best time on the opening day. It was a quite chaotic session. A heavy shower immediately before the start meant that everyone went out on wets, only to discover that most of the circuit — out of sight of the pits — was dry. In they all rushed for slicks, and by the time they had taken anew to the track it was wet everywhere. In they came for wets, etc, etc.

Then the rain abated again. There was even a slice of blue in the sky. The very brave went out again on slicks, and a 'line' began to emerge. It was, Berger admitted, a very narrow one, but enough to make dry tyres momentarily the thing to have. In the eye of the storm, the Ferrari skittered round in 2:06.2. At about the same time Nigel Mansell also broke into the sixes, but for anyone else the moment was gone. The 'line' was down for only three minutes, and then the heavens opened once more.

Spa in recent years had been blessed with untypical weather but few could recall a Spa weekend with quite so many showers. "It's six bloody degrees this morning," Derek Warwick moaned on Friday, and one of the motorhome drivers said be glad you weren't here a couple of days ago when they had arrived, the paddock was thinly coated in white, the temperature minus three . . .

3.

On Saturday morning Prost gloomily surveyed the sky. "I didn't try too hard yesterday, hoping it would be better today. But it looks like being the same."

After the untimed session, though, it did begin to cheer up, and as one o'clock approached the drivers got ready to scramble. By five past, it could be raining again. There had been no dry practice worth the name, so settings, gear ratios and so on were inspired guesswork to a large extent. The track was very busy very soon.

Mansell, fastest in the morning, emerged at once as the man to beat. And it was evident that conditions — cool air and track washed clean — were very fast indeed. Despite the ban on qualifying tyres and the advent of the four bar boost limit, Nigel was quickly below Nelson Piquet's 1986 pole position time of 1:54.3. His fourth flying lap was at 1:53.6, followed immediately by a 52.9.

After 25 mins of the session down came the inevitable shower, but this time it was brief. Mansell was able to go out again, recording a sensational 1:52.026. Then he came in, remaining in the car, belts tight and ready, watching the TV monitor, keeping an eye on the rest. Nelson Piquet went out again, but was having trouble selecting third gear, and could offer no threat.

Which was just as well for Nigel. Shortly before the end of the session it was discovered that a couple of bolts had sheared on the Williams's right-hand driveshaft. He would have been powerless to respond, but he had no need. Pole position was secure, and for the first time in the season it was a new record.

Nelson, still feeling a bit knocked about after his Imola shunt, made sure of second place and next up was Ayrton Senna and the 'active' Lotus-Honda. "The balance is not too bad," Ayrton said, "but the car doesn't feel as stable as I would like at a circuit as quick as this. It's been difficult to evaluate the suspension here, because the conditions have changed constantly". Senna — first in 1985, second in 1986 — likes Spa, and has always excelled in the rain. "Yes, I am quick in the wet, but that doesn't mean I like it," he said. "In the rain two years ago the

Renault engine was perfect here because the power came in so smoothly. The Honda has more power, but arrives more brutally . . ."

Berger and Alboreto, first and third for Ferrari on the opening day, were unable quite to sustain their pace in the dry, but they finished respectably, fourth and fifth. The rumours continued that Michele would quit the team at the end of the season, but at Spa he was content. "The handling is not so good on empty tanks, but otherwise the car is nice to drive

1: Streiff heads out in the Tyrrell for a practice thrown into chaos by quickly changing weather conditions, the bane of Spa.

2: Christian Danner avoided the initial carnage but had his own accident on lap nine.

3: Reviving memories of better times, Andrea de Cesaris was having one of his good days as the Brabham team continued to make progress with their more conventional car.

4: Beautiful one minute, dreadful the next. The capricious weather plays havoc during the qualifying sessions.

4.

here. And I think we will be even more competitive in the race."

Prost said the same, but then Prost always says that about the race. And means it. "Early in the session I set what was the second best time, and the balance wasn't quite right. We made some changes, but I went out again after the rain, and never had a completely dry lap. For Sunday I think we are OK."

And what of the fuel situation? In 1986 Mansell and Senna, first and second, finished with barely a cupful between them. "Well, we were looking good on fuel at Imola," Alain replied, "and we should be all right. But no one knows here, because no one's been able to do any consumption tests in the dry . . ."

The Benettons were expected to excel at this 'downforce' circuit, and indeed Rory Byrne's cars impressed with their stability through the fast corners, but Teo Fabi — not a man who relishes the wet — really came into the picture only in the final session. They finished up seventh and ninth, lower than expected, and a glance at the speed trap figures, taken at the top of the hill, pointed the finger at the Ford V6. Over the winter Cosworth undoubtedly found some more power (at some cost to the previously excellent throttle response), but there was some way to go.

It is a long haul up to Les Combes, and by the top of it Piquet's Williams-Honda was timed at 203.296 mph, with Mansell the only other man to better 200. BMW, TAG and Ferrari came in at 195 and above. Thierry Boutsen and Fabi were pegged at 189-190, slower than Zakspeed and Motori Moderni. You thought about that as you considered Thierry's impressive lap time.

Riccardo Patrese impressed by qualifying ninth in

the Brabham, and Stefan Johansson's McLaren also made the top 10. "Problems? None, really," Stefan said. "Except that bloody Danner ruined my best lap. Not looking in his mirrors, as usual. I had to change down before I got around him. In fact, I'm on my way to see him now . . ."

The Arrows were frustratingly close to the pace, not quite on it, but Warwick and Eddie Cheever both said their times did no real justice to the car. Thanks to the 'light switch' power delivery of the Megatron four-cylinder, it was not easy to drive in the rain. "Car's good," Derek said confidently on Friday, although he confessed to an anxious moment out of Eau Rouge in the wet: "I got into a 'tank slapper' which seemed to last a long time. I can do without too many of those . . ."

"We had to guess at ratios for the dry," commented Cheever, "and top was too low — I was on the limiter for quite a time." Despite that, the Arrows were beaten only by the Williams at the Les Combes trap.

At this, a driver's circuit, it was fine to see the name of Alessandro Nannini consistently in the top six or eight when the conditions were at their most treacherous. Through Eau Rouge — which makes call on most of the qualities a grand prix driver needs — Sandro was very fast, very smooth and controlled. And another who impressed in precisely the same fashion was Ivan Capelli, pole man in the normally-aspirated class.

Mansell was very relaxed on Saturday evening, as one might expect of a man fastest by 1.5 sec. But he summed it up for everyone when he anticipated race day. "Obviously I'd rather it be dry than wet. But one or the other will do. What we really don't want is mixed conditions . . ."

1.

2.

4.

On Sunday afternoon all the action for Mansell and the rest really came in the opening minute. At the start Mansell got away beautifully, tailed by Senna, Piquet, the Ferraris and Prost. Approaching the end of the first lap Nigel was already more than a second to the good. As he accelerated past the pits, though, a Ferrari was having what the Italians are pleased to call an *incidente* behind him. Berger was spinning, and those behind were darting into evasive action. The luckless Boutsen made contact, however, and the Benetton joined the Ferrari in what seemed to be retirement for the day.

Long after the field had gone through, Andrea de Cesaris appeared, right rear tyre missing, to trail into the pits. The Brabham had been clouted by Rene Arnoux's Ligier at La Source. The Frenchman, too, had parked.

Lap two seemed to take an awfully long time, and when Mansell's white car appeared it was crawling, an orderly file of colour and subdued revs behind it. The race had been stopped, and we began queasily to run through our lap charts, to see who was missing. There were no Tyrrells, no Philippe Alliot.

1: *The teams' fleet of motor homes assemble at the mountain circuit. It had been snowing on the first day when they rolled onto the track.*
2: *Prost and the other survivors of the first attempt at the race start return to the pits to try again.*
3: *Johansson chased by Boutsen and de Cesaris. The Swede would move up to make it a McLaren one-two.*
4: *Boutsen continues to show flair in his new team, helped by revisions to the Ford turbo. But a broken CV joint struck him down during the race, when a good result looked on for his home grand prix.*

3.

The absence of Boutsen and Arnoux was otherwise explained.

Out of Eau Rouge Philippe Streiff had crashed massively, and Jonathan Palmer was also involved. Alliot, it seemed had stopped at the scene to see what he could do to help. But quickly it was confirmed from the scene that all were safe.

Palmer revealed the extent of this deliverance. "Caffi was ahead of me, and Philippe in front of him. At that point you're at the brow of the hill, and you can't see immediatley beyond you. I got to the brow and was confronted by somebody having an enormous accident. I sort of recognised it as Streiff's car, broadside across the track, about a quarter of the way from the barrier on the right.

"I started to pull left," Jonathan went on, "and Philippe's car was moving into my path. It was just fragmenting — wheels, engine, gearbox — and a huge dust cloud enveloped everything. I just drove into nothing. Caffi had gone through just as Streiff hit, I suppose.

"I kept aiming left, and couldn't avoid what turned out to be the Tyrrell tub, without engine and with Streiff strapped into it. The right hand front corner of my car came off at once, and I slid on for another 50 yards before stopping. As it did, I moved my legs around, and was very relieved to find everything was still intact . . . As for Phillippe, I was sure he had to be in a bad way, but before I got to him he'd climbed out!"

It was with no little surprise that we saw the spare Tyrrell coming to join the grid for the 'new' race. and with astonishment that the man aboard was Streiff! An unusual breed of man, your grand prix driver. On the grid, too, were spare cars for Berger, Boutsen and Arnoux and 40 mins after the original start, they were flagged away for another formation lap.

Once more a fracas at La Source was avoided, but this time it was the yellow of Senna's Lotus in front, then Mansell, Piquet, Alboreto, Prost Berger and Boutsen.

Ayrton and Nigel were clear of the rest — which was just as well, for there could otherwise have been another multiple accident. As the Lotus went down to the right-hander on the approach to Blanchimont, the Williams flicked left. Into the corner the cars were side by side, and then Mansell nosed slightly ahead. Halfway through the turn the cars touched, and in perfect unison they spun off into the gravel. There the Lotus remained for the duration, bogged down, but Mansell was able to extricate the Williams, rejoining the race a minute and a half adrift of the new leader, Piquet.

"I couldn't believe what he was trying to do — overtake on the outside at a place like that," Senna said. "When I saw what he was doing, I tried to get out of the way, brake as much as possible, but you can only do so much in a situation like that. I was committed to the corner — there was no way I could stop."

Mansell's interpretation, as you might expect, was rather different: "I had no intention of trying to pass him there — especially on the first lap. I was close behind him, and I couldn't believe how early he braked for the corner. I flicked out from behind, and was past him in an instant. I thought I'd get the corner, but he just didn't give way and slid into me . . ."

Unplanned or not, Nigel's move was undeniably an attempted passing manoeuvre, and one which didn't come off. Senna was forced into a very tight line, right on the inside kerbing, and contact was almost inevitable.

Call it 'a motor racing accident', put it into the category of 'these things happen'. What happened later, when Mansell retired from the race with underbody damage, legacy of the incident on the first lap, comes into a different category altogether. Nigel went down to the Lotus pit, and at first Ayrton thought he had come to apologise. Not so. Mansell gave vent to his feelings, and verbal abuse showed signs of giving way to physical. He was, eyewitnesses reported, restrained by members of his own team. Senna, it should be said, behaved with admirable calm and maturity.

Out on the circuit, in the meantime, Prost was quietly going about the business of winning the Belgian Grand Prix, of moving on to his 27th victory,

perhaps a step closer to his third world championship. Standing in his way at this point were Messrs Piquet and Alboreto.

"Mansell and Senna I knew about, of course," he said. "And then on the second lap Berger went . . ." So, too, he did, the Ferrari blowing up hugely on the lonely climb towards the pits. "Then, Alain continued, "I had only Piquet and Alboreto to worry me — although the Benettons were not far behind. Michele was weaving a bit when I tried to pass him once or twice, and Nelson began to get away. But I wasn't

1.

going to risk anything so early in the race. There was plenty of time."

By lap nine Prost was crowding the Ferrari which had closed to within a second and a half of Piquet. and on lap 10 the No. 1 McLaren came through alone. A turbo sensor pipe had become disconnected on the Williams-Honda, and the electronics had gone haywire. Nelson made it to the pits, however, whereas Michele was stopped at the trackside with rear wheel bearing failure. Prost had started sixth, and all those preceding him were now out.

"Nothing to do after that, except hope that the rain would keep away. The sky was always grey." Alain put in a handful of quick laps to draw clear of Fabi, and the issue of the day looked settled. Teo, in fact, would not keep second place for long. In the morning warm-up Johannson's time had been beaten only by Prost. And now Stefan was moving up to make it a McLaren 1-2.

By lap 17 it was just so, and as Fabi lost second place, so team-mate Boutsen came in to retire from fourth. A lap later Prost was in for tyres, rejoining without losing first place, immediately in front of Johansson, who pitted himself on lap 20. Next time round it was Fabi's turn.

The fourth name on the lap charts, though, was a surprise. Patrese's Brabham had gone early, but de Cesaris's sister car was running strongly, Andrea reviving memories of this race four years before, when he led convincingly in an Alfa for a long way. Uniquely among the leading runners, he would go the distance without a tyre stop.

Behind him Cheever's Arrows held fifth, followed by Piercarlo Ghinzani, the impressive Satoru Nakajima and Arnoux. Rene was not having a happy time: "I didn't really look at the fuel read-out for the

first 15 laps or so," he said, "and when I did I realised I had to slow down or run out before the finish. I could see a lot of people were out and I thought I might get a finish in the points, so I turned the boost down to minimum and took it easy. Unfortunately, the tyres and brakes got too cold like that, and the car became very difficult to drive . . ."

Lap 27: Fabi sounding sick. An exhaust pipe had broken, and Teo quickly fell into the clutches of de Cesaris. For a while he was able to keep going, but eventually the oil pressure warning light glowed

2.

bright in front of him, and the Italian had to pull off.

The single truly anxious moment in Prost's Belgian Grand Prix came on lap 37. Alliot, who had spiritedly split the Ligiers with his normally-aspirated Lola, had a spin just as the world champion arrived. Happily, contact was avoided, and Alain continued on his metronome way.

Alliot actually spun twice near race end before taking the Clark Cup for the event. Alliot's Lola and Streiff's Tyrrell were in control of this part of the race, although the spare Tyrrell still suffered from the team's misfire problem and as a result, the car popped and banged to the finish. For a time, Ivan Capelli's March took command, the fastest nor-

mally-aspirated contender, in qualifying, but then the engine began to fail, leaving Alliot to play with the Ligiers until his gyrations.

So the McLaren demonstration came to a close. Nakajima just failed to separate Cheever from fourth place at the line, and de Cesaris — not realising that they had already taken the flag — leaped from his Brabham as it ground to a stop within sight of the line, out of fuel. Absolutely exhausted, he needed a lot of persuading that third place was in the bag, that he had completed 42 laps before Cheever.

1: *A hard working Alboreto in third place after Mansell and Senna went spinning off. He knew Prost was closing quickly.*
2: *Arnoux's Ligier and Nakajima's Lotus sandwich the noseless Zakspeed of Brundle, struggling on. Arnoux had to turn the boost down to conserve fuel and consequently was nabbed by the Japanese.*
3: *De Cesaris on a rare visit to the podium and a pat on the back for Stefan for setting up a McLaren one-two.*

BELGIAN GRAND PRIX

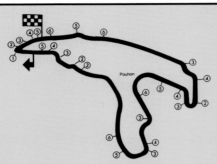

Round 3: May 17, 1987
Circuit: Spa Francorchamps

Race data:	43 laps of 4.312 mile (6.94 km) circuit
Weather:	Dry, overcast
Fastest lap:	Prost, McLaren MP4/3, 1:57.153, 132.513mph
Existing record:	Prost, McLaren MP4/2C, 1:59.282, 130.147mph

ENTRIES

No	Driver (Nat)	Car/Chassis	Engine
1	Alain Prost (F)	McLaren MP4/3-3*	TAG V6 Turbo
1T	Alain Prost (F)	McLaren MP4/3-1	TAG V6 Turbo
2	Stefan Johansson (S)	McLaren MP4/3-2	TAG V6 Turbo
3	Jonathan Palmer (GB)	Tyrrell DG/016-2	Ford Cosworth V8
4	Philippe Streiff (F)	Tyrrell DG/016-1	Ford Cosworth V8
4T	Philippe Streiff (F)	Tyrrell DG/016-3*	Ford Cosworth V8
5	Nigel Mansell (GB)	Williams FW11 B/3*	Honda V6 Turbo
5T	Nigel Mansell (GB)	Williams FW11 B/1	Honda V6 Turbo
6	Nelson Piquet (BR)	Williams FW11 B/4	Honda V6 Turbo
7	Riccardo Patrese (I)	Brabham BT56/3	BMW S4 Turbo
8	Andrea de Cesaris (I)	Brabham BT56/2	BMW S4 Turbo
9	Martin Brundle (GB)	Zakspeed 871/1	Zakspeed S4 Turbo
10	Christian Danner (D)	Zakspeed 871/2	Zakspeed S4 Turbo
11	Satoru Nakajima (J)	Lotus 99T/1	Honda V6 Turbo
12	Ayrton Senna (BR)	Lotus 99T/4*	Honda V6 Turbo
12T	Ayrton Senna (BR)	Lotus 99T/2	Honda V6 Turbo
14	Pascal Fabre (F)	AGS JH22/02-032	Ford Cosworth V8
16	Ivan Capelli (I)	March RT 871/01*	Ford Cosworth V8
16T	Ivan Capelli (I)	March RT 879/01	Ford Cosworth V8
17	Derek Warwick (GB)	Arrows A10/1	Megatron S4 Turbo
18	Eddie Cheever (USA)	Arrows A10/2	Megatron S4 Turbo
19	Teo Fabi (I)	Benetton B187-04	Ford V6 Turbo
20	Thierry Boutsen (B)	Benetton B187-03	Ford V6 Turbo
20T	Thierry Boutsen (B)	Benetton B187-05*	Ford V6 Turbo
21	Alex Caffi (I)	Osella FA1H/01/87	Alfa Romeo V8 Turbo
23	Adrian Campos (E)	Minardi M186-05	Moderni V6 Turbo
24	Alessandro Nannini (I)	Minardi M186-03	Moderni V6 Turbo
25	Rene Arnoux (F)	Ligier JS29B/1	Megatron S4 Turbo
25T	Rene Arnoux (F)	Ligier JS29B/3*	Megatron S4 Turbo
26	Piercarlo Ghinzani (I)	Ligier JS29B/2	Megatron S4 Turbo
27	Michele Alboreto (I)	Ferrari F187-096	Ferrari V6 Turbo
28	Gerhard Berger (A)	Ferrari F187-097	Ferrari V6 Turbo
28T	Gerhard Berger (A)	Ferrari F187-095*	Ferrari V6 Turbo
30	Philippe Alliot (F)	Lola LC87/01	Ford Cosworth V8

* Race car

QUALIFYING

FRIDAY: Wet, cold		SATURDAY: Dry then wet	
Driver		Driver	
Berger	2:06.216	Mansell	1:52.026
Mansell	2:06.965	Piquet	1:53.416
Alboreto	2:07.459	Senna	1:53.426
Piquet	2:08.143	Berger	1:53.451
Senna	2:08.450	Alboreto	1:53.511
Boutsen	2:08.752	Prost	1:54.186
Nannini	2:09.650	Boutsen	1:54.300
Warwick	2:10.946	Patrese	1:55.064
Prost	2:11.203	Fabi	1:55.339
Nakajima	2:11.441	Johansson	1:55.781
Johansson	2:12.063	Cheever	1:55.899
Fabi	2:12.358	Warwick	1:56.359
Patrese	2:12.914	De Cesaris	1:57.101
Alliot	2:13.002	Nannini	1:58.132
Capelli	2:13.355	Nakajima	1:58.649
De Cesaris	2:13.871	Arnoux	1:59.117
Brundle	2:14.432	Ghinzani	1:59.291
Palmer	2:14.931	Brundle	2:00.433
Campos	2:14.945	Campos	2:00.763
Arnoux	2:15.012	Danner	2:01.072
Cheever	2:15.321	Capelli	2:02.036
Ghinzani	2:15.339	Alliot	2:02.347
Caffi	2:16.268	Streiff	2:03.098
Streiff	2:18.900	Palmer	2:04.677
Danner	2:20.610	Fabre	2:07.361
Fabre	2:26.498	Caffi	2:12.086

STARTING GRID

No	Driver	Time
5	Mansell	1:52.026
6	Piquet	1:53.416
12	Senna	1:53.426
28	Berger	1:53.451
27	Alboreto	1:53.511
1	Prost	1:54.186
20	Boutsen	1:54.300
7	Patrese	1:55.064
19	Fabi	1:55.339
2	Johansson	1:55.781
18	Cheever	1:55.899
17	Warwick	1:56.359
8	De Cesaris	1:57.101
24	Nannini	1:58.132
11	Nakajima	1:58.649
25	Arnoux	1:59.117
26	Ghinzani	1:59.291
9	Brundle	2:00.433
23	Campos	2:00.763
10	Danner	2:01.072
16	Capelli	2:02.036
30	Alliot	2:02.347
4	Streiff	2:03.098
3	Palmer	2:04.677
14	Fabre	2:07.361
21	Caffi	2:12.086

RESULTS

Pos	No	Driver	Car	Laps	Time/Retirement
1	1	Prost	McLaren-TAG	43	1-27:03.217
2	2	Johansson	McLaren-TAG	43	1-27:27.981
3	8	De Cesaris	Brabham-BMW	42	
4	18	Cheever	Arrows-Megatron	42	
5	11	Nakajima	Lotus-Honda	42	
6	25	Arnoux	Ligier-Megatron	41	
7	26	Ghinzani	Ligier-Megatron	40	
8	30	Alliot	LC-Cosworth	40	
9	4	Streiff	Tyrrell-Cosworth	39	
10	14	Fabre	AGS-Cosworth	38	
R	19	Fabi	Benetton-Ford	32	Engine
R	9	Brundle	Zakspeed	19	Engine
R	20	Boutsen	Benetton-Ford	18	CV Joint
R	5	Mansell	Williams-Honda	17	Underbody damage
R	16	Capelli	March-Cosworth	14	Engine
R	6	Piquet	Williams-Honda	11	Turbo
R	21	Caffi	Osella-Alfa Romeo	11	Gearbox
R	27	Alboreto	Ferrari	9	Gearbox
R	10	Danner	Zakspeed	9	Accident
R	17	Warwick	Arrows-Megatron	8	Water hose
R	7	Patrese	Brabham-BMW	5	Clutch
R	28	Berger	Ferrari	2	Engine
R	24	Nannini	Minardi-Moderni	1	Turbo
R	12	Senna	Lotus-Honda	0	Accident
NS	23	Campos	Minardi-Moderni	—	Accident
NS	3	Palmer	Tyrrell-Cosworth	—	Accident

FASTEST LAP

Driver	
Prost	1:57.153
Johansson	1:59.015
Piquet	1:59.572
Mansell	1:59.651
Fabi	1:59.927
Alboreto	2:00.017
De Cesaris	2:00.154
Boutsen	2:01.020
Nakajima	2:02.076
Cheever	2:03.091
Warwick	2:03.843
Brundle	2:04.227
Arnoux	2:04.471
Ghinzani	2:04.691
Patrese	2:05.206
Danner	2:05.247
Alliot	2:05.456
Caffi	2:05.825
Capelli	2:06.011
Berger	2:09.474
Streiff	2:09.872
Fabre	2:09.977
Nannini	2:17.571
Senna	

CHAMPIONSHIP POSITIONS

DRIVERS			CONSTRUCTORS	
1	Prost	18	1 McLaren-TAG	31
2	Johansson	13	2 Williams-Honda	16
3	Mansell	10	3 Lotus-Honda	9
4	Piquet	6	4 Ferrari	7
	Senna	6	5 Brabham-BMW	4
6	Alboreto	4	6 Arrows-Megatron	3
	De Cesaris	4	7 Benetton-Ford	2
8	Berger	3		Zakspeed	2
	Cheever	3	9 Ligier-Megatron	1
	Nakajima	3		
11	Boutsen	2		
	Brundle	2		
13	Arnoux	1		

JIM CLARK CUP		COLIN CHAPMAN CUP	
1 Streiff	21	1 Tyrrell-Cosworth	30
2 Alliot	15	2 Lola-Cosworth	15
3 Fabre	12	3 AGS-Cosworth	12
4 Palmer	9		

Monaco

ROUND FOUR: May 31, 1987

TECHNOLOGY CATCHES UP

The Englishman and the Brazilian discussed their differences before the event and buried the hatchet. On the track, the Englishman went for it and retired, the Brazilian was cautious and won.

Ayrton Senna had dropped his cool, professional mask on the victory podium. He was genuinely and boyishly joyful at having won his first Monaco Grand Prix, his first win for almost 12 months, the first for a car with computerised 'active' suspension.

Champagne, from the victor's violently emptied magnum spotted the glasses of Lotus chief Peter Warr, more of it soaked his yellow shirt. It must have been uncomfortable, but he didn't show it, probably didn't even notice it. He wouldn't stop talking over the radio in the closing stages, Warr said of his driver. 'We're going to win it! We're going to do it!' That was the war cry squealed down the radio link to the Lotus pit.

No-one, even the royal family, even Princess Caroline, escaped Ayrton Senna's celebratory shower. This was OK though, as it had been a popular victory. A recently arrived resident of the tax haven of Monaco, the young Brazilian was more popular here than almost anywhere except his homeland.

When he inherited the lead from the boostless Williams-Honda of Nigel Mansell on lap 29, there had been deafening cheers. When he was arrested in the small hours of Monday, for not wearing a helmet on arriving on the back of a friend's motorcycle at a local nightspot, the gendarmes released him apologetically. He had been very naughty but then they realised who he was: winner of the Monaco Grand Prix and immortalised by the historic achievement.

For a time Nigel Mansell looked a winner at the famous, infamous street circuit, wanting to atone for the unbecoming confrontation with Senna at Spa. He was pushing early to establish a lead, Senna claimed, preferring to sit back in a clear second and set his own pace. Behind him Nelson Piquet was having his usual day off at Monaco, intimidated by the barriers, while Alain Prost struggled with a V5 engine that he expected to stop at anytime.

Nigel Mansell was probably by now in the air, making his sorrowful way back to the Isle of Man. He had set the pace throughout qualifying, and had consummately led the first third of the race, but an exhaust primary had broken, robbing the Honda V6 of boost. Shaking his head, he had walked away, then quickly left the circuit for the airport. The lack of disappointment from the thousands of Brits in the crowd suggested that the 'fisticuffs' with Ayrton Senna at Spa had registered.

Especially galling for Nigel must have been the thought that victory had been left in Ayrton's lap. There had always seemed but three possible winners of this race: Mansell, because he is brilliant at street circuits, and because the Williams-Honda was in a class of its own here; Senna, because he shadowed and stalked Nigel through the qualifying days; and Alain Prost, because he is the best racing driver in the world, and had won here the previous three years. Nelson Piquet came next on this list — but only if the others had strife. Nelson is not at his best when the barriers are high and close, and admits it. He qualified third in a car which should have been on the front row.

There was an air of tension draping the Monaco weekend. Time was when this was considered one of the safest grands prix - after all, it was too *slow* for anyone to hurt themselves seriously. But all that changed 20 years before when Lorenzo Bandini's horrific death made headlines around the world.

The 950-horsepower Formula One car of 1987 belongs in the streets like diving boots in Swan Lake.

However, we live in a commercial world, so the anachronism lives on through deals over TV rights and the demands of sponsors. Many people in F1 rejoice — in a whisper — when there is any chance that the race might not go on. It survives though, money, perhaps as much as $US100 mill greasing the wheels. But progress is gradually catching up at Monaco and that has its own implications for a race setting that trades so heavily on tradition and old world charm.

Monte Carlo is changing. The lovely old station has been swept away, its site given over to an ugly hotel. But that was only the start of it, because the Principality has been gripped by demolition fever. Every square inch, it appears, must be made cost-

Previous page: *A crowded street scene in Monaco. The usual 20 starters became 26, then 24 for the race and the leading lights were not happy.*

Left: *Mansell looked the runaway winner after dominating from the first day of practice. Those behind could do nothing but drive for the finish.*

Below left: *Detesting the intimidating layout of Monaco, Piquet continues his quiet Sunday drive, set for third early, getting second finally.*

Below: *With the active suspension coping better on the slow Monaco layout, Senna was content to stay well back and wait.*

1.

2.

3.

effective, and to that end every outward symbol of gentler, more gracious times past, tremblingly awaits the bulldozer.

Since 1986 the developers have concentrated on Casino Square, which looked more like Beirut than the jewel of the Cote d'Azur. The Cafe de Paris was for 1987's event now a bare shell, the gardens above scooped out to make way for an underground car park. When the work is done, they say, all will be replaced exactly as it was. Time will tell.

The roads which make up the circuit, though, are as before, and they still constitute the ultimate test of a grand prix driver's precision and flair. Anyone who gets through three days here without clouting a guardrail had reason to feel pride — especially if he does it at the furious pace set by Nigel Mansell during qualifying.

He has always been in his element at Monte Carlo. As a Formula One novice, six years before, he stunned everyone by qualifying third. Three times since then he had been second fastest; for 1987 he took the pole.

More than that, too. When the track opened, at 10am on Thursday, the No. 5 Williams-Honda was the first car out, and within 10 minutes was going quickly enough to command attention. The pattern of qualifying began to take shape right there: Nigel looked the man to beat, and it stayed that way.

Over the two practice days he put in an incredible number of laps — 41 on Saturday morning alone. Before the last session he was sitting in the pit behind a stack of tyres, holding an oxygen mask to his face. "I'm a bit knackered after this morning,' he smiled, "and I've used this before here. It clears your head, and for about an hour or so improves your vision."

In the final session — only 60 minutes — Mansell managed another 25 laps. The pattern of Monaco qualifying had changed distinctly with the disappearance of Q-tyres: before drivers had to pray for a single clear lap while the tyres were working, where now you could begin a hot lap and afford to abandon it if someone got in your way.

It was less of a lottery, in other words: with two sets of race tyres available, there were many more laps to play with. Conversely, of course, the track was generally much more crowded. No longer were there periods of relative silence in the final session. It was a matter of staying out, getting in a quick lap, cruising to cool the tyres, trying for another, backing off, going for it.

On Thursday, Mansell got down to 1:24.514, three-quarters of a second faster than Senna's Lotus, with Prost third and Piquet fourth. This quartet detached itself from the rest throughout, with Nigel always playing the lead. "Hmmm, Mansell and Senna together on the front row," Piquet said with malicious glee. "I like that . . ."

But the Spa contretemps appeared to be behind them. After the drivers' meeting on Thursday, Nigel and Ayrton had a chat: neither had changed his stance over the cause of the accident in Belgium, but they had at least agreed to disagree, to start over once more. Which was a relief to Prost: "You can't afford to have grudges in this business. They're unhealthy for the sport — and dangerous for everyone, not just the drivers directly involved."

Even so, people wondered, how busy was it going to be at Ste Devote on the first lap? "It's so easy to bang wheels anyway at this place," an uninvolved team manager said. "They're bound to be aware that the whole world is watching them. You'll probably find they'll be walking on eggs."

In qualifying, it was plain that neither man had suffered any loss of confidence. After Thursday, Mansell had predicted that times on Saturday would be *much* quicker — maybe as much as two or three seconds. "I think that might have been a bit optimistic," he said after the morning session. "This place always picks up a lot of speed on the second day, but it's not going to be as much as I thought."

He wasn't far out. Fifteen minutes into the last session, he was down to 1:23.6, and Senna immediately threatened with a 23.7. There was a feeling, though, that Nigel faced no real threat, that whatever time anyone else set, he would be able to respond. With 20 minutes to go, he went round in 1:23.09, and that settled it. More to the point, he followed up with two later laps in the 23s; Senna broke the 24 barrier only once in the entire season.

Twelve months before Mansell looked set for the pole, only for Prost unobtrusively to steal it in the closing minutes. On Thursday, the world champion had found the McLaren's balance not quite *au point*, and also had niggling problems with gear selection and a sticking throttle. But even so he had been third fastest, and one always felt that Alain constituted Nigel's chief opposition. On Saturday morning he was fastest.

That lap, though, was to stand as his best of the two days. In the final session his challenge never materialised. "I did 26 laps," he said, "and not one

4.

was clear. It happens I've been lucky with clear laps in previous years." And any hope of a last-minute improvement evaporated when an electrical problem brought the McLaren to a silent halt in Casino Square. Still, he was fourth on the grid — and he had previously won at Monte Carlo with a lower start position than that. Mansell, two seconds ahead, had no doubts about his main *race* opposition: "Alain," he said without hesitation. "It's the same anywhere, isn't it?"

The Frenchman shared row two with Piquet. Around the streets of Monte Carlo, Nelson simply wasn't in the same class as his Williams team-mate, if appreciably up on the somnolent performance he turned in for 1986. Attitude played a major part. Nigel adores driving at Monaco, Nelson detests it and in the final session any of three of Mansell's laps would have given him pole position. Eight times he bettered 1:25, which Piquet managed only once. At the end there was a second and three-quarters between them, and Nigel probably made up half of that in the swimming pool area alone. This is a scary spot, and Mansell's commitment was simply awesome. In this department only Eddie Cheever came close.

Eddie did a brilliant job for Arrows. The on-or-off power characteristics of the Megatron four-cylinder made it less than ideal for this kind of circuit, yet the American worked his car onto row three, alongside the first of the Ferraris, driven by the courageous Michele Alboreto.

The most remarkable aspect of Michele's performance in qualifying, in fact, was that within half an hour of his terrifying shunt on Thursday he was back out in the spare — and actually improved on his previous best!

Briefly on Thursday there had been dense black smoke towards the top of the hill, and the hazard lights were flashing. The session had been stopped.

What had happened was this: Christian Danner had come out of his pit, set off up the hill. Alboreto was on a hot lap. The Zakspeed was over on the right, so the Ferrari went left — and Michele almost made it through the gap. But his right rear wheel went over Danner's front left, and at perhaps 165mph, the red car was off the deck and into a terrifying sequence of bounces and clouts against the barriers. Bits of Ferrari were strewn over 200 yards.

Alboreto was extraordinarily fortunate. The car could have flipped, but didn't; could have gone over the barrier, but didn't. The impact had torn the gearbox from the engine, and the 'pedal box' was gone. The oil fire was fierce, but brief. Michele stepped out without a scratch, immediately going over to Danner to make his feelings clear. Christian, too, was quite unhurt.

Back in the pits, the German was remarkably phlegmatic about it all: "I was just going up the hill, straight out of the pits, and Alboreto ran into the back of me — wallop! I'm awfully sorry for the guy, but he ought to have used his brakes. I couldn't just vanish, you know. Michele took off, came down again, and there was a huge ball of flame. He's obviously furious, but so am I, quite honestly."

Down in the Ferrari pit, Alboreto's face was a mask of rage. He had had a massive fright: "I think Danner just didn't see me — I was nearly past him when he turned into me. I was up in the air . . . pieces came down over 200 metres . . . then I stopped in the barrier before Casino Square . . ."

"He says the car's absolutely finished," John

Barnard said. "This really is a bloody stupid race, isn't it? Scary."

Others felt the same way. Ever since FISA announced that there would be 26 starters at Monte Carlo, rather than usual 20, Alain Prost and others had been loud in their condemnation, bitter that such a decision had been taken without a word of consultation with the drivers.

Many reasons for the change were put forward, among them that grand prix racing was now a two class formula, and that allowing only the fastest 20 to start would be unfair to the normally-aspirated brigade, three of whom qualified in the top 20, anyway!

A cynic's interpretation might be that here was an instance of sponsor power. Commercially, this race is more important than any other in Formula One, and if your driver doesn't qualify for it, your name and logo are absent from the magic screen.

Perhaps the organisers to some extent took on board the drivers' feelings, and decided to pare down the 26. Why else would they have announced,

1: Can I beat your record, please Jackie? Prost and Stewart, 27 wins apiece, discuss the possibilities of a new record.

2: Berger's mangled Ferrari is hoisted away from the swimming pool after a big accident on Thursday. The Italian team were running out of Ferraris quickly by then as Alboreto had written his off earlier in the session in an incident with Danner.

3: Reflections on Monaco. The fireman on station was a sober reminder that modern F1 cars had outgrown the famous street circuit.

4: The expanded entry ensured the under three litre cars had their chance to peg back the turbos. That's what Capelli did, getting his March into the points, just behind the fellow 'class' car of Palmer.

Below: With Thursday's big accident out of his mind, Alboreto had a trouble-free event to produce his second third place in four races.

Bottom: Berger on the way to more points, although a lap behind team-mate Alboreto. He was not showing up his senior team-mate as some had expected.

Right: Jonathan Palmer drove hard all the way, without a tyre stop, ending up with an amazing sixth place, just two laps in arrears of Senna.

a few hours after the accident, that Danner was to be excluded from the rest of the meeting for ignoring the blue flag? In light of previous events involving far more experienced drivers, this seemed draconian. Absurd, even. There was, after all, considerable doubt that Christian was to blame.

Right behind Alboreto at Ste Devote, the previous corner, was Senna — who backed off. "I could see Danner, and it was one of those situations where you had to decide whether or not it was worth taking a chance. I decided not, but Michele went for the gap. I feel sorry for Danner."

When he had calmed down, so, too, did Alboreto. "I regret his disqualification, I must say. Incidents like this are inevitable occasionally, but this one was very serious — exactly the same as the one which killed Gilles Villeneuve. It's crazy to have 26 cars at this circuit. If there should be a big accident on Sunday, that decision may be seen as a big mistake . . ."

That afternoon was a thoroughly torrid one for Ferrari: later in the session Gerhard Berger seriously damaged his car in an accident by the swimming pool. By Saturday afternoon, though, both red cars were in the top eight, as could have been reasonably expected.

Two Williams, two McLarens, two Ferraris, one Lotus — and the maverick Arrows. They were the pace in qualifying, and it was difficult to see even a possible winner beyond them. Peter Collins of Benetton had predicted that Monaco would be his team's worse race of the season, and practice seemed to prove him right. The Ford V6 had gained horsepower, but there was a substantial trade-off in

throttle response, and that — together with an insoluble understeer problem at Monte Carlo — made life very hard for Thierry Boutsen (ninth) and Teo Fabi (12th).

Riccardo Patrese, whose Formula One career got started at this race 10 years before, should have qualified higher than 10th — and would have done had he not clouted a barrier in the last session. And Derek Warwick's 11th place, too, was perhaps artificially low. He spent the last half-hour making his way back to the pits, having parked the Arrows, engine dead, at Mirabeau.

What else was of note? Well, Sandro Nannini impressed as ever, and so did Jonathan Palmer — 15th overall, and a clear second ahead in the normally-aspirated class! Alex Caffi did a terrific job in the tatty Osella. And four men — Andrea de Cesaris, Rene Arnoux, Philippe Streiff and Pascale Fabre — had cause to rejoice at the enlarged size of the field. In fact, 24 cars — not the original 26 — would start, Danner being excluded and Adrian Campos declared medically unfit after suffering concussion in a shunt at Casino Square on Saturday morning and fainting on the walk back to the pits.

So at 3.30 on Sunday afternoon the 24 starters duly presented themselves on the grid. And there was no problem at Ste Devote because all the front runners got away perfectly, and filed into the corner in orderly fashion. Mansell led, followed by Senna, Piquet, Alboreto, Prost and Cheever. The only man to suffer in the notorious funnel was Satoru Nakajima in his first Monaco GP, whose Lotus was cheekily

pincered into an airborne command by Ivan Capelli and Philippe Alliot.

At the Loews hairpin, though; a couple more cars made contact. and to Guy Ligier's intense distress, they were driven by Piercarlo Ghinzani and Arnoux. "I took a wide line into the corner," Piercarlo said, "and Rene thought I was letting him through. I wasn't . . ." Both blue cars pitted for attention at the end of lap one, thereafter running reliably, if not very quickly, through to the finish.

Mansell put a lot into those early laps, establishing himself in a very firm lead. "He was pushing," Senna said, using his favourite English word, "and I didn't really try to stay with him. From the start, I tried to find a pace, a rhythm, I could keep up for the whole race."

He was safe enough. Piquet was evidently in no mood to go racing seriously, and was falling away in third place. And behind Nelson was the weaving Ferrari of Alboreto, very obviously holding Prost back. It was a surprise, nevertheless, that Alain was not exerting more pressure. There had to be a reason, and there was.

"I think I lost a cylinder very early in the race," he said. "All the way through I could smell oil burning. The engine just had no power at all, and I didn't expect my race to last very long. It was frustrating because I was much quicker than Michele through the corners, but there is only one place to pass — at the end of the pit straight — and he left me behind down there. I was never close enough to outbrake him into Ste Devote."

After 10 laps Mansell was eight seconds up on

Senna, and the rest nowhere. You wondered why the second Williams-Honda was so steadily dropping away, and you realised the extent of Prost's difficulties when Cheever's Arrows began to close on the McLaren. Behind Eddie was the second Ferrari of Berger, Warwick and Patrese. After a considerable gap there was Fabi in the surviving Benetton-Ford — Boutsen's car having broken a driveshaft after only six laps — and starting seriously to embarrass Teo was young Alex Caffi, who makes an Osella move as it has never done before.

Stefan Johansson meanwhile was having a wretched time. From seventh on the grid, he was down in 12th, and struggling. "It was a very peculiar problem, outside my experience. Whenever my revs rose quickly — like in a low gear, or going over a bump — the engine just cut out completely. Dead. I found that by switching the ignition on and off, it would start to run again. And that was my race! It was like that the whole way, until finally it blew altogether."

Emphatically, this was not a McLaren day. No, this looked like a Williams day. Mansell seemed to have the hammer down, although later he said it had been easy, that he hadn't been pushing. On lap 20 there was an anxious moment when he lapped, and very nearly touched, the unhelpful Arnoux, but otherwise he was untroubled. Prost, the one man he had feared, was nearly half a minute back, still penned in by Alboreto.

After 28 laps he was 11 secs ahead, but on the 29th Senna came through only six adrift. Mansell was slowing, and, yes, Senna was through into the lead. The Lotus-Honda computer-controlled suspension and all, was in front, and if it kept going it was going to win, no question.

Looming into the picture now were the tyre stops. Prost finally got to see something other than a Ferrari's tail when Alboreto came in on lap 34. Alain himself stopped next time round, and the McLaren mechanics did him excellent service, getting him out again in seven seconds, and enabled him to rejoin in fourth, well ahead of Michele, who had dropped to sixth.

Nothing else was affected by the stops, however. Piquet was in after 39 laps, and kept his leisurely second place. Three laps later it was Senna's turn, but he was still 25 secs to the good when he went back out.

Attention at this point was focused on Cheever, yet to change. In his mirrors Eddie saw the red and white of No. 1. It isn't often that an Arrows driver gets to lead the world champion's McLaren, and he was determined to savour the moment, stretch it out as long as possible. With his V5 engine hampering him, Alain could not get by, and Eddie was on a high.

His pit really thought he ought to be stopping, and they held out the boards to him. At first these were relatively discreet, suggesting he might come in. After five laps, it was 'Eddie — tyres'. Prost got him at Mirabeau, in any case, so there was nothing more to be lost.

At this point, though, there seemed every chance of at least one Arrows in the points, for Warwick had been within close range of Cheever all the way. Twenty laps from the end, though, Derek pulled off at the exit of Casino Square, gearbox selector finger broken. When the race has been satisfying, though, Warwick is never down afterwards, whatever the result: "The car was terrific today — I could pull in the Ferraris at will, and thought I was in for a good finish."

A lap later Cheever, too, was out. "I'd been overheating for a while," he said, "and it seems like a head gasket went. Still, it was a nice race for me, good fun. I could run with Alboreto and Prost, no problem."

At this point, he knew nothing of Prost's engine problem, yet Arrows were without a doubt the most improved team of the season.

For the late stages of a Monaco Grand Prix, there were a lot of cars still running, and there was little sign of any important place change. For a time Prost had been closing on Piquet's second place, but Alain really didn't like the sounds coming from behind him, turned the boost down to minimum, cut his revs and hoped to make the finish. "Third place was looking pretty good to me — I couldn't believe the way the engine was still running. Every lap I thought would be my last . . ."

1.

2.

His 75th was his last. Just three laps from the flag. As the McLaren came down towards Tabac, there was a wisp of blue smoke, then a cloud. "The oil had burned away, you see," Prost said, more gracious in disappointment than many in victory.

That delivered two Cosworth cars into the top six. Palmer and Capelli had gone the distance without a tyre stop, and had driven hard all the way. World championship points were no less than their due. Among their scalps were Martin Brundle's Zakspeed and Fabi's Benetton. "At last I finished a race," Teo said, "and it has to be at the race where throttle response is important . . ." He didn't enjoy his Monaco Grand Prix too much, but at least he was spared the ignominy of fighting it out with an Osella. The luckless Caffi — surely a man central to the coming seasons — had to quit when the electrics did.

Ken Tyrrell was delighted with Palmer, who scored the first points of his career. Jonathan's fifth place went some way towards consoling him at the loss of yet another chassis. Streiff destroyed a car at Spa, then another during practice at Monaco, then a third in the race. It was a big one, too, into the guardrail just before Casino Square. For a few minutes Philippe, although unhurt, was trapped in the wreckage by his feet. For a lot longer than that, spectators at the spot rejoiced that bits of the disintegrating Tyrrell had somehow missed them.

Senna's final lap was so slow as to cause panic among his supporters, but Peter Warr, on the other end of the radio line, had no worries. He knew that Ayrton was simply taking care. He was waving to the crowds long before he took the flag.

"Towards the end," he said, "I was having some trouble with selection of second and third, and there was one bad moment near the swimming pool. I couldn't get the gear in, and suddenly realised I had to get on the brakes! The car got a little bit sideways, but it was OK, no problem. The car really worked well today . . ."

1: An empty road behind him, Mansell had an eight second lead in just ten laps and was pulling away further with each lap.

2: Alboreto and Prost, in their tussle for fourth, quickly reel in the second-string Lotus of Nakajima. The Japanese, in his first Monaco GP, was rudely tossed out of the pack at the first corner crush.

3: A royal reception for Senna at the finish. It was his first win for almost 12 months and the first for a car with active suspension.

3.

MONACO GRAND PRIX

Round 4: May 31, 1987
Circuit: Monaco

Race data:	78 laps of 2.065 mile (3.32 km) circuit
Weather:	Warm, dry
Fastest lap:	Senna, Lotus 99T, 2:27.685, 84.918mph
Existing record:	Prost, McLaren MP4/2C, 1:26.607, 85.957mph

ENTRIES

No	Driver (Nat)	Car/Chassis	Engine
1	Alain Prost (F)	McLaren MP4/3-3*	TAG V6 Turbo
2	Stefan Johansson (S)	McLaren MP4/3-2	TAG V6 Turbo
3	Jonathan Palmer (GB)	Tyrrell DG/016-2	Ford Cosworth V8
4	Philippe Streiff (F)	Tyrrell DG/016-4	Ford Cosworth V8
4T	Philippe Streiff (F)	Tyrrell DG/016-3*	Ford Cosworth V8
5	Nigel Mansell (GB)	Williams FW11 B/3*	Honda V6 Turbo
5T	Nigel Mansell (GB)	Williams FW11 B/1	Honda V6 Turbo
6	Nelson Piquet (BR)	Williams FW11 B/4	Honda V6 Turbo
7	Riccardo Patrese (I)	Brabham BT56/3	BMW S4 Turbo
8	Andrea de Cesaris (I)	Brabham BT56/2	BMW S4 Turbo
9	Martin Brundle (GB)	Zakspeed 871/1	Zakspeed S4 Turbo
10	Christian Danner (D)	Zakspeed 871/2	Zakspeed S4 Turbo
11	Satoru Nakajima (J)	Lotus 99T/1	Honda V6 Turbo
12	Ayrton Senna (BR)	Lotus 99T/4*	Honda V6 Turbo
12T	Ayrton Senna (BR)	Lotus 99T/2	Honda V6 Turbo
14	Pascal Fabre (F)	AGS JH22/02-032	Ford Cosworth V8
16	Ivan Capelli (I)	March RT 871/02	Ford Cosworth V8
16T	Ivan Capelli (I)	March RT 871/01	Ford Cosworth V8
17	Derek Warwick (GB)	Arrows A10/1	Megatron S4 Turbo
18	Eddie Cheever (USA)	Arrows A10/2	Megatron S4 Turbo
19	Teo Fabi (I)	Benetton B187-04	Ford V6 Turbo
20	Thierry Boutsen (B)	Benetton B187-03	Ford V6 Turbo
20T	Thierry Boutsen (B)	Benetton B187-05*	Ford V6 Turbo
21	Alex Caffi (I)	Osella FA1H/01/87	Alfa Romeo V8 Turbo
23	Adrian Campos (E)	Minardi M186-05	Moderni V6 Turbo
24	Alessandro Nannini (I)	Minardi M186-03	Moderni V6 Turbo
25	Rene Arnoux (F)	Ligier JS29B/1	Megatron S4 Turbo
25T	Rene Arnoux (F)	Ligier JS29B/3*	Megatron S4 Turbo
26	Piercarlo Ghinzani (I)	Ligier JS29B/2	Megatron S4 Turbo
27	Michele Alboreto (I)	Ferrari F187-096	Ferrari V6 Turbo
27T	Michele Alboreto (I)	Ferrari F187-098*	Ferrari V6 Turbo
28	Gerhard Berger (A)	Ferrari F187-097	Ferrari V6 Turbo
28T	Gerhard Berger (A)	Ferrari F187-095*	Ferrari V6 Turbo
30	Philippe Alliot (F)	Lola LC87/01	Ford Cosworth V8

* Race car

QUALIFYING

FRIDAY: Warm, dry Driver		SATURDAY: Warm, dry Driver	
Mansell	1:24.514	Mansell	1:23.039
Senna	1:25.255	Senna	1:23.711
Prost	1:25.574	Piquet	1:24.755
Piquet	1:25.917	Prost	1:25.083
Patrese	1:26.957	Alboreto	1:26.102
Alboreto	1:27.017	Cheever	1:26.175
Boutsen	1:27.082	Johansson	1:26.317
Warwick	1:27.685	Berger	1:26.323
Johansson	1:27.701	Boutsen	1:26.630
Cheever	1:27.716	Patrese	1:26.763
Nannini	1:28.517	Warwick	1:27.294
Alliot	1:29.114	Fabi	1:27.622
Fabi	1:29.264	Nannini	1:27.731
Berger	1:29.281	Brundle	1:27.894
Brundle	1:29.801	Palmer	1:28.088
Palmer	1:30.307	Caffi	1:29.233
Nakajima	1:30.606	Nakajima	1:28.890
Streiff	1:30.765	Capelli	1:29.147
Campos	1:30.805	Ghinzani	1:29.258
Ghinzani	1:31.098	Alliot	1:29.459
Arnoux	1:31.270	De Cesaris	1:29.827
Capelli	1:31.589	Arnoux	1:30.000
De Cesaris	1:32.643	Streiff	1:30.143
Fabre	1:35.179	Fabre	1:31.667
Caffi	1:36.267		

STARTING GRID

No	Driver	Time
5	Mansell	1:23.039
12	Senna	1:23.711
6	Piquet	1:24.755
1	Prost	1:25.083
27	Alboreto	1:26.102
18	Cheever	1:26.175
2	Johansson	1:26.317
28	Berger	1:26.323
20	Boutsen	1:26.630
7	Patrese	1:26.763
17	Warwick	1:27.294
19	Fabi	1:27.622
24	Nannini	1:27.731
9	Brundle	1:27.894
3	Palmer	1:28.088
21	Caffi	1:28.233
11	Nakajima	1:28.890
30	Alliot	1:29.114
16	Capelli	1:29.147
26	Ghinzani	1:29.258
8	De Cesaris	1:29.827
25	Arnoux	1:30.000
4	Streiff	1:30.143
14	Fabre	1:31.667

RESULTS

Pos	No	Driver	Car	Laps	Time/Retirement
1	12	Senna	Lotus-Honda	78	1-57:54.085
2	6	Piquet	Williams-Honda	78	1-58:27.297
3	27	Alboreto	Ferrari	78	1-59:06.924
4	28	Berger	Ferrari	77	
5	3	Palmer	Tyrrell-Cosworth	76	
6	16	Capelli	March-Cosworth	76	
7	9	Brundle	Zakspeed	76	
8	19	Fabi	Benetton-Ford	76	
9	1	Prost	McLaren-TAG	75	Engine
10	11	Nakajima	Lotus-Honda	75	
11	25	Arnoux	Ligier-Megatron	74	
12	26	Ghinzani	Ligier-Megatron	74	
13	14	Fabre	AGS-Cosworth	71	
R	18	Cheever	Arrows-Megatron	59	Engine
R	17	Warwick	Arrows-Megatron	58	Gear linkage
R	2	Johansson	McLaren-TAG	57	Engine
R	30	Alliot	LC-Cosworth	42	Engine
R	7	Patrese	Brabham-BMW	41	Electrics
R	21	Caffi	Osella-Alfa Romeo	39	Electrics
R	8	De Cesaris	Brabham-BMW	38	Accident damage
R	5	Mansell	Williams-Honda	29	Exhaust
R	24	Nannini	Minardi-Moderni	21	Electrics
R	4	Streiff	Tyrrell-Cosworth	9	Accident
R	20	Boutsen	Benetton-Ford	5	Drive shaft

FASTEST LAP

Driver	
Senna	1:27.685
Mansell	1:28.049
Piquet	1:28.642
Prost	1:28.891
Alboreto	1:28.914
Warwick	1:29.048
Berger	1:29.220
Johansson	1:29.758
Cheever	1:29.905
Patrese	1:30.077
Capelli	1:30.502
Palmer	1:30.817
Fabi	1:31.207
Alliot	1:31.271
Boutsen	1:31.300
Nannini	1:31.293
Caffi	1:31.474
De Cesaris	1:31.511
Brundle	1:31.619
Nakajima	1:32.265
Ghinzani	1:32.389
Arnoux	1:32.417
Streiff	1:32.715
Fabre	1:35.699

CHAMPIONSHIP POSITIONS

DRIVERS

1	Prost	18
2	Senna	15
3	Johansson	13
4	Piquet	12
5	Mansell	10
6	Alboreto	8
7	Berger	6
9	Cheever	3
	Nakajima	3
11	Boutsen	3
	Brundle	2
	Palmer	2
14	Arnoux	1
	Capelli	1

JIM CLARK CUP

1	Streiff	21
2	Palmer	18
3	Fabre	16
4	Alliot	15
5	Capelli	6

CONSTRUCTORS

1	McLaren-TAG	31
2	Williams-Honda	22
3	Lotus-Honda	18
4	Ferrari	14
5	Brabham-BMW	4
6	Arrows-Megatron	3
7	Benetton-Ford	2
	Tyrrell-Cosworth	2
	Zakspeed	2
10	Ligier-Megatron	1
	March-Cosworth	1

COLIN CHAPMAN CUP

1	Tyrrell-Cosworth	39
2	AGS-Cosworth	16
3	Lola-Cosworth	15
4	March-Cosworth	6

THE ACTIVITY CONTINUES

Countless times a second the car's computer beat the traction and wear problems. So the driver went on and on, past the time of its pit stop, past the early leader, onto another victory in the streets.

The efforts of street racing had usually left Ayrton Senna's hands blistered, bruised and bloody. Not any more. The Lotus-Honda's 'active' suspension was proving its worth, proving a revelation, proving balm to a driver tossed around and tortured in the turbo area.

It was taking care of the driver's battered hands, just as it was taking care of the tyres and that allowed Senna the luxury of minimising the risks at a track where there were almost too many risks to be tolerated.

Things can go wrong in pitstops so why risk it, he thought, taking on the responsibility of a decision that most drivers leave to the team manager. But this was Ayrton Senna the autocrat, the gifted Brazilian and the young man who was quickly developing tactical skills to match his speed. And in 30 laps or so this would also be the new leader in the world championship.

The seemingly untouchable Nigel Mansell took that extra risk. In the pits at half distance he could only glare and growl under his helmet as one wheel stuck for enough precious seconds to allow Senna, then Alain Prost, to flash by. Ever the lionheart he charged until an unexpected leg cramp had him falling away in agony, even waving through his overshadowed team-mate Nelson Piquet.

Piquet and Prost, who both detest Detroit, charged too, but Senna was simply too far in front, having suckered everyone in. For Piquet, who sleeps in the cockpit through street races, this was a return to his belligerent best, stirred up by an early stop due to a puncture. For Prost, this was simply over the limit stuff in a car running out of brakes and refusing to go into gear.

1.

Another street circuit and streetwise Nigel Mansell was in a class of his own again, just like at Monaco. The parallel continued with Ayrton Senna's Lotus in touch behind, playing the waiting game. At Monaco it was a broken exhaust primary weld that claimed Mansell, this time there was nothing awry, until the tyre stop.

It appeared to be a straightforward pit stop, but it began a whole series of problems. Three out of four wheels were changed in customary Williams good order, but the right rear was troublesome, and that made the stop a long one. Glancing furiously at his pit, Nigel catapulted away down pit lane to chase after his lost lead.

All seemed not to be lost at this point. Yes, Senna and Alain Prost were ahead now, but both had still to make their tyre stops. Hadn't they?

Alain did. Five laps after Nigel he was in for fresh Goodyears, but Ayrton . . . well, Ayrton was another matter. Forty laps came and went, then 50. The Lotus mechanics busied themselves with tyres and air hammers and so on for a while, and then they all relaxed again. No, the yellow car would not be stopping, after all.

For a time it appeared that the bonus of active suspension was really coming home to roost. Obviously, the Lotus was much more sparing of its tyres than more conventional vehicles. Senna and his team had sold everyone a dummy, that was it.

Even more remarkably, Mansell, far from carving into Ayrton's lead, was actually losing ground. Right after his stop he set a new lap record in his immediate pursuit of Prost — causing all to wonder if he might have blistered his new tyres in the process. Thereafter, the gap to Senna grew and grew.

After Mansell's stop the Goodyear technicians inspected his used set, and swiftly came to the conclusion that — on wear, at least — they could almost certainly have gone the full 63 laps. How much grip they would retain over the whole race was another matter, of course, but they would last. And, this information was relayed to all other teams.

The news came too late to be of use to Prost, who was in a few minutes later. "I told them on the radio," Alain said, "that the tyres seemed fine, but I think maybe they didn't understand me. They told me to come in, and so I did."

The McLaren, though, was never a serious challenger for victory in Detroit; Prost was having a hectic time with a long brake pedal, having to pump all the time, which is not what you need at a tight street circuit. As well as that, the gearchanges from third to fourth, and fourth to fifth, were increasingly baulky. A place in the first three at this venue looked good to him.

For Senna, though, such was not the case. "I was intending to stop at half-distance," was his comment afterwards. "Then I decided to stay out another 10 laps. The tyres were still in good shape, so it seemed better to continue on them to the end. Things can go wrong in pit stops — no point in coming in unless it was necessary."

For a while after his stop, Mansell's lap times were all over the place: 1:47.06 on his first lap out of the pits, then a stunning 1:40.5, then 42.0, 42.6, 45.8, 41.6, 40.8 . . . that *had* to be more than traffic. "We don't know what the problem was," Williams personnel insisted immediately after the race. "He didn't say a word over the radio through the second half."

Well, perhaps he had cooked his second set of tyres, thrashed them too hard too soon. The explanation, when it came, was much more unusual, if not bizarre: cramp in the right leg. "I was in so much pain," Nigel said, "that it drastically affected my driving. Every time I came towards the pits, I was tempted to come in, quit. And, because of the pain, I got very tired, very quickly."

Actually, right leg cramp on a street circuit is not a new phenomenon. By the end of the race, Nigel was indeed spent, needing to be lifted from his car. After a medical check, he was then carried up to his nearby hotel room.

No-one could have possibly predicted Mansell's fate after watching him dominate Friday, Saturday and for 34 laps, Sunday. There is nothing hesitant about Mansell on a street circuit, and this separates him from many of his fellows. His sheer commitment

Previous page: Active suspension shows its worth again in the streets. The computer took care of the tyres and Ayrton took care of the opposition.

2.

1: In the shadow of towers built from motor industry money, Senna prepares for the start. The man on his mind, yet again, was Mansell, beside him on the front row.

2: The tyres were OK, Prost insisted on the radio. He was right, but the team still called him in for an unnecessary fresh set, while Senna stayed out.

3: Mansell takes a break from showing everybody else how to drive Detroit to consult team boss and his race engineer, Frank Williams.

4: Piquet — scowl for another track he disliked.

5: With another hat to wear as FISA's marketing chief, the diminutive dynamo, Bernie Ecclestone, talks F1 politics with fellow FISA heavy Max Mosley.

never fails to impress. At the end of the pit straight, for example, he was yards later onto the brakes than team-mate Nelson Piquet, and it was no surprise to find Nelson more than a second adrift during qualifying.

No one even looked like a serious challenger to Mansell for the pole, although Piquet should have made it a Williams front row. Once again, though, the yellow Lotus split them. Honda 1-2-3 in the home of the American motor car.

Ford, though, could justifiably smile, for Thierry Boutsen's Benetton joined Piquet on row two, and the sister car of an off-colour Teo Fabi was but four places further back. There was a lot of pressure to do well here in Henry's backyard. The latest spec ford V6s (with revised turbos) were on hand, and Boutsen

Mansell smiled all the time. Perhaps mindful of his colleagues' distaste for the track, he lost no opportunity to sing its praises, and those of America in general. The locals were much seduced.

It was Alain Prost, more vocal for 1987 in his role of driver spokesman, who distilled the general feeling about the track: "I don't find Detroit satisfying to drive on — and yet it's also very dangerous. I hate it for two reasons: first, the track itself is a joke; second, the whole principle of racing there is wrong. We race there purely because it's in America, nothing else. Everyone says we must race in the United States because it's good for the image of Formula One. I agree. But there's no way it's good for the image of F1 to race at a track like that."

"We want Formula One to succeed in America —

me better than that. No danger of that at all — but it's better to be realistic. For some reason, the McLaren has never been on the pace there. No, I'll be very happy to get some points from Detroit."

Since 1987 a certain amount of resurfacing work had been done on the bumpy streets. Recent high temperatures, though, caused a certain amount of consternation. Would the surface hold up? Happily, the problem never arose. Odd patches bothered the drivers, but not seriously so.

From the first moment of qualifying, Mansell thrived, his deftness of touch on difficult tracks like this immediately coming into its own. But there was a moment to survive before pole would fall to him. "I was on a quick lap, coming down towards Cobo Hall, one of the fastest sections. And when I put the

3.

5.

raved about the transformation. The improved horsepower remained, but gone was the debilitating throttle lag which had partnered it. "Fantastic," Thierry said. "The response is almost like an atmospheric engine." Michael Kranefuss and the Ford hierarchy were very pleased with what they saw.

Boutsen, fourth on the first day, kept his place in the final session, despite quite a serious misfire. As well as that, he found the gearchange getting stiffer all the time, and had to give the throttle an almighty blip each time he changed down — to the point that he got cramp in his right leg! He missed several shifts, he said, adding that a trouble-free run might well have taken him past Piquet. No matter, Benetton was a happy team after practice, even solemn Teo — getting over his bug by Saturday — permitting himself a rationed smile.

but how can it when the Americans' only chance to see the cars is on that circuit? They can have *no idea* of the capabilities of a grand prix car, and that's sad. There are some great tracks in the States: Watkins Glen, for example, if they resurfaced it.

"I tell you this," the world champion concluded, "if I had to race every Sunday on a track like Detroit, I would stop immediately. What I want is fun — to enjoy motor racing. OK, once a year we have to run at a place like that, but once is already too much for me . . ."

Niki Lauda always claimed not to have 'favourite circuits', working on the theory that if he allowed himself to think that way, it would put him at a psychological disadvantage on tracks not in that bracket. Was there not a danger that Prost could be talking himself out of a strong performance at Detroit? "Absolutely not!" Alain retorted. "You know

brakes on, nothing happened! Came off the pedal, pressed it again, and now I had all four wheels locked. Once that happens, of course, you're not really slowing any more. Takes a lot to come off the brakes when you're almost into the corner, you know . . . Anyway, I did, then hit them again — and I've no idea how many times I spun. Thought it was going to be a real big one, but we didn't hit anything. The engine was dead when I'd come to rest, and the marshals could have taken me out of the session, just pushed the car off the road. As it was, they gave me a shove, and I was able to drive back to the pits."

After Monte Carlo, it was remarkable to see that Senna's hands, often bruised and blistered after a street race, were in fine condition. The 'active' 99T, he said, gave the driver a much easier ride. No small thing, this, in a race of this kind.

During the final session Senna was briefly quickest,

but Mansell then eclipsed everyone, moving alone into the 1:39 bracket. Qualifying then came to a temporary halt (a frequent occurrence at Detroit) after an accident to Martin Brundle, and afterwards Ayrton sensibly decided to concentrate on the race car. The only worry was that Piquet might displace him on the front row, but it never came to be: Nelson was having trouble with third gear selection.

Mansell had everyone handled, seemed able at will to pluck out a new fastest time quite beyond the reach of the rest. By the end he was going on 1.5 sec quicker than anyone else, and nearly two up on his team-mate. The only problem with the car, he said, had been a temporary loss of fifth gear.

"The big problem at this place," Mansell commented, "is that it's incredibly slippery if you get off line for any reason. Some of the slower cars insist on keeping to the line, forcing you to go off it to get by them. You do that, think you're OK — and then at the next corner you think you've hit oil or something.

What's happened? Have you missed the apex? Have the tyres suddenly gone off? And what it is, your tyres have picked up so much rubbish that it can take two full laps before they come back to normal again. There's a little space — say the last foot or so up to the barrier — and if you go in there it's like hitting a puddle. So that's the real challenge of this place. You cannot afford to get off the line."

Mansell-Senna-Piquet-Boutsen. And then the world champion, fifth. It hadn't looked that way. With 15 minutes of the last session remaining, Prost was barely into the top 10, and Detroit was fully living up to its reputation for being unkind to McLarens. As bad as you expected? "Worse!" Alain replied on Friday afternoon, putting thumb to chin and rolling his eyes. "No grip, no power..." In the circumstances, this last may have been a blessing, since he went on to speak of wheelspin in fourth gear . . .

It was this absence of traction which was the major problem. An overnight engine change gave

him more horsepower for Saturday, and changes to the set-up improved the car's turn-in, but after experimenting during the morning both Prost and Stefan Johansson decided there was nothing else for it: in the afternoon they would have to run 'heavy', with a lot of fuel aboard, simply to get some traction. "I had 140-150 litres in the car," Alain said. "In the circumstances, I'm happy to be as high as fifth."

On row three, next to him, was Eddie Cheever, once again right up there for Arrows. Eddie was never happy with his car's handling, and ascribed his impressive position to a single banzai lap, during which he was not held up. And during which he clouted the barriers "at least three times." It was a full second faster than any of his other times.

Derek Warwick, like Fabi, feeling distinctly unwell, was consistently quicker than his team-mate through practice — until the last few minutes, when a blown engine prevented any quick laps on his second set of tyres. Grey-faced and unsmiling, he was a picture of frustration.

As always on street circuits, there were innumerable shunts during practice, most of them involving the people who usually have shunts, Andrea De Cesaris kept up his batting average with one each day, and Berger — who trashed a Ferrari during final qualifying at Monaco — did not amuse John Barnard by backing into a wall on Saturday afternoon at Detroit. Philippe Alliot had a couple in the Lola, but much more surprising was that Martin Brundle took a corner off his Zakspeed. Martin probably wished he could have traded places with Jonathan Palmer — for this race, at least.

As at Monaco, Palmer revelled in the response of the Cosworth-engined car, and was a pleasure to watch through the long first turn, steering to a large extent with the throttle and coming off the corner like a slingshot. Fastest of the atmospheric brigade again, he was for a long tiime in the top three during the rainy part of Saturday morning.

The streets were awash at breakfast time on race day, and still very damp as engines were fired up for the 9.45 warm-up session. To no-one's great surprise, Mansell was quickest in this, too, but an encouraging second was Warwick, then Piquet, Palmer (!) and Prost. There were many spins — even Prost revolved at one point — but no one hit anything hard.

By 1.45 the track was quite dry, but high humidity promised an uncomfortable afternoon for all. A race of attrition, everyone reckoned. There were so many things to worry about in this place: brakes holding up, punctures, litter in the radiators, keeping away from the walls.

Satoru Nakajima at least didn't need to worry long. His Detroit Grand Prix lasted less than a minute, but it was an eventful one in which he hit Ivan Capelli and was later clobbered into retirement by Adrian Campos. Scratch one Lotus, one Minardi.

Others, too, were in trouble early. Johansson: "Someone ran into the back of me at the first corner, pushed me into Warwick and that took a wing endplate off." That would be changed later, but a more serious misfire, cured by a change of the Bosch Motoronic box, took a long time. Stefan was distinctly po-faced at the end.

Lap five was bad for Palmer: "Patrese had spun, and I went round the back of his car. But he didn't have his foot on the brake, and rolled into me . . ." That meant a stop to change a broken toe-link in the rear suspension, and put him at the back. Thereafter Jonathan pressed on with all vigour and spirit, his unexpected reward being maximum Jim Clark Trophy points as the first normally-aspirated driver home.

De Cesaris, having distinguished himself in traditional fashion in practice, took no chances in the race. "He came in after two laps, said it was jumping out of second, and he'd had enough," reported Herbie Blash of Brabham. That was it? "Yes," Herbie replied, "that was it . . ."

As early as lap three Piquet was out of third place, into the pits. In his efforts to keep ahead of Cheever's Arrows, he had run wide at a turn, picked up some dirt, which punctured a front tyre. He rejoined in 21st place, and began his most determined drive of the season. And he, too, needed no further change of tyres.

While Mansell pulled away from Senna, and Senna pulled away from everyone else, Cheever fought off the attentions of Fabi, who had started brilliantly from his eighth grid slot. But sadly the battle was brief; on the seventh lap they tangled at turn three. Both made it to the pits, Eddie for tyres (puncture) and Teo for a new nosecone, which could not be made to fit. Boutsen was now the sole Ford representative in the race, but he was looking good in fourth place, having passed Prost and moved up to hassle Michele Alboreto.

The pace of the first two was just astounding. After 10 laps Mansell was five seconds up on Senna, and there were almost half a minute wait for third placed Ferrari to come by. This really was were the 'race' began, for Boutsen, Prost, Berger and Johansson were all in close order behind.

Gradually Michele began to inch away from the rest, for Boutsen was clearly holding up his pursuers.

"My brakes were completely gone after about 10 laps," he reported later. "The pedal was right to the floor, and I was in no real condition to fight with anyone."

At the 30-lap mark, there were the beginnings of a question mark against first place. Mansell still led comfortably enough, but the gap to Senna was down to 13 secs, as against 18 a few laps earlier. On lap 33 Nigel — his tyre stop imminent — responded with a new fastest lap, but it stood only until Ayrton crossed the timing beam.

"Early in the race," the Brazilian said, " I was in trouble with a soft brake pedal, and I backed off. Two years ago I had the same problem, and finished up in the wall, so this time I knew better. And maybe slowing down helped me on tyre wear. The team gave me excellent information on what was happening with the others." Including, presumably, the information that Mansell's set of tyres looked just fine to the Goodyear people.

Above left: There were numerous shunts and incidents in the days leading up to the race. Senna had his moment — without consequence — as did many of his illustrious fellows at a venue nobody liked.

Top: Delayed in the pits, Mansell rockets around in a bid to get the lead back. In front of him were Piquet and Senna, still to stop. Then the Englishman's times started to slip mysteriously.

Above: Cheever moved up the ranking during qualifying and was an influence on the race, leading the bunch immediately behind the leaders. Fabi was to stop him going any further.

73

Right: The boil went off the Brabhams at Detroit after a promising start early in the season on the fast tracks. Patrese did best, in and out of the pits to fix a reluctant seat belt buckle.

Below: Raging Piquet. Frustrated by a puncture, it was the Piquet of old fighting up through the field all afternoon to finish a worthy second.

Inset: Two in a row for Senna and he had taken the lead in the world championship.

Not that there could have been a deal wrong with Senna's. On new rubber, Mansell might have been expected to close impressively on the Lotus, but it was not so. Instead, Ayrton cranked out three stunning consecutive laps, one of which was beneath his qualifying time. And his lead grew.

From lap 45 on, in fact, Nigel began seriously to drop away, losing two, three, four seconds every time around, and falling back into the clutches of Piquet, now third, ahead of Prost. When he saw the second Williams in his mirrors, Mansell waved it through, an action inconceivable in normal circumstances. A few corners later Prost, too, was by him, and then it was Berger's turn.

For a few minutes we saw the real stuff of Alain Prost. Forget all that about 'The Professor', about the cool analytical, point-scoring machine. This was Prost as racer pure. At this, his most hated circuit, in this car with brake and gearchange problems, he began to chase Piquete for second. Three of his laps bettered his qualifying time — one of them by more than a second . . .

When Nelson kicked again, though, Alain accepted that third it had to be. "If I score points at Detroit," he grinned, "I feel as if I have won."

Another fine drive was that of Cheever, who scraped back into the points for Arrows, despite running out of fuel on the last lap. Team-mate Warwick's race ended early after he had clipped a wall, breaking a cv joint.

Several men had stories to tell: Riccardo Patrese spoke of his seat harness buckle, which persistently undid itself through the race; Rene Arnoux of a completely numb right foot, legacy of a 'hard' brake pedal; Philippe Streiff of the disappointment he felt at losing certain victory in the atmospheric class. His Tyrrell shed its right rear wheel right in front of the pits.

That incident gave Senna his nastiest moment of the afternoon. As the wheel bounced its mindless way across the track, one of the first cars through was the number 12 Lotus, in the process of lapping someone. Fortunately Ayrton saw it in time, fell back into line. Won.

"The World Championship starts now," he said after victory, his second in a row. "We have done the street circuits, and now we go on to the fast tracks."

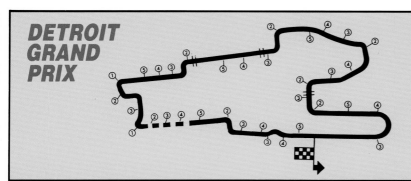

DETROIT GRAND PRIX

Round 5: June 21, 1987
Circuit: Detroit

Race data:	63 laps of 2.5 mile (4.03 km) circuit
Weather:	Overcast, humid
Fastest lap:	Senna, Lotus 99T, 1:40.464, 89.584mph
Existing record:	Piquet, Williams FW11, 1:41.233, 88.904mph

ENTRIES

No	Driver (Nat)	Car/Chassis	Engine
1	Alain Prost (F)	McLaren MP4/2C-3	TAG V6 Turbo
2	Stefan Johansson (S)	McLaren MP4/2C-2	TAG V6 Turbo
3	Jonathan Palmer (GB)	Tyrrell DG/016-3	Ford Cosworth V8
4	Philippe Streiff (F)	Tyrrell DG/016-5	Ford Cosworth V8
5	Nigel Mansell (GB)	Williams FW11 B/3	Honda V6 Turbo
6	Nelson Piquet (BR)	Williams FW11 B/4	Honda V6 Turbo
7	Riccardo Patrese (I)	Brabham BT56/3	BMW S4 Turbo
8	Andrea de Cesaris (I)	Brabham BT56/2	BMW S4 Turbo
9	Martin Brundle (GB)	Zakspeed 861/2*	Zakspeed S4 Turbo
9T	Martin Brundle (GB)	Zakspeed 871/1	Zakspeed S4 Turbo
10	Christian Danner (D)	Zakspeed 871/2	Zakspeed S4 Turbo
11	Satoru Nakajima (J)	Lotus 99T/1	Honda V6 Turbo
12	Ayrton Senna (BR)	Lotus 99T/4	Honda V6 Turbo
14	Pascal Fabre (F)	AGS JH22/02-032	Ford Cosworth V8
16	Ivan Capelli (I)	March 871/1	Ford Cosworth V8
17	Derek Warwick (GB)	Arrows A10/1	Megatron S4 Turbo
18	Eddie Cheever (USA)	Arrows A10/2	Megatron S4 Turbo
19	Teo Fabi (I)	Benetton B187-02	Ford V6 Turbo
19T	Teo Fabi (I)	Benetton B187-04*	Ford V6 Turbo
20	Thierry Boutsen (B)	Benetton B187-06	Ford V6 Turbo
21	Alex Caffi (I)	Osella FA1H/02/87	Alfa Romeo V8 Turbo
23	Adrian Campos (E)	Minardi M186-02	Moderni V6 Turbo
24	Alessandro Nannini (I)	Minardi M186-03	Moderni V6 Turbo
25	Rene Arnoux (F)	Ligier JS29B/4	Megatron S4 Turbo
26	Piercarlo Ghinzani (I)	Ligier JS29B/2	Megatron S4 Turbo
27	Michele Alboreto (I)	Ferrari F187-098	Ferrari V6 Turbo
28	Gerhard Berger (A)	Ferrari F187-095	Ferrari V6 Turbo
30	Philippe Alliot (F)	Lola LC87/02	Ford Cosworth V8

* Race car

QUALIFYING

FRIDAY: Hot, dry Driver		SATURDAY: Overcast, muggy Driver	
Mansell	1:42.223	Mansell	1:39.264
Senna	1:42.985	Senna	1:40.607
Piquet	1:43.152	Piquet	1:40.942
Boutsen	1:44.686	Boutsen	1:42.050
Berger	1:45.054	Prost	1:42.357
Warwick	1:45.234	Cheever	1:42.361
Cheever	1:45.296	Alboreto	1:42.684
Alboreto	1:45.437	Fabi	1:42.918
Prost	1:46.067	Patrese	1:43.479
Nannini	1:46.449	Warwick	1:43.541
Johansson	1:46.623	Johansson	1:43.797
Patrese	1:46.932	Berger	1:43.816
Palmer	1:47.010	Palmer	1:44.350
Fabi	1:47.064	Streiff	1:45.037
Alliot	1:47.470	Brundle	1:45.291
De Cesaris	1:47.670	Danner	1:45.740
Streiff	1:47.963	De Cesaris	1:46.046
Arnoux	1:48.338	Nannini	1:46.083
Ghinzani	1:48.661	Caffi	1:46.124
Danner	1:48.867	Alliot	1:46.194
Brundle	1:48.932	Arnoux	1:46.211
Capelli	1:49.969	Capelli	1:46.269
Campos	1:50.495	Ghinzani	1:47.471
Nakajima	1:51.355	Nakajima	1:48.801
Caffi	1:55.787	Fabre	1:53.644
Fabre	1:57.475	Campos	3:26.319

STARTING GRID

No	Driver	Time
5	Mansell	1:39.624
12	Senna	1:40.607
6	Piquet	1:40.942
20	Boutsen	1:42.050
1	Prost	1:42.357
18	Cheever	1:42.361
27	Alboreto	1:42.684
19	Fabi	1:42.918
7	Patrese	1:43.479
17	Warwick	1:43.541
2	Johansson	1:43.797
20	Berger	1:43.816
3	Palmer	1:44.350
6	Streiff	1:45.037
9	Brundle	1:45.291
10	Danner	1:45.740
8	De Cesaris	1:46.046
24	Nannini	1:46.083
21	Caffi	1:46.124
30	Alliot	1:46.194
25	Arnoux	1:46.211
16	Capelli	1:46.269
26	Ghinzani	1:47.471
11	Nakajima	1:48.801
23	Campos	1:50.495
14	Fabre	1:53.644

RESULTS

Pos	No	Driver	Car	Laps	Time/Retirement
1	12	Senna	Lotus-Honda	63	1-50:16.358
2	6	Piquet	Williams-Honda	63	1-50:50.177
3	1	Prost	McLaren-TAG	63	1-51:01.685
4	28	Berger	Ferrari	63	1-51:18.959
5	5	Mansell	Williams-Honda	62	
6	18	Cheever	Arrows-Megatron	60	
7	2	Johansson	McLaren-TAG	60	
8	10	Danner	Zakspeed	60	
9	7	Patrese	Brabham-BMW	60	
10	25	Arnoux	Ligier-Megatron	60	
11	3	Palmer	Tyrrell-Cosworth	60	
12	14	Fabre	AGS-Cosworth	58	
R	20	Boutsen	Benetton-Ford	52	Brakes
R	26	Ghinzani	Ligier-Megatron	51	Running
R	4	Streiff	Tyrrell-Cosworth	54	Lost wheel
R	30	Alliot	LC-Cosworth	38	Accident
R	27	Alboreto	Ferrari	25	Gearbox
R	24	Nannini	Minardi-Moderni	22	Gearbox
R	9	Brundle	Zakspeed	16	Turbo fire
R	17	Warwick	Arrows-Megatron	12	CV Joint
R	16	Capelli	March-Cosworth	9	Electrics
R	19	Fabi	Benetton-Ford	6	Accident damage
R	21	Caffi	Osella-Alfa	3	Broken gear lever
R	8	De Cesaris	Brabham-BMW	2	Gearbox
R	23	Campos	Minardi-Moderni	1	Accident
R	11	Nakajima	Lotus-Honda	0	Accident

FASTEST LAP

Driver	
Senna	1:40.464
Mansell	1:40.535
Piquet	1:41.196
Prost	1:41.340
Berger	1:42.238
Boutsen	1:42.292
Johansson	1:42.332
Cheever	1:43.951
Palmer	1:44.048
Patrese	1:44.255
Arnoux	1:44.813
Alboreto	1:45.016
Alliot	1:45.869
Streiff	1:46.048
Nannini	1:47.069
Warwick	1:47.260
Ghinzani	1:47.477
Danner	1:47.532
Fabi	1:48.325
Brundle	1:48.744
Capelli	1:49.341
Fabre	1:50.309
Caffi	1:53.496
De Cesaris	1:53.860
Campos	2:16.237

CHAMPIONSHIP POSITIONS

DRIVERS		CONSTRUCTORS	
1 Senna	24	1 McLaren-TAG	35
2 Prost	22	2 Williams-Honda	30
3 Piquet	18	3 Lotus-Honda	27
4 Johansson	13	4 Ferrari	17
5 Mansell	12	5 Arrows-Megatron	4
6 Berger	9	Brabham-BMW	4
7 Alboreto	8	7 Benetton-Ford	2
8 Cheever	4	Tyrrell-Cosworth	2
De Cesaris	4	Zakspeed	2
10 Nakajima	3	10 Ligier-Megatron	1
11 Boutsen	2	March-Cosworth	1
Brundle	2		
Palmer	2		
14 Arnoux	1		
Capelli	1		

JIM CLARK CUP		COLIN CHAPMAN CUP	
1 Palmer	27	1 Tyrrell-Cosworth	48
2 Fabre	22	2 AGS-Cosworth	22
3 Streiff	21	3 Lola-Cosworth	15
4 Alliot	15	4 March-Cosworth	6
5 Capelli	6		

France

ROUND SIX: July 5, 1987

NO STOPPING HIM NOW

The bugs, both mechanical and personal, had been blown away. With such single-minded determination, nothing would get in his way this time.

It had to happen eventually: Nigel Mansell dominated every moment. There had been the customary, imperious qualifying performance for the fourth race out of five, but this time, back on a fast track, nothing went seriously awry with the car or driver when it mattered, when the points were handed out.

Even renewed vigour from his eternally overshadowed team-mate did not faze the Englishman. Nelson Piquet, more motivated, more determined than for a long time, salivated hungrily at Mansell's exhausts early. Nigel continued to control the situation though and the challenge faded initially when Piquet, with unforced errors now part of his driving repertoire, slipped out of the Mansell-Alain Prost sandwich. Then, when the Brazilian angrily, perhaps overhastily, rocketed away from his tyre stop, Mansell, on fresher tyres, reeled him in and charged through a hole that shouldn't have been there.

From then on it was racecraft to the fore, Mansell calculating correctly that he could pace it to the end on one set of tyres while Piquet, unable to get by, couldn't, and would realise it much too late to be a further threat.

Behind that exaggerated expression of Williams-Honda superiority, way behind, was the outclassed McLaren of Alain Prost, in the most frustrating race of his career. There was also, further back, Ayrton Senna's Lotus, no longer a winning proposition. Neither McLaren nor Lotus could live with the Williams-Honda on power early but worse was to come — Prost just circulating in the T-car that became as sick as the race car he discarded before the start, while Senna cursed his car's sudden, alarming lack of downforce and balance away from the street circuits.

In the overall scheme of things, Senna did hang onto the championship lead with a drive for points, however Mansell was now on a rush up the points table, a genuine championship contender again in season two of his glorious re-birth.

The Circuit Paul Ricard, bisected in 1986 after the fatal testing accident to Elio de Angelis, amounts to little more than a club circuit. And not an especially interesting one at that. A lap required little more than a minute, the only plus point being that you get to see them 81 times on Sunday afternoon, when the real interest begins. So guess who was fastest in qualifying?

Nigel Mansell had put a lock on pole position in a manner unknown since Niki Lauda's greatest Ferrari year of 1975. Five times in six races he had taken it, and the one that got away — Imola — was lost only because Mansell was sent out for full tank testing while Ayrton Senna was going for it.

At Ricard, where he was a comfortable winner twelve months before, Nigel topped the lists in all four sessions. You had the impression that whatever anyone else produced, the No. 5 Williams-Honda had the answer.

On acceleration Frank's cars were awesome. "On one lap," Derek Warwick reported, "I came out of the slow corner onto the back straight a good hundred yards up on Piquet. And by the time we got to Signes, at the end of the straight, he was 150 yards ahead of me! That's no exaggeration. Just drove straight past me. Those things go away from you out of a corner like nothing else, believe me."

Add in that Mansell was well satisfied with the

balance and grip from his FW11B and that mechanical problems were confined to the small and niggly, and the picture came more sharply into focus. His commitment to the job was never in doubt, and his confidence was a match for it. He expected to be quickest. The car was the fastest in the business, and he spared it nothing.

From most drivers, the best times came on the first day. In the south of France the weather was hot and mighty sticky, but at midday on Friday the sun took a break for a while. As the sky blackened, thunderclaps boomed in from the surrounding hills, and a downpour seemed on the cards. It never came. But the absence of sun cooled the day, and it was in these conditions that the drivers — fearful of a heavy shower — dashed out, trying to set a quick lap — what Nigel calls a "banker" — while the track was bone dry.

For most of the session he looked quite beyond reach, going on a second and a half faster than anyone else. Senna and Nelson Piquet were stuck in the pits, having gear ratios changed, and Alain Prost, inevitably the man Mansell most feared, was unhappy with his race car, which was bottoming too much.

In the last few minutes the world champion abandoned his own McLaren, and took out the spare car. And soon he confirmed Nigel's opinion that here lay his chief opposition. The McLaren T-car had a baulky gearchange, but Alain preferred to use it, anyway. And even though the track was by now very greasy — legacy of several blown engines — and though he 'buzzed' the engine while changing down from fourth to first, Prost got himself within four-tenths of the Williams, and onto the front row.

That got everyone's attention, and afterwards Alain was brimming with quiet confidence. "Several problems today, but all small ones, really — ride height, brake balance, gear change, things like that. Basically, though, I can tell you that the car feels as good as it ever has." As good as at Spa? "Yes, definitely. We should be strong in the race."

The fact that Prost set his time in less than ideal circumstances, registered with Mansell, but in the hotter and slower conditions on Saturday afternoon he was again fast man. Although nearly three-tenths off his Friday time, he alone got under 1:07, and he reckoned he should have gone quicker. "I was on a quick lap — and found a couple of marshals in the road at Signes . . ."

Still in terms of the grid, this latest piece of Ricard nonsense had no effect on the grid. Indeed, even Mansell's Saturday time would have given him the pole.

It was, however, only qualifying. Nigel needed no reminding of that: five poles, one win. "These have been two good days for us, but I'd like to have been a bit quicker on full tanks, I must say. And Alain's time yesterday was impressive. The McLaren seems to be working awfully well in race spec here . . ."

Even in its abbreviated state, Ricard's Mistral Straight is long by Formula One standards. Two years before, when last the full circuit was used for the grand prix, heat build-up in the tyres was a major problem, and a blow-out caused Mansell to have a huge accident. Mindful of past problems, Goodyear produced a new rear tyre, of more rounded profile. Essentially, the purpose was to minimise heat build-up, allow the tyre shoulders to relax and cool on the straight. And there were no problems of any kind.

Mind you, in the Friday qualifying session, you could have run whatever you wanted — and as many sets as you liked. The officials duly stencilled all the tyres before the session (as the word of FISA decreed), then failed altogether to check them as the cars took to the track. Should not some penalty have been exacted from the Circuit Paul Ricard?

The track surface at Ricard is abrasive, and there were suggestions during practice that Williams would be following the 1986 plan of two tyre stops. This they were understandably unwilling to confirm or deny, but Peter Warr said Lotus anticipated only one stop for Senna.

Ayrton had not been at all pleased with the 99T on the opening day, despite placing, as ever, in the first four. Nearly a full second from Mansell's pole time, he was yet fastest of all — at better than 205 mph — down the Mistral. There, in fact, lay the clue to the problem: the car, he said, was very short on

downforce, undriveable. Attention to the gearbox used up the first half of the timed session, and then he slid off at Signes while out on his first set. On the second, the Lotus-Honda behaved waywardly, thanks to a pressure imbalance on the 'active' system.

On Saturday, though, Senna was more content. Despite the slower conditions he found another three-tenths, moving ahead of Piquet on the grid, and he thought there was more to be had: he would go for Prost's time. As he began the lap, however, he felt the engine begin to tighten up, and immediately switched off and parked. Third it would have to be.

Piquet dropped a place, therefore, despite himself improving in the final session. Nelson, as usual, had no answer to the absolute pace of his team-mate, but a lot of people reckoned him for the race. The only member of the leading quartet without a win, he was due to come back into the picture.

Logically, you had to go for someone from the first couple of rows: Mansell, Prost, Senna, Piquet. You looked at row three — Thierry Boutsen's Benetton and Gerhard Berger's Ferrari — and took aboard the bald fact they were nearly a second away. And this over a 66-second lap.

Fifth he may have been on the grid, but Thierry was in a rage by the end of practice. From an engine point of view, the qualifying days had been disastrous: turbo failure, then blow-up on Friday afternoon;

blow-up on Saturday morning; dire misfire in the last session. And with Teo Fabi's engine failure in the first timed session, exit both turbos in the last. The Ford V6 may be giving good power, even accompanied by excellent response at last, but longevity was not its strong suit. A pity, because predictably both drivers were well pleased with the balance of their B187 chassis.

Such, however, was not the case with the Ferrari drivers. Berger qualified sixth, yes, but complained strenuously about his car's appalling understeer. Michele Alboreto, a couple of tenths slower, was more concerned about poor traction out of the slow corners. On full tanks, he said, the car was much better. A reasonable race finish was their best hope.

Absent from the scene on Friday was John Barnard. He was away, Marco Piccinini said, "doing something else."Had he walked out, or had perhaps

been fired by the Old Man? On Saturday morning there were headlines to this effect in the Italian papers. And on Saturday morning, also, there was John in the Ferrari pit!

All in all, the profile of the grid was much as usual, although Stefan Johansson, ninth, should have been higher — and would have been had he not lost most of Friday's quicker session, a consequence of being pushed off the road by Adrian Campos's Minardi in the morning. "I'm happy enough with the car," Stefan said, "but I'd like a bit less understeer, I must say."

Race day was hot and humid, a true Riviera day. Yet again it was Nigel who set fastest time in the warm-up, and behind him were more Hondas, the Williams of Piquet, the Lotus of Senna. Prost was fourth, having switched to the McLaren T-car after his own car had started misfiring.

"They changed the plugs, and I tried it again at the end," Alain said. "It was definitely better, but they knew from the graph that something else was definitely wrong — maybe something in the turbos. Still, we decided to use it for the race because it was set up better. Big mistake . . ."

Warwick was the quicker of the Arrows drivers throughout practice, and had a couple of relatively untroubled days. "No real problems," he commented on Friday afternoon. "I've driven it into the ground, and that's it! Don't think there's anything more to come."

On Friday morning the time keepers made him third fastest, with a time he was never to duplicate when it mattered. "Just my luck, right? First time in my life I get a bum time — and it has to be in an untimed session!"

On Saturday afternoon Derek went for the boost switch, but hit the extinguisher button instead, temporarily freezing his assets. But the sun swiftly thawed him, and he was one of very few to improve his time. Eddie Cheever, more than a second slower, was four places back of him.

Elsewhere Riccardo Patrese prepared for his 150th grand prix, his team for the second anniversary of their last grand prix win. Rene Arnoux said that new Ligier mods had made the JS29 less tail-heavy, and Martin Brundle wondered where all that Zakspeed horsepower — so impressive in winter testing — had gone. And on this high speed track, Messrs Jonathan Palmer and Philippe Streiff looked in frustration at the straight-line speed of their Tyrrells — nearly 10 mph down on Pascal Fabre's AGS! Ivan Capelli's March and Philippe Alliot's Lola were the clear leaders in the Cosworth class here.

At the green light Mansell got away to perfection, but it was Piquet, not Prost, who followed him by at the end of the first lap. The McLaren was third, tailed by Senna, Boutsen and Fabi. And already both Ferrari drivers were in trouble, one of them knowingly. Berger, having completely muffed his start, was back in 19th place. And Alboreto, clutch dragging on the line, had left quite a while before anyone else. For that, he received a one minute penalty.

Others, too, had problems. At the first corner Johansson's car had been clouted by the inevitable Andrea de Cesaris, who approached the turn as if on a lap of the old, long circuit. That left Stefan without a right front wing, and he came in for a new one.

Piquet's determination in the early laps was plain to see, but quite soon Mansell began to edge away. Ten laps in, the gap between them was almost three seconds, but soon afterwards Nelson began closing again. That was unexpected.

By now Johansson's replacement front wing had broken up, fluttered away, and he had pitted for a third. No problem for him, save the loss of further time. Not until much later, however, did we learn that Stefan's errant wing had hit Mansell's front wing, damaging it slightly, and giving him an instant understeer problem . . .

"I'd been pulling away quite nicely," Nigel said, "but now I had no choice but to slow down, at which Piquet of course closed in again. My first thought

was to come in, have it changed, but I knew I was going to have a stop for tyres anyway, and didn't want to come in twice. So I decided to stay out, try and keep in front, but at a slower pace."

Nelson tried it on a couple of times, then settled back to tail Nigel. By now, though, Prost was firmly into the picture, closing on the pair. His path was smoothed by Piquet, who missed his braking point at the first turn, and slid wide into a half-spin. In a trice he was on his way again, with little time lost, but now he had the McLaren in front of him.

For many laps they ran together, these three, but Prost was clearly unable to get on terms with Mansell, being literally left behind down the long Mistral straight.

"It was very frustrating, I must say, trying to fight against two perfect cars, perfect engines, perfect drivers, like that. On acceleration, I was 'opeless. There is really a big difference in power between the Honda engine and mine. I think my *chassis* was better than theirs — particularly during the first part of the race, when they seemed a bit short of grip, but I was never close enough at the end of a straight to try to pass — and if I had, I couldn't have kept ahead. They would have just passed me in the straight again . . ."

These three were the race. Senna ran a distant fourth, and might well have lost the place to Boutsen, had not the Benetton died of electrical problems out on the circuit. Fabi inherited fifth from his team-mate, and Berger had put in a fine comeback drive after his dreadful start, climbing back to sixth. Going well, too, were Alboreto (forgetting the penalty of effectively a lap), Warwick and Arnoux. But none of these would finish.

At the front, it seemed that the game would be decided by the stops — how many, and how long? Piquet set the thing in motion by coming in at the end of his 30th lap. Senna followed on the 32nd but the Lotus was too far back to be considered a factor. Ayrton had been dissatisfied with the balance of the car from the start, and was thinking of this race solely in terms of points towards his world championship lead.

Lap 34: Prost, and the tyre change was copybook. Lap 35: Mansell. This stop was also good, but such had been Piquet's pace on his new set that he took the lead while his rivals were in. On lap 36 it was Nelson, Alain, Nigel.

"After my stop," Prost said, "the engine went from poor to useless. It was like in Monaco — I could smell that something in the engine was burning. The wastegate or exhaust or something. I don't know yet. I could do nothing against Nigel, and after that I just turned down the boost, and hoped I would get to the finish. But it was the most frustrating race I can remember. I really wanted to win this one."

Having dealt with the McLaren in short order, Mansell had now to get on terms with Piquet, nearly five seconds ahead. Clearly Nelson was on the hook, but getting by, Nigel knew, would not be a breeze. By lap 45 the two Williams were right together and Mansell, in fact, got by Piquet only when Nelson made a mistake, getting off line into a right-hander.

Was that the end of the game? Not by a long way. Piquet, justifiably aggrieved with himself, did not fall away, but stayed with Mansell. After the race he claimed that he had had to run wide, to let Nigel through, otherwise, he said, they would have touched, and that would have been the end of the race for both.

Now a fascinating game of cat-and-mouse began. Would one stop again for tyres? Or both? No one knew, including the drivers, although Nigel was sure in his own mind that he had made his last stop. "I was pretty sure *he* was going to stop again," Mansell said later, "but I'd done a lot of running in practice, thinking about this situation, and I knew that a new set of tyres started going off after only 10 laps or so. At this point of the race I could have gone quicker, but I was hoping that if Nelson thought he could still stay with me, he might delay making his second stop until it was too late."

If this was the plan, it worked to perfection. Piquet finally came in on lap 64, leaving himself only another 16 to the finish. The gap, when he came back out, was almost 25 seconds: simply, there wasn't enough French Grand Prix left for him.

Nelson put everything into the attempt, however.

By the end he was less than eight seconds adrift, but Nigel knew exactly what was happening. The victory could hardly have been more satisfying.

"The aim today," Mansell said, "was to win the race at the slowest possible speed. That had to be the plan, because ideally I knew I didn't want to make two tyre stops. Apart from that damaged front wing, the only problem was that the gearlever knob came off, making the palm of my hand a bit raw. A good day, that."

For him, yes. But hardly any other driver was pleased with the race. Prost was decidedly upset. "At least I wasn't lapped this year," he said on Sunday. His tone was ironic, but he wasn't his usual smiling self. "The difference," he said, "between the Honda horsepower and ours is just a joke. Very difficult to fight like that — even when the engine is working properly. But today . . ."

And Senna was none too impressed with an uncompetitive drone to fourth place. Nor can he have much enjoyed being lapped by Mansell in the course of it. But Fabi got pleasure from a rare finish, and Streiff was delirious at taking a point in his home grand prix.

Far left: Nakajima and Patrese about to be lapped by the Ferrari of Michele Alboreto. Of those three, only Nakajima was running at the end, although not classified as a finisher.

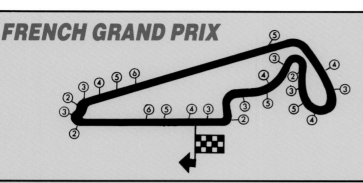

FRENCH GRAND PRIX

Round 6: July 5, 1987
Circuit: Paul Ricard

Race data:	80 laps of 2.37 mile (3.8 km) circuit
Weather:	Very hot, dry
Fastest lap:	Piquet, Williams FW11, 1:09.548, 122.811mph
Existing record:	Mansell, Williams FW11, 1:09.993, 122.573mph

ENTRIES

No	Driver (Nat)	Car/Chassis	Engine
1	Alain Prost (F)	McLaren MP4/3C-3	TAG V6 Turbo
2	Stefan Johansson (S)	McLaren MP4/3C-2*	TAG V6 Turbo
2T	Stefan Johansson (S)	McLaren MP4/3C-1	TAG V6 Turbo
3	Jonathan Palmer (GB)	Tyrrell DG/016-2	Ford Cosworth V8
4	Philippe Streiff (F)	Tyrrell DG/016-5	Ford Cosworth V8
5	Nigel Mansell (GB)	Williams FW11 B/3*	Honda V6 Turbo
5T	Nigel Mansell (GB)	Williams FW11 B/2	Honda V6 Turbo
6	Nelson Piquet (BR)	Williams FW11 B/4*	Honda V6 Turbo
6T	Nelson Piquet (BR)	Williams FW11 B/1	Honda V6 Turbo
7	Riccardo Patrese (I)	Brabham BT56/3	BMW S4 Turbo
8	Andrea de Cesaris (I)	Brabham BT56/2*	BMW S4 Turbo
8T	Andrea de Cesaris (I)	Brabham BT56/1	BMW S4 Turbo
9	Martin Brundle (GB)	Zakspeed 871/3	Zakspeed S4 Turbo
9T	Martin Brundle (GB)	Zakspeed 871/1*	Zakspeed S4 Turbo
10	Christian Danner (D)	Zakspeed 871/2	Zakspeed S4 Turbo
11	Satoru Nakajima (J)	Lotus 99T/1	Honda V6 Turbo
12	Ayrton Senna (BR)	Lotus 99T/4*	Honda V6 Turbo
12T	Ayrton Senna (BR)	Lotus 99T/5	Honda V6 Turbo
14	Pascal Fabre (F)	AGS JH22/02-032	Ford Cosworth V8
16	Ivan Capelli (I)	March 871/02	Ford Cosworth V8
17	Derek Warwick (GB)	Arrows A10/1	Megatron S4 Turbo
18	Eddie Cheever (USA)	Arrows A10/2	Megatron S4 Turbo
19	Teo Fabi (I)	Benetton B187-07	Ford V6 Turbo
20	Thierry Boutsen (B)	Benetton B187-04	Ford V6 Turbo
21	Alex Caffi (I)	Osella FA1H/01/87	Alfa Romeo V8 Turbo
21T	Alex Caffi (I)	Osella FA1H/03/86*	Alfa Romeo V8 Turbo
23	Adrian Campos (E)	Minardi M186-02	Moderni V6 Turbo
24	Alessandro Nannini (I)	Minardi M186-03	Moderni V6 Turbo
25	Rene Arnoux (F)	Ligier JS29C/5	Megatron S4 Turbo
26	Piercarlo Ghinzani (I)	Ligier JS29C/4	Megatron S4 Turbo
26T	Piercarlo Ghinzani (I)	Ligier JS29C/2*	Megatron S4 Turbo
27	Michele Alboreto (I)	Ferrari F187-097	Ferrari V6 Turbo
28	Gerhard Berger (A)	Ferrari F187-099	Ferrari V6 Turbo
30	Philippe Alliot (F)	Lola LC87/02	Ford Cosworth V8

* Race car

QUALIFYING

FRIDAY: Very hot, dry		SATURDAY: Very hot, dry	
Driver		Driver	
Mansell	1:06.454	Mansell	1:06.705
Prost	1:06.877	Senna	1:07.024
Piquet	1:07.270	Piquet	1:07.140
Senna	1:07.303	Prost	1:07.843
Boutsen	1:08.077	Boutsen	1:08.176
Berger	1:08.198	Berger	1:08.335
Fabi	1:08.293	Warwick	1:08.800
Alboreto	1:08.390	Alboreto	1:08.916
Johansson	1:08.577	De Cesaris	1:08.949
Warwick	1:09.256	Patrese	1:08.993
Arnoux	1:09.430	Johansson	1:09.095
Patrese	1:09.458	Nannini	1:09.868
De Cesaris	1:09.499	Cheever	1:09.869
Cheever	1:09.828	Arnoux	1:09.970
Nannini	1:10.388	Nakajima	1:10.652
Ghinzani	1:10.798	Ghinzani	1:10.900
Brundle	1:11.451	Brundle	1:11.170
Danner	1:11.456	Danner	1:11.389
Caffi	1:12.167	Fabi	1:11.815
Nakajima	1:12.268	Campos	1:12.551
Alliot	1:13.026	Caffi	1:12.555
Campos	1:13.145	Capelli	1:12.654
Capelli	1:13.204	Palmer	1:13.474
Palmer	1:13.443	Streiff	1:13.525
Streiff	1:13.553	Alliot	1:14.422
Fabre	1:14.699	Fabre	1:14.787

STARTING GRID

No	Driver	Time
5	Mansell	1:06.454
1	Prost	1:06.877
12	Senna	1:07.024
6	Piquet	1:07.140
20	Boutsen	1:08.077
28	Berger	1:08.198
19	Fabi	1:08.293
27	Alboreto	1:08.390
2	Johansson	1:08.577
17	Warwick	1:08.800
8	De Cesaris	1:08.949
7	Patrese	1:08.993
25	Arnoux	1:09.430
18	Cheever	1:09.828
24	Nannini	1:09.868
11	Nakajima	1:10.652
26	Ghinzani	1:10.798
9	Brundle	1:11.170
10	Danner	1:11.389
21	Caffi	1:12.167
23	Campos	1:12.551
16	Capelli	1:12.654
30	Alliot	1:13.026
3	Palmer	1:13.443
4	Streiff	1:13.525
14	Fabre	1:14.699

RESULTS

Pos	No	Driver	Car	Laps	Time/Retirement
1	5	Mansell	Williams-Honda	80	1-37:03.839
2	6	Piquet	Williams-Honda	80	1-37:11.550
3	1	Prost	McLaren-TAG	80	1-37:59.094
4	12	Senna	Lotus-Honda	79	
5	19	Fabi	Benetton-Ford	77	
6	4	Streiff	Tyrrell-Cosworth	76	
7	3	Palmer	Tyrrell-Cosworth	76	
8	2	Johansson	McLaren-TAG	74	
9	14	Fabre	AGS-Cosworth	74	
R	28	Berger	Ferrari	71	Spun off
NC	11	Nakajima	Lotus-Honda	71	Running
R	27	Alboreto	Ferrari	64	Engine
R	17	Warwick	Arrows-Megatron	62	Turbo
R	30	Alliot	LC-Cosworth	57	Transmission
R	16	Capelli	March-Cosworth	52	Engine
R	23	Campos	Minardi-Moderni	52	Turbo
R	25	Arnoux	Ligier-Megatron	33	Exhaust
R	20	Boutsen	Benetton-Ford	31	Electrics
R	10	Danner	Zakspeed	26	Turbo
R	26	Ghinzani	Ligier-Megatron	24	Engine
R	24	Nannini	Minardi-Moderni	23	Engine
R	7	Patrese	Brabham-BMW	19	Transmission
R	9	Brundle	Zakspeed	18	Lost wheel
R	21	Caffi	Osella-Alfa Romeo	18	Gearbox
R	8	De Cesaris	Brabham-BMW	2	Turbo
R	18	Cheever	Arrows-Megatron	0	Electrics

FASTEST LAP

Driver	
Piquet	1:09.548
Mansell	1:10.405
Prost	1:11.324
Berger	1:11.675
Johansson	1:11.874
Fabi	1:12.101
Senna	1:12.231
Alboreto	1:12.457
Boutsen	1:12.567
Warwick	1:13.245
Arnoux	1:13.845
Patrese	1:13.984
De Cesaris	1:14.098
Nannini	1:14.248
Nakajima	1:14.524
Ghinzani	1:15.367
Brundle	1:15.549
Alliot	1:15.984
Danner	1:16.133
Palmer	1:16.256
Capelli	1:16.290
Streiff	1:16.433
Caffi	1:17.147
Fabre	1:17.499
Campos	1:17.836

CHAMPIONSHIP POSITIONS

DRIVERS		CONSTRUCTORS	
1 Senna	27	1 Williams-Honda	45
2 Prost	26	2 McLaren-TAG	39
3 Piquet	24	3 Lotus-Honda	30
4 Mansell	21	4 Ferrari	17
5 Johansson	13	5 Arrows-Megatron	4
6 Berger	9	Benetton-Ford	4
7 Alboreto	8	Brabham-BMW	4
8 Cheever	4	8 Tyrrell-Cosworth	3
De Cesaris	4	9 Zakspeed	2
10 Nakajima	3	10 Ligier-Megatron	1
11 Boutsen	2	March-Cosworth	1
Brundle	2		
Fabi	2		
Palmer	2		
15 Arnoux	1		
Capelli	1		
Streiff	1		

JIM CLARK CUP

1 Palmer	33
2 Streiff	30
3 Fabre	26
4 Alliot	15
5 Capelli	6

COLIN CHAPMAN CUP

1 Tyrrell-Cosworth	63
2 AGS-Cosworth	26
3 Lola-Cosworth	15
4 March-Cosworth	6

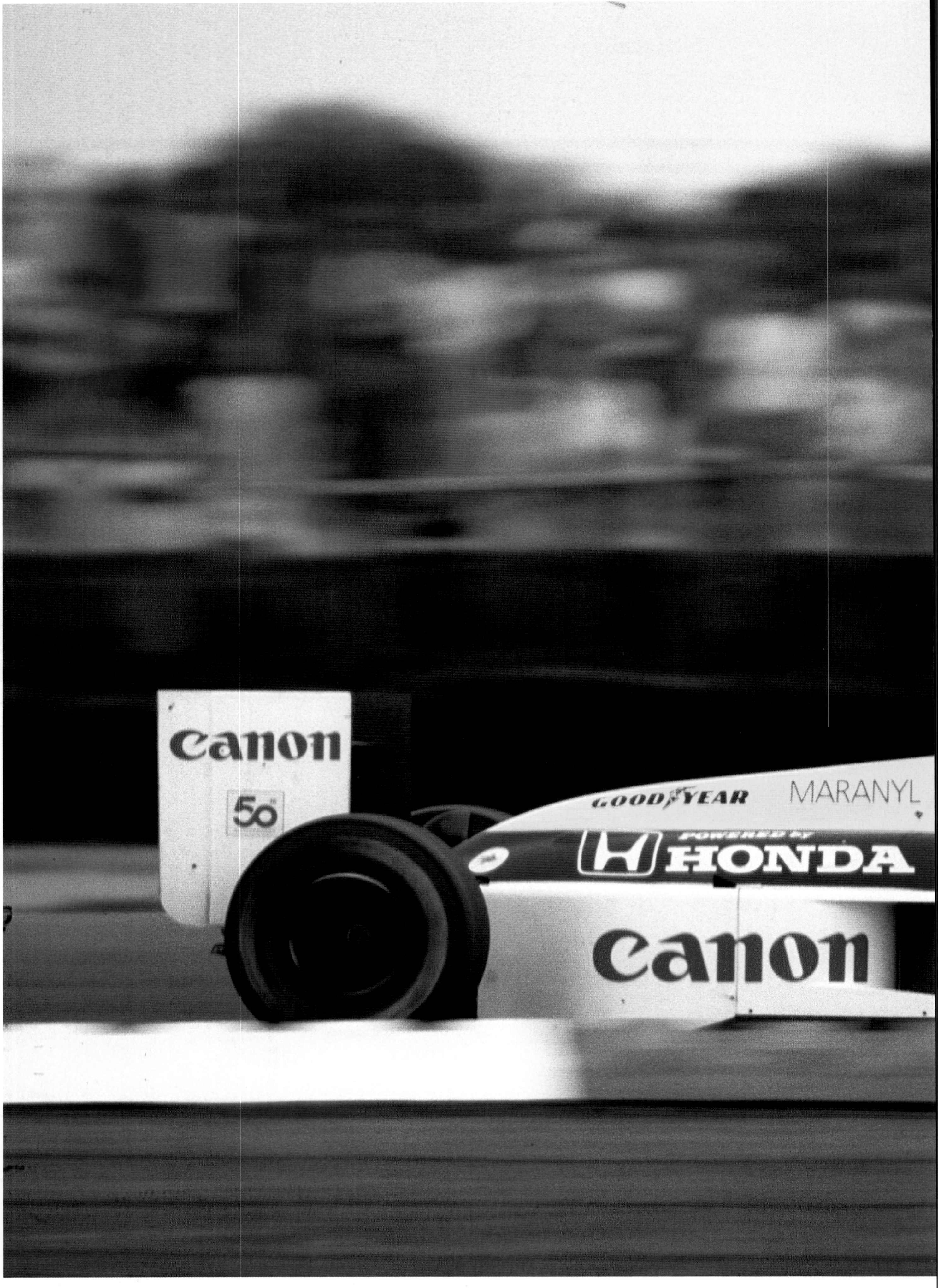
Canon
50
GOODYEAR
MARANYL
POWERED by
HONDA
Canon

Britain

ROUND SEVEN: July 12, 1987

CARRIED AWAY AT HOME

His fellow countrymen were with him, spiritually, in the driver's seat. Their clearly audible support sustained him in the chase that left the lap record in tatters and his resurgent team-mate back in his place.

The gap to race leader Nelson Piquet was almost half a minute when Nigel Mansell returned from the pits with new tyres that his team had earlier reckoned he wouldn't need. It seemed all over, but nobody had figured on the emotional power Mansell was about to be charged with as he blasted around harder than he had previously dared on such a fast track.

For 20 risky, breathtaking laps, Mansell had the muffled sounds of inspiration ringing in his helmet and at the corners of his vision he caught the banners fluttering wildly to exhort him on to his second straight British Grand Prix victory.

This was what Nigel needed to counter a sudden dose of the Nelson Piquet of old. Stung out of complacency by torrential public criticism of his motivation, and also by the delicious prospect of keeping his rival and team-mate from winning a second grand prix at home, the Brazilian hammered around in the lead for 62 laps in a race that was just two Williams-Hondas blowing the rest away on sheer speed and acceleration.

However Piquet had opted for conventional pre-race strategy which dictated no tyre stop, while Mansell, worried about fuel, opted to go with minimal wing. At a distinct disadvantage on full tanks, Mansell trailed early, then when a wheel balance flew off, sending the car vibrating and his vision blurring, he went for a new set of tyres.

With three laps to go, and economy the last thing on his mind, he tagged Piquet and swiftly and supremely dispatched him. Those final three laps were too much for those who shared the victory. The emotion bubbled over the barriers and helped carry home the hero who was now just one point behind the world championship leader.

Previous page: Nigel Mansell on a charge, carried home by the chorus of support from the crowd. With each lap there was a new lap record and just up the road, race leader Piquet.

Above: The acclaimed Nannini in a characteristic Minardi pose — waiting for the engine to be tended.

For seven grands prix the upper hand at Williams had indubitably been Nigel Mansell's. In France Nelson Piquet at least ran close, now at Nigel's home grand prix, the time had come for Nelson to wake up.

During qualifying the Brazilian responded in the way one would expect of a driver of real stamp. The desire was back, rumours of retirement seemed just vicious gossip, for he desperately wished to have the pole for this grand prix, to keep Mansell from it.

It was the other Williams driver at the pole position press conference, and the signs were that for one not big on media communications, he therefore rather enjoyed it. Certainly he stayed longer than is his custom.

He had been unable to match Mansell during the first half of the session, he said, because the handling had been off. "This morning we ran with full tanks, of course, and when the car is like that — heavy — you put packers in the dampers, to keep the car from bottoming. Well, we forgot to take out the packers for the qualifying session, and for the first 35 minutes I had to fight the car — it was very slow.

"Finally we realised, took out the packers, lowered the car, and it was much better. But by this stage I'd already used up one set of tyres, and had a spin at Becketts. Fortunately I put the act together right at the end, and did the same time as Nigel." A hair quicker, in fact.

"This year," Nelson went on, "I've been very slow. You know, we've had a choice of car: long wheelbase or short. At Imola I tried the 'short' one, and liked it very much. It was quick there — and also much easier to drive. And I stayed with it all the time until Ricard last week. There I decided to try the long wheelbase car again — and found that one better for that circuit.

"It was still much more difficult to drive, but it was quicker. Here I did a back-to-back test very carefully, and again the 'long' car was quicker. And I think one of the reasons I've been slow was that I stayed too long in the wrong car."

Piquet concluded by firmly denying rumours of his impending retirement. "If you're happy to be second, to stay in just because the money is good, better you should stop racing. But that's not my case: I want to race, I want to be at the front, and maybe I still have the thing inside me to be able to do that."

Predictably, nothing was remotely in range of the Williams-Hondas at Silverstone. The fight for pole position was exclusively between Piquet and Mansell. While neither expressed much enthusiasm for the new chicane at Woodcote, it worked undeniably to their advantage, for now the next stretch — down to Copse — became a sheer blitz of acceleration, right up through the gearbox. And what you needed here was a Honda V6.

Over the finish line Mansell was beamed at 189.418 mph, and the No. 5 Williams was still accelerating. Next up were Senna and Piquet, Honda men both, at 186 plus, and then you found the McLarens at 181, and on down.

"I don't mind the new corner," Alain Prost commented. "It provides a place to pass, and I think it's been quite well done. But certainly it hasn't helped anyone but the Hondas. On handling and grip we're good. Top speed, too. But on acceleration we can't get near them."

The world champion, like Ayrton Senna, hovered behind the Williams pair throughout the two days of practice, without remotely offering serious threat.

Piquet was fastest in each of the time sessions. After the first day, though, most expected Mansell to vault ahead, for his had been a trying session — first set of tyres out of balance, sudden puncture at Becketts, damaged undertray, into T-car for the last minutes — and he was only a tenth away.

For much of the final session Nigel sat in the pits, waiting for someone to beat his new fastest time. Nelson did it, and thereafter Mansell was unable quite to come back, although he was but seven-hundredths away. Finally, at 1.55, a supreme final effort from Nigel ended with a wild spin into the Woodcote chicane: "We took off the front cooling ducts, and I lost the brakes a little bit." Performing one of his dramatic full-throttle spin turns, Mansell

Above: *Greg Norman and Nigel Mansell in mutual admiration. A few hours on the golf course after qualifying did wonders for Nigel.*

Below: *What's this? Prost steals the first corner from the Williams pair. It was a short-lived glory.*

proceeded down the escape road, and thence to the pits. Before the chequered flag fluttered, he was leaving the circuit for 18 holes with buddy Greg Norman.

Senna was third, but a clear second distant. On a fast circuit, once again, the 'active' Lotus-Honda was quick, but not quick enough. On Friday Ayrton was distinctly unhappy with the car's balance. The team tried different settings, but any hopes of quick lap at the end were lost when a sizeable chunk of metal (probably from Christian Danner's Zakspeed, which shed a portion of sidepod . . .) was flicked up by Mansell. It hit Senna's left front wing. It could have hit Senna.

Peter Wright and his men came up with a better answer on Saturday, enabling Ayrton to find more than a second, and to move a place ahead of Prost. But the Brazilian had his doubts about being on the pace for the grand prix.

Prost, by contrast, looked to Sunday with more optimism, despite a final session disastrous by his own standards, in which he placed only ninth. In both race and spare McLarens, he said, the engines were well down on power, and grip and balance could have been better. But he liked it on full tanks,

and expressed reasonable confidence in the fuel consumption achieved in the untimed sessions.

This was not a factor at Ricard, but very much one at Silverstone. "Tyres are the only consideration here," Piquet insisted. "You cannot control them — if you get a blister, it's finished, you have to come in. The fuel you can control." Others were less convinced. Clearly, what Prost had to do was push the Honda men into lapping faster than they wished. As Alain pointed out, though, that meant using the TAG hard, and on recent evidence that could be dangerous.

Friday for the Benetton team was unusually trouble-free. Not a single Ford V6 blew up, and both Thierry Boutsen and Teo Fabi were in the first eight. By Saturday each was in the top six, and looking worth it. The cars' balance and grip delighted the drivers, and the engines — so long as boost was in relative check — gave acceptable reliability and power. The team was establishing itself after a slow start to the season.

Ferrari, too, were in better shape than for some while, Michele Alboreto seventh, Gerhard Berger eighth. There has never been a lot wrong with the F187's handling in fast corners, nor with the horse-

power from the latest 90 deg V6, and at Silverstone each could be seen to relative advantage. Only at the Woodcote chicane did the car's chronic problems — too little front end bite into the corner, too little traction out — manifest themselves. More than two seconds off the Williams pace, the red cars were at least in the picture.

Thereafter it was mainly gloom, in varying degrees, although Andrea de Cesaris pleased himself — and amazed everyone else — by keeping his Brabham on the road long and fast enough to lap quicker than team-mate Riccardo Patrese. Neither Arrows man was high-spirited, though, Derek Warwick unable to get the set-up right, Eddie Cheever bedevilled with engine problems. And Martin Brundle had two thoroughly dispiriting days, which included an alarming trip down the Woodcote escape road after the failure of a rear suspension rose-joint, and a turbo fire of some magnitude.

Philippe Alliot topped the Cosworth runners, but this was not a race for any of them to relish. Jonathan Palmer, his Tyrrell very slow in a straight line, spoke of the frustrations of qualifying at Silverstone: "It might sound ridiculous, with only 500-odd horsepower, but what I need is a clear lap! Seriously, you have to spend all your time looking in your mirrors, moving over for the turbos — and when they come by, with 900 bhp plus, they all but blow you off the road . . ."

On race morning logic dictated that probably no one would fluster the Williams-Hondas. But there were possibilities to be borne in mind. After a bright start to the day, clouds drifted over, and there were a few drops of rain. One wild card right there. And in the morning warm-up Prost was second fastest, between Piquet and Mansell, with Stefan Johansson fourth. The McLarens looked like being quick.

The opening seconds promised more of the same. While the Williams drivers worried about each other, taking off with a little too much wheelspin, Prost got the revs absolutely right, saw a gap on the left about as wide as the McLaren, and went for it. to the surprise of all — including Piquet and Mansell — it was the red and white car which led into Copse.

By the next turn, however, Piquet was past the Frenchman, and it was all done with the right foot. Down to Stowe a few seconds later, and it was Mansell's turn to shoot past. Nothing was to head a Williams for the rest of the afternoon.

Piquet was very quickly into his stride, showing all the resolution seen in qualifying. Within three laps he was a couple of seconds up on Mansell, and this he gradually stretched. But it was a matter of a tenth here and there, and obviously Nigel was far from out of it.

Equally obviously, he was using more road than Nelson, drifting right out the kerbing, and sometimes beyond. It was a gamble; mindful of the importance of fuel efficiency here, he had opted to run less wing than his team-mate, knowing that this would put him at a particular disadvantage during the first fuel-heavy half of the race. But if he could keep in touch in these conditions, he might be better fixed on fuel in the closing laps. That was the hope.

The Williams drivers, like virtually everyone else, had gone into the race in the expectation of going the distance on one set of Goodyears. But within 10 laps Mansell knew that was out for him. There was a worsening vibration through the steering, and he was finding it difficult to stay with Piquet. A front wheel balance weight had gone, as it turned out, but Nigel thought he might simply have blistered the tyres.

"The vibration got so bad," he reported, "that I literally couldn't see clearly. I radioed the pits, and told them I was going to have to come in at some stage. We settled on lap 35, and until then I just tried to keep as close to Nelson as possible.

That he did to some effect. Despite the problem, he was going well enough to set new fastest laps on 17 and 18. By lap 20 the two cars were separated by only a second and a half. And already there were 10 cars on the lead lap.

Prost could do nothing. He had fought off Senna successfully, but by now was 12 seconds adrift. "As early as lap five I knew from the read-out that we were using way too much fuel, for some reason. Nothing to do. I could not, in any case, fight with the Williams, so I turned the boost down."

1.

2.

Thus it was that we witnessed Prost driving, in his terms, almost raggedly, using the kerbs, brushing the grass. To compensate for the reduced power, he and the car were putting in the hard work. But that, inevitably, took its toll of the tyres. Wear was not a problem, but Alain knew that the grip would go away. On lap 29 he came in, the first to change, and in so doing dropped to fifth, behind Senna and Alboreto.

Yes, there were other cars in this race, although they went largely unnoticed by the spectators, who had eyes only for the lead battle. Alboreto impressed in the Ferrari, keeping within striking distance of Senna, and giving the team something about which to enthuse: for Berger it had been another poor day, the Austrian making a poor start, then spinning spectacularly into retirement after only seven laps.

And Senna, of course, never gave up. As Lotus had feared, their Honda fuel consumption was no match for the Williams' figures, and for Ayrton it was Ricard all over again: a matter of keeping going as hard as possible, hoping for points to keep the world championship lead intact. But this is not how Senna likes to go racing.

Others had faded rather more. Johansson, after running strongly in sixth during the early laps, had blown up massively — which did not bode well for Prost. The Benetton-Fords, impressive qualifiers,

And how the crowd worked for Nigel in those closing minutes! All round the circuit people waved their banners, yelled their support in great gusts of sound clearly audible above the engine noise. "It was an extraordinary feeling," he later said. "I drove maybe the last 20 laps at ten-tenths, right on the limit, and I don't really like to do that on such a quick circuit. But I knew that was what it was going to take to beat Nelson, and support like that really inspires you!"

The pace was something quite incredible. For the record, Mansell put in no fewer than 12 laps which were beneath his team-mate's fastest — and no one else was within a second of Piquet's best. By lap 49 Nelson had lapped fourth-placed Prost, and soon, for the second time in a week, the same indignity befell Senna.

Still, Ayrton did make it to the finish, which was not true of Alain. The McLaren pulled silently off onto the grass with 12 laps to go: "After I knew we had the consumption problem, I just hoped to finish as well as possible. Then, after my tyre stop, I lost the clutch. And then, finally, the engine just cut out. Electrics somewhere, I suppose."

In sight, though, was win No. 10 for Mansell. "If Nelson had stopped for tyres earlier, when I first started catching him," he said afterwards, "I think he would have won, quite honestly. But he stayed out…"

"The tyres were still good, with 15 laps to go," Piquet commented, "but during the last 10 laps they really began to go off in a big way, and I didn't expect that."

Now there was no way Mansell could be resisted. With 10 laps left, the gap was 7.6, after which it came down like this: 6.5, 3.9, 2.0, 1.4, 0.8, nothing. As they set off on lap 63 Nelson was clearly on the ropes, and Nigel was keen to dispatch as quickly as possible, not allowing him the luxury of working out a plan to keep him back.

He did the thing supremely. On the thrash down to Stowe he jinked left — and Piquet instantly countered. By now, though, Mansell had gone right.

1: Last man home, Pascal Fabre, nevertheless took second points in the normally aspirated class.
2: It was a long way down the list before a non-Honda powered car appeared. It was Derek Warwick's Arrows-Megatron in fifth.
3: Dead. Streiff abandons his silent Tyrrell and falls to third in the standings for the Jim Clark Cup.
4: Nice day for a walk in the English countryside. Rene Arnoux's Ligier was one of the first cars to retire on this day for the local hero.
5: Kaboom. Turbo fire consumes the back of the Andrea de Cesaris Brabham after just eight laps. The Italian was OK.

3.

4.

were running fuel-conscious races with low boost, and were only just in the top dozen, although both would be around at the end. The Arrows of Warwick and Cheever circulated in tandem for a long while, but Eddie had to quit with a blown engine. Gone, too, were both Brabhams.

Focus on the front. Mansell's aim of keeping in touch with Piquet was still on target. As the race neared the halfway point, indeed, the two Williams were right together, and on lap 35 came the pivotal point of the race: Nigel came in for that new set of tyres, was stationary for a fraction more than nine seconds.

He had driven down the sinuous pit entry road perhaps as quick as ever it has been done, but even so faced a huge task. With 30 laps to go, he was almost half a minute behind Piquet. Nelson looked to have it locked away, and he thought so himself.

"Everything was fine. The car was working well, and the tyres were in good shape. We took the decision not to stop." On lap 37 Mansell set a new fastest lap on his fresh Goodyears; on lap 40 Piquet beat it on his old ones. Yes, everything seemed on course for Nelson.

With 20 laps to go, though, Mansell really began to cut loose. Nearly every time around, it seemed, they were announcing a new fastest lap for him. One second, sometimes two, were chopped from Piquet's lead, and now the calculations got serious. At their present rate, they would be running together in the last two or three laps.

5.

87

Nelson had been sold the dummy, and Nigel, always deeper into Stowe than his rival, had the inside line.

The situation was hopeless for Piquet, but for old times' sake he gave Mansell a fairly unsubtle chop at the entry to the corner. It was wasted. This was a man pumped up after 20 flat-out laps, this was Silverstone, with less than eight miles to go. Nigel never flinched, and it was Nelson who had hastily got out of the way again.

Two more laps, and Mansell was home, winner of the British Grand Prix for the second year running — and in a style more remarkable than his victory at Brands in 1986.

The charge was calculated to perfection too, for during the course of the slowing down lap he ran out of fuel, coasted to a halt and was immediately engulfed by the appreciative crowd.

Mansell recalled the moment before the crowd swallowed him up. "Coming out of Club on the last lap, the engine cut. I don't mean it misfired, I mean it died! What fuel that remained all sloshed to the left, and that was it — *nothing*! I really thought I was going to lose the British GP in the last seconds of the race, for the sake of a pint of fuel.

"Fortunately," he continued, "it caught again, and got me to the flag. But then I got to Copse on my cooling-down lap, and it cut again. Once more it restarted, and I got as far as Becketts . . . and so on, until it finally stopped for good . . ."

Piquet did not offer him sanctuary, a ride back on the sidepod of No. 6, but afterwards was rather more cordial to Nigel than has sometimes been the case. In the press room they shook hands, for example, and spoke well of each other.

Nakajima and Warwick took fourth and fifth respectively. This was far and away Satoru's most competitive Formula One drive to date, and Derek was delighted with a finish at last: "I'm so happy I feel as if I won the race!"

Behind all the emotion of the day, however, a stark fact confronted 22 of the 266 grand prix runners: there were four Honda engines in the British Grand Prix, and they finished 1·2·3·4.

Right: This is for all of you! Mansell acknowledges the crowd for playing their role in his second straight British Grand Prix victory.

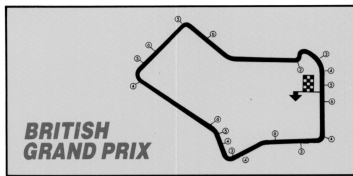

BRITISH GRAND PRIX

Round 7: July 12, 1987
Circuit: Silverstone

Race data:	65 laps of 2.969 mile (4.78 km) circuit
Weather:	Sunny, dry
Fastest lap:	Mansell, Williams FW11B, 1:09.832, 153.059mph
Existing record:	Prost, McLaren MP4/2B, 1:09.886, 151.035mph (old circuit)

ENTRIES

No	Driver (Nat)	Car/Chassis	Engine
1	Alain Prost (F)	McLaren MP4/3C-4	TAG V6 Turbo
2	Stefan Johansson (S)	McLaren MP4/3C-2	TAG V6 Turbo
3	Jonathan Palmer (GB)	Tyrrell DG/016-2	Ford Cosworth V8
4	Philippe Streiff (F)	Tyrrell DG/016-3	Ford Cosworth V8
5	Nigel Mansell (GB)	Williams FW11B/3*	Honda V6 Turbo
5T	Nigel Mansell (GB)	Williams FW11B/5	Honda V6 Turbo
6	Nelson Piquet (BR)	Williams FW11B/4*	Honda V6 Turbo
6T	Nelson Piquet (BR)	Williams FW11 B/1	Honda V6 Turbo
7	Riccardo Patrese (I)	Brabham BT56/3	BMW S4 Turbo
8	Andrea de Cesaris (I)	Brabham BT56/2	BMW S4 Turbo
9	Martin Brundle (GB)	Zakspeed 871/3	Zakspeed S4 Turbo
10	Christian Danner (D)	Zakspeed 871/2	Zakspeed S4 Turbo
11	Satoru Nakajima (J)	Lotus 99T/5	Honda V6 Turbo
12	Ayrton Senna (BR)	Lotus 99T/4	Honda V6 Turbo
14	Pascal Fabre (F)	AGS JH22/02-033	Ford Cosworth V8
16	Ivan Capelli (I)	March 871/02A	Ford Cosworth V8
17	Derek Warwick (GB)	Arrows A10/4	Megatron S4 Turbo
18	Eddie Cheever (USA)	Arrows A10/2	Megatron S4 Turbo
19	Teo Fabi (I)	Benetton B187-07	Ford V6 Turbo
20	Thierry Boutsen (B)	Benetton B187-06	Ford V6 Turbo
21	Alex Caffi (I)	Osella FA1H/01/87*	Alfa Romeo V8 Turbo
21T	Alex Caffi (I)	Osella FA1I/01/87	Alfa Romeo V8 Turbo
23	Adrian Campos (E)	Minardi M186-02	Moderni V6 Turbo
24	Alessandro Nannini (I)	Minardi M186-03	Moderni V6 Turbo
25	Rene Arnoux (F)	Ligier JS29C/5	Megatron S4 Turbo
27	Michele Alboreto (I)	Ferrari F187-098	Ferrari V6 Turbo
28	Gerhard Berger (A)	Ferrari F187-099	Ferrari V6 Turbo
30	Philippe Alliot (F)	Lola LC87/02	Ford Cosworth V8

* Race car

QUALIFYING

SATURDAY: Sunny, dry Driver		RACE: Sunny, dry Driver	
Piquet	1:07.110	Mansell	1:09.032
Mansell	1:07.180	Piquet	1:10.632
Senna	1:08.181	Senna	1:11.605
Boutsen	1:08.972	Alboreto	1:12.846
Fabi	1:09.246	Prost	1:13.346
Alboreto	1:09.274	Nakajima	1:13.780
Berger	1:09.408	Fabi	1:13.885
De Cesaris	1:09.475	Brundle	1:14.102
Prost	1:09.492	Boutsen	1:14.162
Johansson	1:09.541	Warwick	1:14.210
Patrese	1:10.020	Cheever	1:14.346
Warwick	1:10.781	Johansson	1:14.380
Nakajima	1:10.998	Patrese	1:14.814
Cheever	1:11.310	Berger	1:14.879
Nannini	1:12.293	De Cesaris	1:15.401
Arnoux	1:12.402	Caffi	1:17.347
Brundle	1:12.632	Nannini	1:17.383
Danner	1:13.337	Arnoux	1:17.552
Campos	1:13.793	Campos	1:18.059
Caffi	1:15.558	Palmer	1:18.543
Alliot	1:15.868	Streiff	1:18.745
Streiff	1:16.524	Alliot	1:18.924
Capelli	1:16.692	Capelli	1:18.999
Palmer	1:17.105	Fabre	1:19.784
Fabre	1:18.237	Danner	1:19.848

STARTING GRID

No	Driver	Time
6	Piquet	1:07.110
5	Mansell	1:07.180
12	Senna	1:08.181
1	Prost	1:08.577
20	Boutsen	1:08.972
19	Fabi	1:09.246
27	Alboreto	1:09.274
28	Berger	1:09.408
8	De Cesaris	1:09.475
2	Johansson	1:09.541
7	Patrese	1:10.012
11	Nakajima	1:10.619
17	Warwick	1:10.654
18	Cheever	1:11.053
24	Nannini	1:12.293
25	Arnoux	1:12.402
9	Brundle	1:12.632
10	Danner	1:13.337
23	Campos	1:13.793
21	Caffi	1:15.558
30	Alliot	1:15.868
4	Streiff	1:16.524
3	Palmer	1:16.644
16	Capelli	1:16.692
14	Fabre	1:18.237

RESULTS

Pos	No	Driver	Car	Laps	Time/Retirement
1	5	Mansell	Williams-Honda	65	1-19:11.780
2	6	Piquet	Williams-Honda	65	1-19:13.698
3	12	Senna	Lotus-Honda	64	
4	11	Nakajima	Lotus-Honda	63	
5	17	Warwick	Arrows-Megatron	63	
6	19	Fabi	Benetton-Ford	63	
7	20	Boutsen	Benetton-Ford	62	
8	3	Palmer	Tyrrell-Cosworth	60	
9	14	Fabre	AGS-Cosworth	59	
R	4	Streiff	Tyrrell-Cosworth	57	Engine
NC	9	Brundle	Zakspeed	54	
R	1	Prost	McLaren-TAG	53	Electrics
R	27	Alboreto	Ferrari	52	Rear suspension
R	18	Cheever	Arrows-Megatron	45	Engine
R	23	Campos	Minardi-Moderni	34	Fuel pump
R	21	Caffi	Osella-Alfa Romeo	32	Engine
R	10	Danner	Zakspeed	32	Gearbox
R	7	Patrese	Brabham-BMW	28	Engine cut
R	2	Johansson	McLaren-TAG	18	Engine
R	24	Nannini	Minardi-Moderni	10	Engine
R	8	De Cesaris	Brabham-BMW	8	Fire
R	28	Berger	Ferrari	7	Spun off
R	30	Alliot	LC-Cosworth	7	Transmission
R	25	Arnoux	Ligier-Megatron	3	Engine
R	16	Capelli	March-Cosworth	3	Gearbox damage

FASTEST LAP

Driver	
Piquet	1:07.596
Mansell	1:07.725
Prost	1:08.577
Senna	1:09.255
Boutsen	1:09.724
Patrese	1:10.012
Johansson	1:10.242
Fabi	1:10.264
Berger	1:10.328
Alboreto	1:10.441
Nakajima	1:10.619
Warwick	1:10.654
De Cesaris	1:10.787
Cheever	1:11.053
Arnoux	1:12.503
Brundle	1:12.852
Ghinzani	1:13.381
Nannini	1:13.737
Campos	1:15.719
Danner	1:15.833
Palmer	1:16.644
Alliot	1:16.770
Capelli	1:17.122
Streiff	1:17.208
Caffi	1:18.495
Fabre	1:19.163

CHAMPIONSHIP POSITIONS

	DRIVERS			CONSTRUCTORS	
1	Senna	31	1	Williams-Honda	60
2	Mansell	30	2	McLaren-TAG	39
	Piquet	30	3	Lotus-Honda	37
4	Prost	26	4	Ferrari	17
5	Johansson	13	5	Arrows-Megatron	6
6	Berger	9	6	Benetton-Ford	5
7	Alboreto	8	7	Brabham-BMW	4
8	Nakajima	8	8	Tyrrell-Cosworth	3
9	Cheever	4	9	Zakspeed	2
	De Cesaris	4	10	Ligier-Megatron	1
11	Fabi	3		March-Cosworth	1
12	Boutsen	2			
	Brundle	2			
	Palmer	2			
	Warwick	2			
16	Arnoux	1			
	Capelli	1			
	Streiff	1			

JIM CLARK CUP		COLIN CHAPMAN CUP	
1 Palmer	42	1 Tyrrell-Cosworth	72
2 Fabre	32	2 AGS-Cosworth	32
3 Streiff	30	3 Lola-Cosworth	15
4 Alliot	15	4 March-Cosworth	6
5 Capelli	6		

Germany

ROUND EIGHT, July 26, 1987

OH, LUCKY DAY

In the lonely patch of clear road between the two at the front and the walking wounded behind, he waited. It was to be his lucky day and a familiar name moved conclusively into the championship lead.

The world champion went racing this day in Germany, so did Nigel Mansell, and they were unthreatened by the rest. Mansell felt he had the other covered, but it didn't look that way and this was a novelty: Alain Prost's McLaren catching Mansell's Williams on this fastest of tracks and holding the lead through the tyre stops.

Prost raced confidently knowing fuel was not a problem and in the belief that the recent spate of engine reliability had ended following changes to the engine by Porsche. Mansell, not so sure about fuel, had let Prost past early in the hope that he could sit behind in the draft. The tactics became academic when the Honda engine seized.

That elevated a distant Nelson Piquet to his customary second place. And there he ran until four laps to go, in no shape to reel in Prost. Past the No. 1 McLaren went Piquet: the TAG engine problem hadn't been solved after all.

Piquet was lucky. Everybody said it and the Brazilian agreed. He had been without a fuel readout in the first half of the race due to a loose connection. As well, the car darted and weaved under brakes with a spooky handling problem that was not comforting on such a daunting track.

It was is first win of the season and at a time when his thirst for victory had been questioned. By winning, after so many quiet seconds, he had jumped into the lead in the world championship. He had done it that way before to win a championship and was on course to do it again.

After being temporarily inconvenienced by Nelson Piquet at Silverstone, during qualifying, Nigel Mansell came back at Hockenheim to take his sixth pole position in eight races. Next to him was Ayrton Senna, and then came Alain Prost and Piquet. The Modern Racing Quartet. It seemed a long time since anyone else had seriously threatened.

Hockenheim — two long blasts, three chicanes and a fiddly 'stadium' section — is always a compromise. Ideally, you need as little wing as feasible for the endless straights, as much as possible for the stadium. And there are other considerations, too. "We can get the car as good as perfect," Mansell said of his Williams-Honda on Friday afternoon. "In fact, we've *had* it like that. But for the race that set-up's out of the question because we wouldn't make it to the end on the fuel available . . ."

Fuel was much on everyone's mind at Hockenheim, just as at Imola and Silverstone. This is a place where consumption is critical. Mansell had his fears about fuel. "If it's dry tomorrow," he remarked on Saturday afternoon, "it's going to be a big problem, I think."

For others, the weather had little to do with it. On Saturday it poured down for most of the day, and Lotus, it was said, were getting worse mileage in the wet than in the dry. Eddie Cheever reported that the same was true of his Arrows: "In the rain you run more wing, right? So that uses more fuel, for a start. Plus, in the rain you're spinning the wheels everywhere, and *that* wastes a lot . . ."

Wet or dry, though, you had to favour Mansell and Williams-Honda to make it three on the trot. Nigel was less than delighted with his FW11B on Friday morning — initially it was bottoming quite severely, where it hadn't been during testing — but as soon as the problem was put to rights, No. 5 went to the top of the list, and there it stayed.

"There was an error," he said slowly, picking his words carefully. "A misunderstanding, if you like, between the test and coming here for the race. We supposedly had the car set up exactly as it had been for the test — and when I got in, it just wasn't the same. Something, let's say, hadn't been relayed properly down the line . . .

"At first we couldn't understand the problem, but then eventually we realised. The nice thing, though, is that we know the car pretty well inside out. We made the necessary alteration, and bang! It was quick. And it's all right now, fine."

For most of Friday morning, Prost was fastest, but towards the end of the session Mansell beat his time. And in the afternoon, on a far from clear lap, he was again quickest. The spiteful elements throughout Saturday ensured that the Williams was on the pole.

Hockenheim was at its deadliest on the second day, recalling that appalling day five years before, when Didier Pironi suffered the accident which ended his career. In absolute terms, there was little point in venturing out in the final session, but some weather reports suggested more rain on Sunday, so Nigel agreed with Patrick Head it was as well to give the car a run, however brief.

He did only three laps — and once again the Williams topped the chart, with Thierry Boutsen's Benetton a couple of seconds back. "The biggest problem," Mansell said, "was keeping the thing pointed forwards on the straights . . ." For the record, he passed through the speed trap before the first chicane, the fastest point in the circuit, just a fraction shy of 190 mph. In the dry, on Friday, he had recorded 211 plus at the same point, team-mate Piquet 213!

The straights at Hockenheim give everyone the 'heebies', for the cars are flat out for an unusually long time. Possibilities of tyre failure are always in the mind. Ayrton Senna, in particular, had cause to ponder the consequences of such a thing.

Lotus, together with McLaren and Ferrari, were running at Hockenheim on the Wednesday following the British GP. Senna was into a string of quick laps: on the run down to the first chicane, the fastest part of the circuit, he passed through Ferrari's speed trap at 332 kph (about 206 mph). But immediately afterwards the left rear tyre disintegrated with such violence that the entire corner of the Lotus broke up. "The driveshaft flew off into the woods somewhere," related Peter Warr. "In fact, we never found it . . ."

In a way it was a blessing that the left rear of the car departed *in toto*. "At least there was no upright there," Warr said, "nothing to dig in."

About 350 metres further down the road, Ayrton brought the 99T to a safe halt. Shaken, he reported back to the pits: left rear tyre. And at once Warr was on the telephone to Goodyear in Akron, warning that they might have a problem at the German GP.

A day later, Lotus were in a position to allay Goodyear fears. Analysis of the computer data revealed that, for some time before the incident, the ride height on that corner of the car had been going down. "Through the hydraulic actuator on that corner, the computer was compensating for the problem," Warr continued. "In effect, it was keeping the platform level. That indicates that the tyre had been going down for some distance before it failed altogether.

This discovery was a relief to everyone: the tyre had failed, not because of any inherent fault in construction or manufacture, but because Senna had picked up a puncture, probably along the pit straight. It was definitely *not* a spontaneous blow-out.

There was, of course, another way of looking at this. On the one hand, it was good that the active system had allowed analysis of the incident, but was it also conceivable that, in compensating for the tyre deflation, it had masked the problem, kept it from the attention of the driver?

"No," said Peter firmly. "We don't think that's the case. The construction of the current tyre is such that the driver can't feel a puncture too well. At Silverstone, you know, Mansell had a puncture during practice, which gave him a huge moment at Becketts. Now he came past the pits *twice* with the tyre going down — the second time actually running on the white letters of the sidewall. A Goodyear engineer spotted it from the other end of the pits, and began running down to the Williams pit to warn them. But by the time he got there, it was too late . . ."

The fact that the Hockenheim incident occurred to the Lotus, rather than the conventionally-suspended Ferrari or McLaren, effectively staved off the need for a last-minute investigative panic for Goodyear. Had it been Alboreto or Prost who had suffered the failure, the Akron men would have had to assume the worst, for proving otherwise would have been well-nigh impossible. "It would have meant looking for bits of the tyre," Warr concluded, "which were spread all over the woods . . ."

The testing was to check out some recent advances in the 'active' system. A new programme improved the Lotus-Honda's balance considerably, Ayrton said, and he was well pleased with the car on Friday. The timed session, though, was hectic. The qualifying car came in after half an hour, its undertray damaged. "As I came into the second chicane, the car jumped out of fourth. I arrived therefore in neutral, and had to go over the kerb . . ."

That meant using the race car for the last 20 minutes, and it was not so well set up, bottoming badly enough for Senna to spin in the stadium. For all that, though, he was second fastest, only a couple of tenths from Mansell, and optimistic for the race. On Saturday morning, in almost dry conditions, he was quickest, and felt that pole in the afternoon was a real possibility. But the rain took care of that.

During the Hockenheim tests, the world champion had lost two engines. Depressing, after the problems at Monaco, Ricard and Silverstone, but there was some cause for optimism: Porsche believed they found — and solved — the reliability problems with the TAG V6.

"I cannot say what they have done," Alain said, "but they have made a . . . mechanical change, which will not help us on power, but should make the engines last much better. I feel much happier about everything than at Silverstone." The first of the revised engines, for Prost's use, arrived on Friday night, and the following afternoon two more were delivered for use in the race.

During the first unofficial session Stefan Johansson was very little slower than Alain, but in the one and only dry timed session, an engine problem with the race car meant going out in the spare — which was down 500 revs. Stefan started eighth, disappointed to be so far down.

The same was true of Piquet, fourth. A broken turbo pipe clip cost him 20 minutes of Friday's dry session, and he never got the car handling to his taste, complaining of way too much oversteer through the stadium section. Mansell, by whom the Brazilian is inevitably judged, was more than a second quicker. But no one discounted Nelson for the race.

Michele Alboreto's Ferrari was only a couple of

tenths slower than the second Williams, and Michele reported that it felt really quite good. Even the traction out of slow corners, for so long a Ferrari bugbear, was reasonable, he said. "The biggest problem is not enough power — we can't get near the Hondas"

Gerhard Berger had a more immediate problem at 1.20 on Friday afternoon. At the first corner, the Austrian, beginning a hot lap, came into view. At close to 180 mph, he put the brakes on for the turn — and the left hand front suspension collapsed. The Ferrari snapped instantly into a spin, across the run-off area and hit the tyre barrier very hard. Berger

93

1.

was quickly out of the car and striding back to the pits, helmet still on, visor still down. Left front? "Yes," Gerhard said, "You saw it?"

Back in the pit, he made his feelings graphically clear to Marco Piccinini, who reportedly suggested he should say he had made a mistake. In every way, this was not a happy team. Time was when you heard Ferrari mechanics burst joyously into song as they worked on the cars. Not any more.

Much on the cars was new in Germany: turbo inlet tracts, underbodies, rear bodywork. There were also new rear wings, one for each driver, and they worked well. One of them was on Berger's car when he crashed, and it survived the accident without damage. But when the mechanics went down to collect No. 28, there was no trace of the rear wing. Several light fingers had whisked it away!

Thierry Boutsen again qualified well, sixth fastest in the Benetton-Ford. In the only dry session the Belgian had the benefit of new, larger turbos, which had shown up favourably, during a test at Silverstone. Unfortunately, though, there was only one set at Hockenheim, and Teo Fabi was due to have them for Saturday — when the rains came, of course. Ninth on the grid, the Italian reckoned he could have picked up at least a second.

On the fringe were the Brabhams (Andrea de Cesaris up there, as he invariably is on fast circuits), Rene Arnoux's Ligier and the Arrows of Derek Warwick and Eddie Cheever.

After the warm-up on Sunday, something interesting had happened. The world champion was in great spirits, he had set fastest time, and said that the McLaren felt great. More, their consumption tests were telling them what they wanted to hear: all being well, there would be no repeat of the previous year's pushing towards the line.

Mansell, too, was relaxed enough, although a little concerned about the way the Williams had bottomed on full tanks. Senna, though, was thoroughly upset: the balance had gone awry overnight somehow, and

2.

the engine was down on power, gutless. During the pre-race laps he found the problems still there, and decided to switch to the spare Lotus.

At the green light Mansell moved off well enough, but the Honda V6 went to the rev limiter in first gear, then nearly died. But this time Senna was away into the lead, and Prost also snicked by before the first corner.

Not a problem for Nigel. A great waft of horsepower took him by the McLaren on the first lap; and on the second he dealt with Senna. But soon after Prost also passed the Lotus, and the two of them quickly distanced themselves from the rest. The race, it seemed already, lay with them. Piquet, in the meantime, moved Senna down to fourth on lap three. Perhaps he could keep in touch with Nigel and Alain.

Ayrton, though, quite obviously could not. "Right from the start we were hopeless on top speed. They all passed me on the straight, and I could do nothing about it. Then I found that the boost control switch had no effect on the boost! And all the time I had terrible understeer . . ."

Behind the Lotus, Alboreto and Boutsen had a brief, but exhilarating scrap over fifth place, which the Ferrari driver appeared to have won — until lap 10, when the red No. 27 crawled into the pits, turbo gone. Berger, well off Michele's pace all weekend, retired for the same reason a few laps later.

Already Hockenheim was to be no repeat of Silverstone, Williams-Honda were not going to walk off with this one. After seven laps, indeed, Prost had closed right up on Mansell — so much so that at the last corner they gave Nigel the blue flag!

Once or twice the Frenchman jinked out of the tow, making as if to go by, but Mansell had him covered, made sure that the piece of road needed by the McLaren was full of Williams. But he was unsure as to how long he could hold on like that, and radioed his pit to that effect. Finally, he decided he was going to let Prost by, try and sit behind him, save some fuel in the draft.

On lap 11, therefore, Alain took the lead on the approach to the first chicane, and soon began to inch away. But there was nothing conclusive about it, for Nigel seemed comfortably able to stay in reasonable touch. By now Piquet was seven secs down to them, Senna a similar distance behind him. Boutsen continued in a strong fifth place, followed by Johansson, who was hampered by poor straight-line speed.

"Don't know what the problem was," Stefan said. "We had it in the warm-up — I was slower than all the turbos apart from the Minardis, so there had to be something wrong . . . They checked it out afterwards, and couldn't find anything, but in the race it was just the same. It was a pity, because the handling was great."

By lap 18 Prost had the lead out to nearly four secs, and at the end of his next he was in for tyres, the first of the leading runners to stop. It was copybook, but any thoughts of a straight-forward cruise to victory were dispelled by the announcement of a new fastest lap to Mansell, now in the lead.

Lap 20 saw Piquet in for tyres, and Mansell followed on the 22nd. Between Prost's stop and his own, Nigel had really charged, hoping to build enough of a cushion to come in for fresh Goodyears, rejoin without losing the lead. But Alain, too, had similar thoughts. As the Williams accelerated away from its pit, the McLaren was hurtling down the road alongside, heading into the first turn, back in the lead once more.

Senna pitted at the end of lap 23 for his new tyres, and the moment was ill chosen. In front of him, coming in for attention to a misfire, was the tardy Zakspeed of Christian Danner. Through the little chicane in the pit entry road, the Lotus was all but going over the top of the German car, and a few metres further on Ayrton accelerated past it, arriving at his pit a little fast, wheels locked. Was overtaking in the pit lane permitted? No one could ever recall a previous instance of it, so nobody knew.

Senna's hastiness availed him little. Two laps later he was in the pits again: "I heard a hissing noise behind me somewhere, and thought it must be a problem with the hydraulics for the suspension." But such was not the case; a turbo mounting bolt

3.

4.

1: Nakajima awaits his Lotus-Honda. The Japanese was to be let down by the suspension and spoil his good finishing record.
2: The Lola protests through the first chicane as Philippe Alliot gets the better of the close-following Tyrrells.
3: The local team, Zakspeed, had a dreadful home grand prix. Warwick did finish but in last place.
4: After his tyre stop Mansell begins to catch Prost, then he felt the engine tighten.

had come loose, and it was this which had rendered useless Ayrton's cockpit boost control.

He had other problems, too. During his fight for fourth place with Boutsen, he had found the Lotus's understeer so extreme that he became convinced there had to be a blockage in the Pitot heads at the front of the car. These, in fact, were found to be clear, but a nose wing was damaged, and this the mechanics changed. As the yellow car left the pits for the last time, however, they noticed a stream of hydraulic fluid in its wake. Before the end of the race, indeed, the 99T was devoid of its 'active' suspension — in fact, devoid of much in the way of suspension at all. During the closing laps, Senna passed the pits in a cloud of sparks, the Lotus now settled on its conventional slave springs. Ayrton said it was like driving a kart. At which, of course, he is adept.

Lap 24 had brought a big change in the condition of the race track. Warwick, who had been running a strong seventh in the Arrows, came into the stadium with fingers of flame at the rear of the car. By the time he was through the Sachskurve, it had become something of a conflagration, and the car, on now molten rubber, was sliding all over the place. It was a turbo fire of immense proportions, and Derek was looking for somewhere quick and safe to park, finally pulling off before the fast turn. But a lot of oil had unavoidably gone down, and now the Sachskurve was like glass. For a while, the only safe line through the corner was a wide one, and speeds throughout the stadium fell considerably.

After his tyre stop Mansell had rejoined around five secs behind Prost. He began to catch Alain, but not at a dramatic rate. And on lap 26 the Williams was barely moving as it entered the stadium. "I felt the engine begin to go," he said, "and half a lap later it just seized completely." Disconsolately, he parked next to the guardrail behind the paddock. Prost, it seemed, was home free, nearly 40 secs up on Piquet.

Nelson was going better now. During the first half of the race, it transpired, he had been without a fuel readout. "After his pit stop, it was OK," Patrick Head said later. "It must have been a loose wire, which somehow jiggled back to work again after his tyre stop." Piquet also complained of a front end instability, which made the Williams weave and dart under braking. He now began to gain on Prost, but at a barely perceptible rate. No, it was going to be second again, for the sixth time in the season.

Or maybe not. On lap 37 Alain led by 26 secs, but next time around it was 21, then 17, then . . . nothing. All waited for the red and white car to flash into the stadium again, but it was Piquet's Williams which eventually appeared. With less than five laps to go, the McLaren's alternator belt had broken, and with it had gone that remarkably elusive 28th record victory.

"The car was perfect," Prost said. "Then suddenly I got a bad misfire. The green and red lights on the dash came on at the same time, and that was it. I was lapping the Tyrrells when it started, and I was hardly able to pass them in a straight line . . . I had the same problem at Imola, and Stefan had it at Ricard . . ." It should *not* have happened again, in other words.

Thus, both main protagonists were gone, and with it the prospect of an enthralling duel. Mansell: "I was going to catch him, I know it." Prost: "I don't believe anyone would have beaten me today." Piquet: "This was my lucky day."

Indeed, Nelson now had less than 20 miles to the flag, and new second man Johansson worried about his engine, had turned the boost down to minimum, looking for his first finish in a long time. Senna, limping along, was nevertheless third now, and looking at four points. And fourth and fifth, incredibly, were the Tyrrells of Philippe Streiff and Jonathan Palmer, which had run in tandem from the start.

Earlier in the race Jonathan had been ahead, dropping behind his team-mate when he was unlucky enough to find Warwick's oil. He was then to see a pit signal from his boss, telling him to hold station behind Streiff.

During the opening laps both Tyrrells had been headed by Philippe Alliot's Lola, now sixth. "After 20 laps or so," team boss Gerard Larrousse said, "the rev limiter began cutting in early — at 9000. Otherwise the car ran perfectly. It's a pity, but we are consoled by scoring our first point . . ."

Three normally-aspirated cars then in the first six — and this at Hockenheim, one of the quick places.

The final drama came after Piquet had taken the flag. All waited a long time for Johansson to appear, and when he did it was at a very much reduced pace. Out of fuel? No, not that. As the McLaren came more sharply into focus, its right hand tyre was seen to be flailing. Through the stadium it was disintegrating, and so, too, was the suspension. Stefan crossed the line to a wall of applause comfortably greater than that accorded the winner.

"The tyre began to go down immediately after the first corner, would you believe? So I had to do virtually a whole lap like that. It finally went in a big way on the approach to the first chicane, but I had to keep going. The car was all over the place! And I had to drive as hard as possible because I didn't know how far ahead I was of the next guy. The suspension was gone, and everything, for most of the lap . . ." How fast on the straight, Stefan? He laughed, perhaps a little sheepishly. "Oh, I don't know. Two-fifty kph, I suppose . . ."

Left: After that string of seconds, Piquet finally lucks one and jumps to the top of the championship tables.

Below left: Johansson survives into second place, having done almost all the last lap on three wheels.

GERMAN GRAND PRIX

Round 8: July 26, 1987
Circuit: Hockenheim

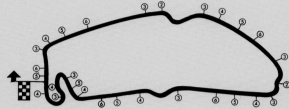

Race data:	44 laps of 4.223 mile (6.79 km) circuit
Weather:	Dry, overcast
Fastest lap:	Mansell, Williams FW11B, 1:45.716, 143.854mph
Existing record:	Berger, Benetton B186, 1:46.604, 142.625mph

ENTRIES

No	Driver (Nat)	Car/Chassis	Engine
1	Alain Prost (F)	McLaren MP4/3C-3*	TAG V6 Turbo
1T	Alain Prost (F)	McLaren MP4/3C-1	TAG V6 Turbo
2	Stefan Johansson (S)	McLaren MP4/3C-2	TAG V6 Turbo
3	Jonathan Palmer (GB)	Tyrrell DG/016-2	Ford Cosworth V8
4	Philippe Streiff (F)	Tyrrell DG/016-3*	Ford Cosworth V8
4T	Philippe Streiff (F)	Tyrrell DG/016-5	Ford Cosworth V8
5	Nigel Mansell (GB)	Williams FW11B/3	Honda V6 Turbo
6	Nelson Piquet (BR)	Williams FW11B/4*	Honda V6 Turbo
6T	Nelson Piquet (BR)	Williams FW11 B/1	Honda V6 Turbo
7	Riccardo Patrese (I)	Brabham BT56/4	BMW S4 Turbo
8	Andrea de Cesaris (I)	Brabham BT56/1*	BMW S4 Turbo
8T	Andrea de Cesaris (I)	Brabham BT56/3	BMW S4 Turbo
9	Martin Brundle (GB)	Zakspeed 871/3	Zakspeed S4 Turbo
10	Christian Danner (D)	Zakspeed 871/2*	Zakspeed S4 Turbo
10T	Christian Danner (D)	Zakspeed 871/1	Zakspeed S4 Turbo
11	Satoru Nakajima (J)	Lotus 99T/3	Honda V6 Turbo
12	Ayrton Senna (BR)	Lotus 99T/4*	Honda V6 Turbo
12T	Ayrton Senna (BR)	Lotus 99T/5	Honda V6 Turbo
14	Pascal Fabre (F)	AGS JH22/02-032	Ford Cosworth V8
16	Ivan Capelli (I)	March 871/01	Ford Cosworth V8
16T	Ivan Capelli (I)	March 871/03*	Ford Cosworth V8
17	Derek Warwick (GB)	Arrows A10/4	Megatron S4 Turbo
18	Eddie Cheever (USA)	Arrows A10/2	Megatron S4 Turbo
19	Teo Fabi (I)	Benetton B187-07	Ford V6 Turbo
20	Thierry Boutsen (B)	Benetton B187-06*	Ford V6 Turbo
20T	Thierry Boutsen (B)	Benetton B187-04	Ford V6 Turbo
21	Alex Caffi (I)	Osella FA1H/87-01	Alfa Romeo V8 Turbo
23	Adrian Campos (E)	Minardi M186-02	Moderni V6 Turbo
24	Alessandro Nannini (I)	Minardi M186-03	Moderni V6 Turbo
25	Rene Arnoux (F)	Ligier JS29C/5	Megatron S4 Turbo
26	Piercarlo Ghinzani (I)	Ligier JS29C-4	Megatron S4 Turbo
27	Michele Alboreto (I)	Ferrari F187-098	Ferrari V6 Turbo
28	Gerhard Berger (A)	Ferrari F187-099	Ferrari V6 Turbo
30	Philippe Alliot (F)	Lola LC87/03*	Ford Cosworth V8
30T	Philippe Alliot (F)	Lola LC87/02	Ford Cosworth V8

* Race car

QUALIFYING

FRIDAY: Dry, warm Driver		SATURDAY: Wet Driver	
Mansell	1:42.616	Mansell	2:00.832
Senna	1:42.873	Boutsen	2:02.981
Prost	1:43.202	Berger	2:03.172
Piquet	1:43.705	Cheever	2:04.003
Alboreto	1:43.921	Alboreto	2:05.139
Boutsen	1:45.066	Palmer	2:06.769
De Cesaris	1:45.411	Fabi	2:06.857
Johansson	1:45.428	Caffi	2:07.753
Fabi	1:45.497	Ghinzani	2:09.992
Berger	1:45.902	Streiff	2:10.404
Patrese	1:46.096	Danner	2:11.115
Arnoux	1:46.323	Alliot	2:11.588
Warwick	1:46.525	Brundle	2:12.913
Nakajima	1:46.760		
Cheever	1:47.780		
Nannini	1:47.887		
Ghinzani	1:49.236		
Campos	1:49.668		
Brundle	1:51.062		
Danner	1:51.448		
Alliot	1:52.760		
Streiff	1:53.528		
Palmer	1:54.491		
Capelli	1:54.616		
Fabre	1:54.977		
Caffi	6:04.561		

STARTING GRID

No	Driver	Time
5	Mansell	1:42.616
12	Senna	1:42.873
1	Prost	1:43.202
6	Piquet	1:43.705
27	Alboreto	1:43.921
20	Boutsen	1:45.066
8	De Cesaris	1:45.411
2	Johansson	1:45.428
19	Fabi	1:45.497
28	Berger	1:45.902
7	Patrese	1:46.096
25	Arnoux	1:46.323
17	Warwick	1:46.525
11	Nakajima	1:46.760
18	Cheever	1:47.780
24	Nannini	1:47.887
26	Ghinzani	1:49.236
23	Campos	1:49.668
9	Brundle	1:51.062
10	Danner	1:51.448
30	Alliot	1:52.760
4	Streiff	1:53.528
3	Palmer	1:54.491
16	Capelli	1:54.616
14	Fabre	1:54.997
21	Caffi	2.07.753

RESULTS

Pos	No	Driver	Car	Laps	Time/Retirement
1	6	Piquet	Williams-Honda	44	1-21:25.091
2	2	Johansson	McLaren-TAG	44	1-23:04.682
3	12	Senna	Lotus-Honda	43	
4	4	Streiff	Tyrrell-Cosworth	43	
5	3	Palmer	Tyrrell-Cosworth	43	
6	30	Alliot	Lola-Cosworth	42	
7	1	Prost	McLaren-TAG	39	Alternator
8	9	Brundle	Zakspeed	34	
R	26	Ghinzani	Ligier-Megatron	32	Engine
R	23	Campos	Minardi-Moderni	28	Engine
R	20	Boutsen	Benetton-Ford	26	Engine
R	5	Mansell	Williams-Honda	25	Engine
R	24	Nannini	Minardi-Moderni	25	Engine
R	17	Warwick	Arrows-Megatron	23	Turbo
R	10	Danner	Zakspeed	21	Driveshaft
R	28	Berger	Ferrari	19	Turbo
R	19	Fabi	Benetton-Ford	18	Engine
R	21	Caffi	Osella-Alfa Romeo	17	Engine
R	8	De Cesaris	Brabham-BMW	12	Engine
R	27	Alboreto	Ferrari	10	Turbo
R	14	Fabre	AGS-Cosworth	10	Engine
R	18	Cheever	Arrows-Megatron	9	Throttle linkage
R	11	Nakajima	Lotus-Honda	9	Suspension
R	16	Capelli	March-Cosworth	7	Electrics
R	25	Arnoux	Ligier-Megatron	6	Electrics
26	7	Patrese	Brabham-BMW	5	Engine

FASTEST LAP

Driver	
Mansell	1:45.716
Prost	1:46.807
Piquet	1:47.517
Senna	1:49.187
Alboreto	1:49.509
Brundle	1:49.742
Johansson	1:49.778
Boutsen	1:49.864
De Cesaris	1:50.436
Warwick	1:50.608
Berger	1:50.667
Fabi	1:50.758
Cheever	1:51.014
Nakajima	1:51.054
Nannini	1:52.382
Ghinzani	1:52.512
Patrese	1:53.002
Arnoux	1:53.433
Streiff	1:54.228
Palmer	1:54.294
Danner	1:54.464
Campos	1:54.705
Alliot	1:54.771
Caffi	1:55.549
Capelli	1:57.292
Fabre	1:58.770

CHAMPIONSHIP POSITIONS

	DRIVERS			CONSTRUCTORS	
1	Piquet	39	1	Williams-Honda	69
2	Senna	35	2	McLaren-TAG	45
3	Mansell	30	3	Lotus-Honda	41
4	Prost	26	4	Ferrari	17
5	Johansson	19	5	Tyrrell-Cosworth	8
6	Berger	9	6	Arrows-Megatron	6
7	Alboreto	8	7	Benetton-Ford	5
8	Nakajima	6	8	Brabham-BMW	4
9	Cheever	4	9	Zakspeed	2
	De Cesaris	4	10	Ligier-Megatron	1
	Palmer	4		Lola-Cosworth	1
	Streiff	4		March-Cosworth	1
13	Fabi	3			
14	Boutsen	2			
	Brundle	2			
	Warwick	2			
17	Alliot	1			
	Arnoux	1			
	Capelli	1			

JIM CLARK CUP			COLIN CHAPMAN CUP		
1	Palmer	48	1	Tyrrell-Cosworth	87
2	Streiff	39	2	AGS-Cosworth	32
3	Fabre	32	3	Lola-Cosworth	19
4	Alliot	19	4	March-Cosworth	6
5	Capelli	6			

Hungary
ROUND NINE: August 9, 1987

THE BENEFICIARY OF MORE

His future with another team secured, it was time to concentrate on compiling the points for another championship. Then a sure second place turned into another victory.

The man who came away empty-handed — again — was Nigel Mansell, who started from pole and was never headed until lap 71. The Williams-Honda suddenly twitched, weaved and Mansell pulled off. He parked the uncatchable Williams, minus one wheel nut, beside the barrier and watched sadly as Nelson Piquet pinched another win.

Piquet was resigned to his usual second, once the Ferraris, finding a new lease of life on this slick, quirky track, but not improved reliability, left the scene. The Brazilian did try determinedly to close the gap on the English lion as the race grew old, he even broke the lap record, but Mansell, always in control of the situation, lowered the record further and that was it.

By this time Piquet claimed he was having trouble with a car vibrating violently. With the race nearing conclusion, there was no time, and his car in no shape, to attack again. Second, and a bigger points lead in the championship would have to do. Then he flashed by the stricken Mansell, saw him leaning on the barrier, and even said he felt sorry for him.

There was no-one to pressure Piquet and he reeled off the final six laps for this second win in a row. Ayrton Senna, in an inherited second, hanging in for points also, had no grip to speak of and plenty of tyre vibration, the active suspension having no answer to the car's lack of bite on such a capricious surface.

Alain Prost really struggled. The re-designed alternator set-up did away with the McLaren's previous habit of not finishing, but this time the misfire of previous races was back and the defending champion was fortunate not to be lapped.

The ambitious Prost was not impressed. He was quickly becoming tired of being handicapped by his car in his defence of the title. And the circumstances of the winner didn't help his demeanour after the race: "He led the last four laps in Germany, the last six here, Eighteen points . . ."

2.

1.

Saturday was Nigel Mansell's 33rd birthday, and he gave himself a fine present, in the shape of pole position — his seventh in nine races. But his big present had been unwrapped a day early: the news that Nelson Piquet was leaving Williams for Lotus at the end of the season.

It had been a long time since one topic so dominated the paddock conversation. Everywhere the question was: "So what d'you think of that, then?" Only much later would someone absent-mindedly venture, "By the way, who's quickest?"

Twelve months before the Hungaroring seemed distinctly virginal and new, but for this second grand prix the place was more familiar and complete. The pits, immaculate as they were, bore traces of previous use; the grass was less sparse, the atmosphere less regimented and formal. The circuit itself, though, was no less quirky than before. True, we had three members of the Modern Racing Quartet in the first couple of rows, but there were anomalies in the grid too.

For the first time in two years there was a Ferrari — Gerhard Berger's — on the front row. And three Cosworth runners in the top sixteen, heading such as Satoru Nakajima's Lotus-Honda. The grid in Hungary was topped and tailed by Mansell and Pascal Fabre, as usual, but in between Williams and AGS there was much of note.

This is a *wonderful* place to watch race cars, and it has nothing to do with the layout of the circuit, which is somewhat ponderous and pedestrian, with a 100 mph lap barrier breached by only three cars in qualifying. No, the attraction is that Hungarian asphalt is apparently very low on grip, and, Lordy, Lordy, the cars actually *slide* on it! They behave as in a Formula One designer's nightmare. And as in days long ago, when 'real' men steered with the throttle.

Today's drivers are no different from those of time gone by; they can powerslide a car as well as any, but so rarely can they do it for other than a moment's fun, for in this era a sliding car is a car losing time. Except, that is, at the Hungaroring, where a driver whose car never steps out of line is a driver not trying. There were spins galore during qualifying, and from end to end in pit lane there was a chorus of "No grip . . ."

If grip was low, a good balance in the car remained essential. If you had a 'dog' like the Zakspeed, which appeared to be on its own 'wet line' on a hot and cloudless afternoon, you were lost. "The thing is," Martin Brundle said, "I've got no idea whether I'm on a reasonable lap or a terrible one. If you just happen to catch the thing at the right moment, and on a bit of track where there's *some* grip, that's lucky. But each lap's just a blurr of opposite lock and wheelspin . . ."

That was an extreme case, but everyone, to some degree, had the same problem. "It's a bit quicker than last year," remarked Mansell, "but only so long as you stay absolutely on line. Once you get off it, though, it's *unbelievably* slippery. It's like a moving target, this track. And the worst of it is, if you have to go off line, your tyres pick up dust and dirt — and you're off the pace for another couple of laps before they're clean again. You can't avoid it, either: most of the circuit is so tight that overtaking's very difficult, so sooner or later you're going to have to go off line to get by someone . . ."

Nigel took the pole on the first day, in a session which initially did not promise quick times. Friday was distinctly cool and overcast, and as one o'clock approached rain was steadily falling. At first few drivers ventured out, but then the clouds passed, and the track began to dry out. Mansell was among the first to try a run on slicks, and towards the end of the session — line dry now — he produced a breathtaking sequence: 1:29.924 was reduced to 1:28.567, then finally to 1:28.047.

No one else managed to beat 1:30, leaving the Williams-Honda fastest by two clear seconds. But it was good that Nigel put in that last flyer on what was his only clear lap, for the following day Berger turned in a scintillating 1:28.549 — quicker than Mansell's best for the session.

Nigel wasted his first set of tyres on Saturday afternoon by spinning before he had registered a quick time but did a 1:28.6 on the second set. More

3.

to the point, perhaps, was that over the two days he managed four laps in the 1:28 bracket. Gerhard got down there just once, and no one else was close.

"This place is something else," Mansell said on Saturday afternoon. "One minute it's slow, the next it's quick. Really, all you can do is stay out as long as you can. But I'm happy with the car, I must say." And the spin? "Well," he explained, "this place is very hard on brakes, and this morning I did a lot of full tank running. The (carbon fibre) discs were getting very thin by this afternoon which sometimes causes grabbing. Twice I went off because of that, actually. Both times it just swapped ends, but fortunately it was at the chicane each time, and there was no damage to the car."

He was less surprised than most, he said, to find a Ferrari next to him on the grid: "I've always believed they would come good this season, and that car's been getting better and better. In fact, I have the feeling this might be a *very* close race. It's very hard to overtake, and it's not at all what I'd call a normal race circuit. Usually you can slide off line and still find there's quite a lot of grip, so you don't lose a lot of time, and you just go on to the next corner. Here you can't do that — literally it's like a dry line on a wet circuit . . ."

Berger's performance — not before time — was especially remarkable since the Austrian was one of several drivers to be feeling distinctly below par. "Don't come too close," he smiled after qualifying. "I've got . . ." and the symptoms sounded like 'flu. "I feel much better than I did earlier in the week, but the main problem is that I'm weak — I get tired quickly." And the car? "Oh, the car feels good here, really good. What we don't understand is that everyone else said the track was slower than yesterday, but it seemed to me there was *more* grip today."

Right up there, too, was Michele Alboreto, fifth. "My second set of tyres," he said on Saturday afternoon, "were not properly pre-heated. I feel I could have gone quite a lot quicker. This could be a very good race for us."

Certain Italian elements naturally ascribed the Ferraris' step up the grid to the absence of John Barnard, who was back in Surrey, hard at work on the F188, which will use Maranello's forthcoming 3.5-litre V12. In charge at the Hungaroring was Ing Harvey Postlethwaite.

Piquet, despite being delighted with his new career prospects, was another man feeling peaky on Friday. But his health was much improved the following morning, and so, too, was the understeer

4.

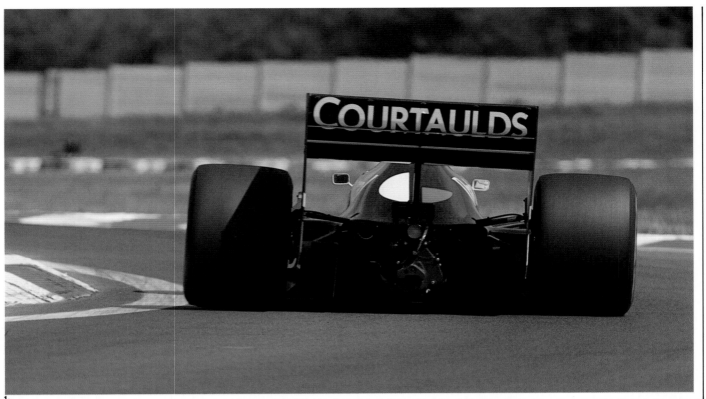

1.

of which he had previously complained. But Nelson was never within shouting distance of Mansell, and only once beat 1:30.

Alain Prost never did it, although he came close on the first day. Through the morning session on Friday, indeed, the world champion looked like the man to beat, heading the time sheets virtually throughout. "I'm very surprised," he admitted. "This is the kind of track which usually doesn't suit the McLaren, yet we're quick here."

Using their high-downforce 'Detroit' double rear wing, the cars looked very stable and secure through the quick corners — on the first day. On the second, both Prost and Stefan Johansson were bewildered by the change in conditions: "Just hopeless today," Alain shrugged. "No grip at all."

In worse trouble, though, was Ayrton Senna. For Hungary, Ayrton had the latest Lotus 99T, with revised rear bodywork. In an attempt to clean up airflow, the engine cover and sidepods had been lowered, and the Brazilian had few complaints — save that, you've guessed, there was no grip . . . And certainly it looked that way, the yellow car among the most skittish on view. As well as that, Senna was in pop-off trouble during the final session, his engine's valve cutting in too early. Sixth fastest, he was almost a full second from his 1986 pole time in the 'passive' Lotus-Renault.

Twelve months previously, the Ford V6 turbo engine performed competitively for the first time, Patrick Tambay qualifying sixth in Carl Haas's Lola. This time around, the quickest Ford — that in Thierry Boutsen's Benetton — started seventh. Thierry was fourth on the opening day, despite pop-off problems, but failed, like so many others, to improve on Saturday.

If an award for sheer heroism had been awarded during practice, it must surely have gone to Derek Warwick, who looked ill, and felt dreadful. He, too, had the 'flu bug, and was also suffering from conjunctivitis in his left eye. By Saturday, the eye was virtually closed, and he ran only a handful of laps in the last session.

"I feel terrible," he said. "Worse than yesterday. I missed a couple of braking points, and decided it would be safer to stop. The eye's a problem, but the worst thing is that I've no strength in my arms and legs. After four or five laps, I'm exhausted. If I'm like this tomorrow, I may have to withdraw, I think." In the circumstances, his Friday time — ninth fastest — was a considerable achievement.

Philippe Streiff, often impressive on a 'scratcher's track' like this, was consistently fastest among the Cosworth's, qualifying 14th overall, and tailed by Philippe Alliot's Larrousse Lola and Jonathan Palmer in the other Tyrrell. Their times suggested a promising race-within-a-race — and maybe a share in the points hand-out. Round the Hungaroring, they had comfortably the measure of the lesser turbo machinery.

Sunday morning was hot, dry, blue and the 30-minute warm-up merely served to confirm what had gone before: Mansell clearly fastest, then the Ferraris of Berger and Alboreto, then Prost, Boutsen and Piquet. Nigel was entirely happy, Gerhard and Michele, too. Alain, though, said the McLaren was slithering all over the place. Senna, down at eighth, said the Lotus was worse than that.

At the green light, the No. 5 Williams got away well, but Berger did it all wrong, creeping before the signal to go, then braking just as the lights changed. It was Piquet who followed Mansell into the first turn — but by the end of it both Ferraris had gone by him on the outside. Nelson was not impressed: "They took a very big risk doing that . . ." he scowled later.

After one lap Mansell had a respectable lead over Berger, but it was soon obvious he was not about to get away. Gerhard, pale and feverish on the grid, closed up on the second lap, and behind them ran Alboreto, Piquet, Senna and Prost. Already it seemed that the world champion had strife.

"Already from the warm-up, I had a bad misfire," he confirmed later. "On the grid they changed the Motronic box, but it made no difference. In the beginning, I was in really good shape! Engine 'opeless, and no grip . . ."

On lap three Boutsen pushed him down to seventh, and a lap later Johansson, too, was by.

On lap seven, a Ferrari looked set to take the lead. As Mansell began it, Berger was right with him, and momentarily thought to try a move on the Williams into the first turn, effectively the Hungaroring's only overtaking spot. He thought better of it, however, and was never so close again.

Mansell began to stretch out the lead, and only odd traffic problems would occasionally reduce the gap. After 12 laps the Williams was a second and a half clear, and after 13 the biggest threat was gone. Berger pulling off with a broken diff.

"I didn't feel so good," Gerhard said, "but I could have run the whole race, I'm sure. While it lasted, the car was great — I'm sure we were quicker through

1: This is the only view Eddie Cheever saw of his team-mate Warwick. The Englishman did his hero act, weak with flu and half blind with an eye infection.

2: With Mansell and Berger gone, Piquet heads the snake line in the early stages.

3: Just five laps to go and another victory for Mansell, but already the wheel nut was hanging by a single thread.

4: Adrian Campos — portrait of a young Spaniard trying to cut it in the toughest game there is.

the corners than the Williams, but on the straights . . . Mansell just went away." There had been no warning of the diff's impending failure, he added. Had there been, he would have taken the car to its pit.

Nigel still had scarlet in his mirrors, though, for Alboreto was running strongly, apparently well able to keep Piquet at bay. By now this was a three-car race, for Senna, battling with the ever-impressive Boutsen, was already more than 10 secs behind. The two McLarens, Johansson in front, ran in tandem behind.

Not for long. "I'd had a repeat of my Monaco problem: the engine was fine up to ten-eight — then

just died completely. Each time you have to restart it," Stefan said. "That was one thing. But then something funny happened to the diff. It sort of locked momentarily, and spun me . . ."

It spun him right in front of his leader. "It wasn't his fault," Prost commented, "but I was obliged to spin, to miss him. How we did not hit each other, I don't know." For Alain, it meant delay, but Stefan's race was through.

This is like no other race track on the Formula One schedule: timing gaps is almost a fruitless exercise, so often and so dramatically do they change. Lapping a slower car — especially should it

Nigel was always able to respond. Nelson's only hope of getting on terms was a really bad break for Mansell in the traffic. As it was, the gap wavered between 11 and 14 secs for lap after lap.

At three-quarter distance, though, Piquet had it down to a little over six secs, and there it stayed for a while. But on lap 55 Mansell plucked out a new fastest lap, pulled two more seconds out, and that was the end of Nelson's challenge. "I picked up a big tyre vibration in the car around then," he said, "and decided to settle for second place. I wasn't going to catch him. The car was shaking like a hot banana . . ."

So Nigel began peeling away the last 20 laps, then

Below: That hard-earned single world championship point within grasp, an exhausted Derek Warwick drives by memory in the final laps.

Bottom: March's Ivan Capelli — eyes on a bright F1 future.

be driven by one so uncooperative as, say, Rene Arnoux — can take an age. After 15 laps Mansell led Alboreto by 6.2 secs; next time round it was 2.5.

Although Nigel looked under no threat whatsoever, the snake dance behind him was closing up. Boutsen was pressuring Senna hard, and that, in turn, was moving the Lotus closer to Piquet's third place. Or was it merely traffic problems? Yes, it probably was, for on lap 20 Ayrton dropped three secs to Nelson.

Prost's McLaren came alive when a ribbon of rubber went down on the track. "After a few laps I had fantastic grip — but the misfire was so bad I couldn't make any progress. There was one short period — maybe five or six laps — when the misfire cleared, and then the car was great. I closed quickly on Boutsen and Senna, but then back it came. We don't know what the problem was, maybe a sensor in the management system. Anyway, it was something new . . ."

Lap 29 brought a big change: Alboreto ran wide at the exit of the second turn, allowing Piquet the opportunity to use his 'instant power' button, squirt by into three. Michele did not concede until the last moment, looking up as Nelson moved across his bows to claim the apex.

So now, could Piquet make any impression on Mansell? Tyre stops were unlikely to come into the reckoning on the slick surface of the Hungaroring, so it was a matter of two drivers in equal cars racing it out to the flag. And quite soon it was clear that Nigel was more than equal to anything Nelson might be able to offer.

For all that, the Brazilian was certainly giving it a go. On lap 35 Mansell set a new fastest lap, but it stood for only 12 seconds or so — until Piquet crossed the line. He was charging, certainly, but

the last 10, then . . . "The car was perfect," he said. "Absolutely not a problem with it." Until lap 71.

At first it looked as though the rear suspension had failed. A top link, maybe? As Mansell flicked through a left-hander, the right rear wheel lurched outwards under load, and looked like coming away. Once out of the turn, however, it somehow stayed on while Nigel sawed at the wheel, stopped the car weaving, got it slowed down, parked it. "Wheel's come off," was his curt radio message to the pits before he climbed out, walked away.

"It was a problem with the lugs on the hub — the locating pins on which the wheel sits," Mansell said later. "In the days before we had planned tyre stops, the fit was very tight indeed, with no backwards and forwards play whatever. Then tyre stops arrived, and they found that the more clearance there was, the easier it was to take the wheel off, and to fit the new one on — especially when it got hot.

"It seems that, over a period of time, we hadn't caught on to the fact that the tolerances had grown a little bit — and when I say a little bit, we're probably talking in terms of ten thou, which is not a lot. But it was enough so that every time you accelerated or decelerated, you got a tiny amount of movement of the wheels on these lugs. And it was just enough, over a grand prix distance, to slacken the wheel nut off. Every time you accelerate, ten thou, next time, maybe twelve thou . . . and it adds up and adds up, until eventually it's a quarter of a wheel turn — and then the next time you accelerate hard, the nut flies off."

"I saw Mansell's car by the side of the track," Nelson said of the incident, "and I felt very sorry for him . . ." In light of their 'difficult' relationship, the remark was greeted with ironic laughter by the surrounding media.

"I've made my move for 1988 yes, but now I want

to concentrate on the championship," Nelson concluded.

Senna arrived at the line well over half a minute behind Piquet, but second nevertheless. He, too, had picked up a severe tyre vibration. "Everything in the car got tired, including me," Ayrton said. "I'm amazed that the car held together, actually. I had a big pain in my back and side . . ."

He enjoyed his battle with Boutsen, which looked lost until the Belgian's turbo boost began to go away in the late stages: "He had more grip than me, I think, but my engine was stronger than his . . ."

"It was a good race for both our drivers, wasn't it?"

Peter Warr said, butting in with a smile. Good for Nakajima? He retired on the first lap? "I wasn't referring to Satoru . . ."

Another lap or two and Prost would have been lapped. Third he may have been, but it is difficult to recall a race in which the Frenchman played so minor a role. And afterwards it was clear that he was becoming bored with trying to defend a world championship with one had tied behind his back.

Boutsen's fourth place was no less than he deserved, and Riccardo Patrese, too, had a good, sound run through to fifth. But perhaps the real hero in Hungary was Warwick, "I've set the car up to be

comfortable, rather than quick," he had said before the start, when he looked in no condition to drive a grand prix car.

Derek drove beautifully, perhaps spurred for much of way by the sight of Eddie Cheever's sister Arrows in his mirrors. At one point, indeed, Eddie clouted the back of his car, sending him to the pits with a puncture.

Warwick drove the last part of the race on autopilot, the leading Cosworth runer. But he made it to the flag, sixth, and never was a point harder earned.

HUNGARIAN GRAND PRIX

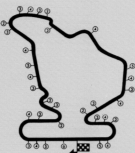

Round 9: August 9, 1987
Circuit: Hungaroring (H)

Race data: 76 laps of 2.494 mile (4.02 km) circuit

Weather: Hot, dry

Fastest lap: Piquet, Williams FW11B, 1:30.149, 99.60mph

Existing record: Piquet, Williams FW11, 1:31.001, 99.669mph

ENTRIES

No	Driver (Nat)	Car/Chassis	Engine
1	Alain Prost (F)	McLaren MP4/3C-3*	TAG V6 Turbo
1T	Alain Prost (F)	McLaren MP4/3C-1	TAG V6 Turbo
2	Stefan Johansson (S)	McLaren MP4/3C-2	TAG V6 Turbo
3	Jonathan Palmer (GB)	Tyrrell DG/016-6*	Ford Cosworth V8
3T	Jonathan Palmer (GB)	Tyrrell DG/016-3	Ford Cosworth V8
4	Philippe Streiff (F)	Tyrrell DG/016-5	Ford Cosworth V8
5	Nigel Mansell (GB)	Williams FW11B/3*	Honda V6 Turbo
5T	Nigel Mansell (GB)	Williams FW11B/1	Honda V6 Turbo
6	Nelson Piquet (BR)	Williams FW11B/4	Honda V6 Turbo
7	Riccardo Patrese (I)	Brabham BT56/4*	BMW S4 Turbo
7T	Riccardo Patrese (I)	Brabham BT56/3	BMW S4 Turbo
8	Andrea de Cesaris (I)	Brabham BT56/1	BMW S4 Turbo
9	Martin Brundle (GB)	Zakspeed 871/3	Zakspeed S4 Turbo
9T	Martin Brundle (GB)	Zakspeed 871/1*	Zakspeed S4 Turbo
10	Christian Danner (D)	Zakspeed 871/2	Zakspeed S4 Turbo
11	Satoru Nakajima (J)	Lotus 99T/3	Honda V6 Turbo
12	Ayrton Senna (BR)	Lotus 99T/5	Honda V6 Turbo
14	Pascal Fabre (F)	AGS JH22/02-032	Ford Cosworth V8
16	Ivan Capelli (I)	March 871/02	Ford Cosworth V8
17	Derek Warwick (GB)	Arrows A10/4	Megatron S4 Turbo
18	Eddie Cheever (USA)	Arrows A10/3	Megatron S4 Turbo
19	Teo Fabi (I)	Benetton B187-07	Ford V6 Turbo
20	Thierry Boutsen (B)	Benetton B187-06	Ford V6 Turbo
21	Alex Caffi (I)	Osella FA1H/87-01	Alfa Romeo V8 Turbo
23	Adrian Campos (E)	Minardi M186-02	Moderni V6 Turbo
24	Alessandro Nannini (I)	Minardi M186-03	Moderni V6 Turbo
25	Rene Arnoux (F)	Ligier JS29C-5	Megatron S4 Turbo
26	Piercarlo Ghinzani (I)	Ligier JS29C-4	Megatron S4 Turbo
27	Michele Alboreto (I)	Ferrari F187-100	Ferrari V6 Turbo
28	Gerhard Berger (A)	Ferrari F187-099*	Ferrari V6 Turbo
28T	Gerhard Berger (A)	Ferrari F187-097	Ferrari V6 Turbo
30	Philippe Alliot (F)	Lola LC87/03	Ford Cosworth V8

* Race car

QUALIFYING

FRIDAY: Wet, drying out		SATURDAY: Hot, dry	
Driver		Driver	
Mansell	1:28.047	Berger	1:28.549
Prost	1:30.156	Mansell	1:28.682
Alboreto	1:30.472	Piquet	1:29.724
Boutsen	1:30.748	Alboreto	1:30.310
Piquet	1:30.842	Prost	1:30.327
Berger	1:31.080	Senna	1:30.387
Johansson	1:31.228	Boutsen	1:30.810
Senna	1:31.387	Johansson	1:31.940
Warwick	1:31.416	Patrese	1:32.422
Patrese	1:31.586	Fabi	1:32.639
Cheever	1:32.336	Cheever	1:33.700
Fabi	1:32.452	Palmer	1:33.895
De Cesaris	1:32.628	Alliot	1:34.014
Streiff	1:33.644	Streiff	1:34.383
Alliot	1:33.777	Warwick	1:34.386
Nakajima	1:34.297	Capelli	1:34.426
Palmer	1:34.398	Nakajima	1:34.476
Nannini	1:34.796	Arnoux	1:34.518
Capelli	1:34.950	Nannini	1:34.770
Arnoux	1:35.346	Caffi	1:35.594
Brundle	1:35.754	Brundle	1:35.818
Danner	1:35.930	Ghinzani	1:36.109
Campos	1:36.067	Danner	1:36.371
Ghinzani	1:36.411	Fabre	1:37.730
Caffi	1:36.693	Campos	1:37.948
Fabre	1:38.803	De Cesaris	1:43.913

STARTING GRID

No	Driver	Time
5	Mansell	1:28.047
28	Berger	1:28.549
6	Piquet	1:29.724
1	Prost	1:30.156
27	Alboreto	1:30.310
12	Senna	1:30.387
20	Boutsen	1:30.748
2	Johansson	1:31.228
17	Warwick	1:31.416
7	Patrese	1:31.586
18	Cheever	1:32.336
19	Fabi	1:32.452
8	De Cesaris	1:32.628
4	Streiff	1:33.644
30	Alliot	1:33.777
3	Palmer	1:33.895
11	Nakajima	1:34.297
16	Capelli	1:34.426
25	Arnoux	1:34.518
24	Nannini	1:34.770
21	Caffi	1:35.594
9	Brundle	1:35.754
10	Danner	1:35.930
23	Campos	1:36.067
26	Ghinzani	1:36.109
14	Fabre	1:37.730

RESULTS

Pos	No	Driver	Car	Laps	Time/Retirement
1	6	Piquet	Williams-Honda	76	1-59:26.793
2	12	Senna	Lotus-Honda	76	2-00:04.520
3	1	Prost	McLaren-TAG	76	2-00:54.249
4	20	Boutsen	Benetton-Ford	75	
5	7	Patrese	Brabham-BMW	75	
6	17	Warwick	Arrows-Megatron	74	
7	3	Palmer	Tyrrell-Cosworth	74	
8	18	Cheever	Arrows-Megatron	74	
9	4	Streiff	Tyrrell-Cosworth	74	
10	16	Capelli	March-Cosworth	74	
11	24	Nannini	Minardi-Moderni	73	
12	26	Ghinzani	Ligier-Megatron	73	
13	14	Fabre	AGS-Cosworth	71	
R	5	Mansell	Williams-Honda	70	Wheel nut
R	21	Caffi	Osella-Alfa Romeo	64	Out of fuel
R	25	Arnoux	Ligier-Megatron	57	Electrics
R	30	Alliot	Lola-Cosworth	48	Spun off
R	9	Brundle	Zakspeed	45	Turbo
R	27	Alboreto	Ferrari	44	Engine
R	8	De Cesaris	Brabham-BMW	44	Gearbox
R	2	Johansson	McLaren-TAG	14	Differential
R	19	Fabi	Benetton-Ford	14	Gearbox
R	23	Campos	Minardi-Moderni	14	Accident
R	28	Berger	Ferrari	13	Differential
R	10	Danner	Zakspeed	3	Electrics
R	11	Nakajima	Lotus-Honda	1	Driveshaft

FASTEST LAP

Driver	
Piquet	1:30.149
Mansell	1:30.298
Prost	1:31.602
Senna	1:32.426
Boutsen	1:32.524
Cheever	1:32.603
Alboreto	1:32.679
Berger	1:33.826
De Cesaris	1:34.039
Warwick	1:34.613
Patrese	1:34.387
Nannini	1:34.519
Palmer	1:34.824
Johansson	1:34.843
Capelli	1:34.926
Streiff	1:35.069
Alliot	1:35.210
Fabi	1:35.210
Fabre	1:36.043
Ghinzani	1:36.045
Brundle	1:36.195
Caffi	1:37.046
Arnoux	1:37.169
Campos	1:39.486
Danner	1:39.650
Nakajima	2:30.651

CHAMPIONSHIP POSITIONS

DRIVERS		
1	Piquet	48
2	Senna	41
3	Mansell	30
	Prost	30
5	Johansson	19
6	Berger	9
7	Alboreto	8
8	Nakajima	6
9	Boutsen	5
10	Cheever	4
	De Cesaris	4
	Palmer	4
	Streiff	4
14	Fabi	3
	Warwick	3
16	Brundle	2
	Patrese	2
18	Alliot	1
	Arnoux	1
	Capelli	1

CONSTRUCTORS		
1	Williams-Honda	78
2	McLaren-TAG	49
3	Lotus-Honda	47
4	Ferrari	17
5	Benetton-Ford	8
6	Arrows-Megatron	7
7	Brabham-BMW	6
8	Zakspeed	2
9	Ligier-Megatron	1
	Lola-Cosworth	1
	March-Cosworth	1

JIM CLARK CUP		
1	Palmer	57
2	Streiff	45
3	Fabre	35
4	Alliot	19
5	Capelli	10

COLIN CHAPMAN CUP		
1	Tyrrell-Cosworth	102
2	AGS-Cosworth	35
3	Lola-Cosworth	19
4	March-Cosworth	10

Austria

ROUND TEN: August 16, 1987

NO INHERITANCE FOR HIM

This time he held back, conserving his car in the opening stages. When he applied the pressure to the front runners, they folded, and he was conclusively back on the winner's list.

In this his 100th grand prix, Nigel Mansell had the luck with him. It took luck to survive two aborted starts on a narrow ribbon called a grid, the second due to the overheating clutch in his Williams-Honda, and it took luck to prevail to the flag with a tired clutch.

For 15 laps he let his team-mate make the front-running, take the heat from Thierry Boutsen in one of the races of his life and Gerhard Berger with a lot to live up to in front of his home crowd at this the fastest of grand prix circuits.

Then with clutch cooled, tyres and fuel conserved, Nigel applied the pressure. He was in third now, the Ferrari's turbo gone in a flash of Berger brilliance and applied himself to pressing the Boutsen Benetton. On this circuit the Benetton-Ford turbo found nirvana, a track made for it, and the lanky Belgian felt he had Nelson Piquet on the hook, until a troublesome gearshift forced him to relinquish the role of hustler to the Englishman.

Soon after it was the familiar sight of Williams-Honda in tandem and rampant. Not for long though and this was Nigel's grand prix anniversary, seven years since he began his F1 career. He would celebrate it by humbling the world championship leader into submission on lap 20.

Piquet had no response to make. Neither did anybody else. Ayrton Senna, Michele Alboreto and Alain Prost, had tried, oh how they tried, storming in a group from their own pit lane grid in the second re-start. Alboreto turned the clock back to the days before the Ferrari drought as he ruthlessly sliced Senna not once, but twice. In short time however, the realities of 1987 had brought the Italian back to the pits. And Prost did his best to nibble at Piquet's sure second, to keep his slim championship hopes alive, before he too began to fall away and into line with recurring theme of 1987. One point is all he salvaged and that was that for the championship, he concluded.

Some strange things were happening in the practice days in Austria, a race that some prayed would be ditched from the Formula One calendar. You had to look to seventh on the grid before you found Ayrton Senna and ninth for Alain Prost, sandwiched by the Brabhams. But the strangest thing of all came before the end of the Friday morning session.

Stefan Johansson crested the blind brow before the Rindtkurve to find a large deer running across the road. Stefan swerved to avoid the unfortunate animal, but could not. The impact shattered the McLaren's nearside front suspension, and the car then hit the guardrail, still travelling at close to 150 mph.

Johansson, shaken and sickened, climbed from the wreckage more or less uninjured, although he was later taken to hospital for X-rays. Nothing was broken, but for the rest of the day he had a severe headache, and all weekend his neck was stiff, shoulders and ribs bruised and sore. All weekend, too, men with shotguns probed the foliage and forest around to give the wildlife a message.

"I got a massive fright," Johansson said, "and I was so lucky it hit the suspension. If it had been head on — just a few centimetres to the right — I reckon that would have been it for me . . ."

That had been a morning of high drama. At 10.30, Nelson Piquet and Pascal Fabre came

Above: *The narrow grid at the Osterreichring takes its toll. Cars lie across the track, bent, twisted and broken. The acrobat is Pascal Fabre, sandwiched by Capelli's March and Alliot's Lola.*

Left: *All hands are called on to get the track ready for the re-start. The brooms and buckets were active again within half an hour.*

Above right: *The fast men get away not realising that all hell has broken loose behind them. The flags were about to come out.*

Previous pages: *Oh no! Not again. Expensive debris is sprayed everywhere as Mansell's crawl off the line causes a chain reaction down the cramped grid.*

together, after being separated by 17 secs in lap times. Coming out of the Rindtkurve onto the pit straight the left rear suspension of Nelson's Williams hit the right front of the AGS, then bounced and ground its three wheeled way along for an alarming distance before the Brazilian could bring it to a safe halt.

The immediate assumption was that Fabre had not been looking in his mirrors, but Piquet accepted the blame: "I passed too close to him. It's true he was more in the middle of the road than he needed to be, but I should have allowed for that . . ."

Nelson did not take the pole until the closing minutes of Friday's timed session, setting the time on his 17th lap. Until then, Mansell looked set for his eighth of the season, his best lap his fourth. A succeeding lap, he had no doubts, would have been far quicker — "Under 1.23, I'm sure . . ." but at the Rindtkurve he came across an obstructive Piercarlo Ghinzani, and that was that.

"I went onto full tanks after that," Nigel said. "We know there's a strong possibility of rain for Saturday, so at least we've done some homework, got some pointers for the race. I've had seven pole positions this year, but only won three races, so I know what I'm concentrating on in future. I still think I'd have got the pole, mind you, if Ghinzani had bothered to look in his mirrors, but there you are. Right at the end, we

mumbled, holding an ice pack to his face. "And I didn't realise how much pain I'd been in today. There was no choice, though. It had to come out. The main problem is that it jars every time you go over a bump here. To be honest, I feel absolutely bloody dreadful today, I just hope it'll improve as the weekend goes on."

What didn't improve was the weather. In Styria the elements are utterly capricious, and where Friday had been warm and dry, Saturday found the Oster-reichring enveloped in mist. By 9.30 there was heavy rain, and the track opened for untimed practice in virtual silence. Towards the end of the session conditions improved a little, but only seven drivers lapped in under two minutes.

Fastest of these was Gerhard Berger, maintaining Ferrari's return to contention. Such crowd as there was cheered the local boy on, as they had the previous day, when he was beaten only by the Williams pair. Fully over the flu bug which weakened him in Hungary, Gerhard also set third best time in the final wet-drying session, being among the first brave enough to venture out on slicks.

Wet or dry, the Ferraris — Michele Alboreto, too, made the top six — were clearly in with a serious shot on race day. But would they last?

Mansell, incidentally, headed the times in that last session, and by four clear seconds. But even so he was not encouraged by his car's behaviour when it

tricted boost, remember — was just the thing for this circuit. This time around, with Ford V8 power, the cars were not quite so fleet, but Teo and Thierry Boutsen both qualified in the first five, the Belgian again the quicker of the two, and raving about the balance of the car.

He was also raving — in the opposite direction — about the quality of the marshalling and general safety standards at the Osterreichring. Towards the end of Friday's dry timed session Derek Warwick's Arrows spun off at the Glatzkurve, coming to rest, with minor bodywork damage, at the edge of the track, only just off line. Boutsen, on a quick lap, came through shortly after, and got a big fright: "It was just scandalous, you know, because it's very quick there, and there were no flags — nothing — to warn us. The safety at this place is starting to worry me."

Messrs Prost and Senna, team mates-to-be, were getting quite enough fright from their cars. "The balance is poor here," Ayrton said of the 'active' Lotus-Honda, "and the car feels unstable on some parts of the circuit." And Alain was in sardonic frame of mind: "Good progress, huh? Two years ago I was on pole here, with a 25-something, and last year I did 24.3. This time it's 26.1!"

So what was the problem? "Oh, there are many. The engine is not very good, for one thing. We are short of power, and at the top end — over 11,000

pumped the fuel out, and I tried to set another quick time but . . ."

Mansell paused at this point, taking care over his words. Quite obviously, his team-mate's incessant whingeing about "being shafted by the Williams team" had begun seriously to get on his nerves.

"I want to make a point here: only having one car available, and trying to do everything with it — quick laps, full tanks running, pump 40-odd gallons of fuel in, then pump most of it out — all within an hour is quite something. My mechanics have almost twice as much work to do as Piquet's. And if anyone should get pole position every time, and win every race, it ought to be him. I think my lads deserve more credit than they get sometimes."

Nigel was not too concerned about starting second, therefore. A bigger problem by far was the constant pain from his left lower jaw, legacy of a wisdom tooth removed on Thursday evening. "I started to get an abcess about a week ago," he

was very wet: "If it rains tomorrow, I reckon we're in trouble: understeer, oversteer, the front's floating all over the place . . ."

"If it's dry," Piquet said, "the big worry here is always the engine. The fuel you can control, and tyres are not so marginal this year. But we have 600 metres here where we've absolutely flat out, where the turbochargers are working very hard. For sure there will be a lot of blown engines. The important thing is to have a good set-up, to be in condition to race the last 10 or 20 laps."

And, after the freak non-stop race in Hungary, tyre changes were back. "We're planning one stop, said Nelson. "The surface here is very abrasive, and it's fast corners all the way. On wear maybe you can go the distance, but on grip you'd lose a lot of time in the second half of the race."

Twelve months before, the Benetton team had control in qualifying, Teo Fabi and Berger finding that the 'upright' BMW four-cylinder — with unres-

— it's not clean. But the biggest thing is that the back end of the car is jumping up and down. I tell you, going flat out in a straight line is already for me . . ." and he made a gesture, universal among racing drivers, pointing to his rear.

Prost's humour was good, as it nearly always is, but one sensed a degree of resignation in the world champion. The McLaren-TAG was now neither out-and-out competitive nor notably reliable and his thoughts were on 1988.

The car behaved no better in the wet, he said, after running a few laps on Saturday afternoon, and he *really* didn't want a wet race here. "No, really, it would be impossible. You get deep puddles lying every-where, and you can't see anything."

In light of his horrifying experience on Friday, Johansson's performance the following day was more heroic. Fifth fastest in the last, wet, session, Stefan said he was actually quite relieved that the conditions had given his battered body an easier time.

Second in the rain was Eddie Cheever, as ever excelling in conditions like these. But the day before Eddie had been shaded by team-mate Warwick, in much better health and spirits than at the Hungaroring. "I can see out of both eyes this weekend," Derek said, gleefully. At this, the fastest circuit on the grand prix trail . . .

Sunday was dry throughout, so that was one worry out of the way. But the Osterreichring is a spooky place in most conditions, fast and difficult enough to have a degree of 'edge' rarely found in the grand prix racing of the eighties. It is not a place for mistakes.

That much the drivers can handle. They are less at peace with the haphazard marshalling, and to a man they loathe the narrow hemmed-in pit straight, which makes the start in Austria perhaps the most perilous half-minute in a grand prix season. More

often than not, there is an accident in the opening seconds, a red flag, a delay.

At 2.30 they faced the starter, got the green light, and this time they seemed to have got away with it. The 26 cars were unscathed as they set off up the hill to Hella-Licht — but suddenly there was a car veering left into the guardrail, bouncing off it again, a cloud of dust as others spun in avoidance.

The errant car was Brundle's Zakspeed. Had it flicked out of contronl, under power, on the bumps? "Don't think so," Martin said. "It simply turned sharp left, as if something had broken — a driveshaft, maybe."

To avoid him, Jonathan Palmer had stood on the brakes, the Tyrrell then snapping sideways —to be collected by Philippe Streiff's sister car. And on the other side of the road Ghinzani had a little shunt in sympathy. Red flag.

Scene: the same, 40 minutes later, with T-cars pressed into service, a full field lined up, and Mansell clearly wanted the lead as soon a possible.

Away from the line he had the drop on Piquet, but the No. 5 hesitated, hung back. As the pack bore down on it, all winced and waited . . .

Alboreto jinked left around the Williams, nearly hit Senna's Lotus, but got away with it. The real problem arose when Cheever, committed to a gap between Mansell and the pit wall, found it suddenly full of Riccardo Patrese's Brabham. A chain reaction began, and in seconds there was wreckage everywhere, the track completely blocked.

This one really looked unpleasant, and it was a surprise to learn that, again, no one had been hurt. Some drivers — Brundle, Ghinzani, Streiff — had been through two accidents in less than an hour. Red flag again.

There was a lot of anger now. In words of one syllable. Alboreto made his feelings about the Osterreichring known to Jean-Marie Balestre: and the FISA President, showing that implacable calm which has marked his whole career, proceeded to scream at the agitated Italian.

1.

Indisputably, it was Mansell's hobbled Williams which had involuntarily triggered the accident. Had a driveshaft failed? Had the engine simply bogged down, as turbos sometimes do? "No," Nigel answered, "it was the clutch. When I hooked second, it just went away, then came back when it cooled..."

When they lined up for the third time, it was 4.10, some 20 minutes after the race had been originally scheduled to finish. And even now things were going awry. As the pack had moved away for the final formation lap Prost's McLaren crawled to the side of the road and stopped, engine dead. "Don't know what it was," Alain said later, "Battery or something..."

The mechanics brought the engine back to life, and the world champion prepared to start from pit lane. Here, in fact, was a little grid on its own: already there were Senna (now in the spare Lotus, his own having broken a CV joint during the brief second 'race'), Cheever (out too late to make the grid) and Fabre. And, astonishingly, they were shortly joined by Alboreto, who rushed in at the *end* of the formation lap. Michele's steering wheel had not been put on straight and, rather than start sixth and race with the wheel like that, he opted to have it to his liking, and start from the back!

The third start was OK. This time Mansell purposely got away gently, content to be third, behind Piquet and Boutsen. Following the clutch problem, Williams people had tried to persuade him to switch to the spare FW11B, but Nigel said no, it would be alright, he preferred to stick with his own car.

The opening laps were stirring, with Boutsen really hustling Piquet, Berger running ahead of a contented Mansell, then Fabi, Patrese and Warwick. And towards the back amazing things were happening, as Senna, Alboreto and Prost — three great drivers, each a little angry — hastened to make up for their delayed getaways.

Johansson's dreadful weekend was getting worse. After two laps he was in with a rear puncture, and they changed all four tyres. After three laps he was back again — on three wheels. In his hurry to get Stefan under way as soon as possible, Ron Dennis had given him the signal to go before the wheel-changing was complete. The mechanic working on the right front was bowled down the road, and the McLaren left with a loose wheel nut. Thereafter Johansson drove a stormer of a race, deserving much more than an eventual seventh place.

After five laps the Austrian Grand Prix had come down to a Williams-Benetton fight, for Berger's Ferrari was out with a blown turbo, and it was Piquet, Boutsen, Mansell, Fabi. This was already the most competitive Formula One race of Thierry's life, and he was relishing it, dropping little, if anything to Nelson. And Nigel continued to look entirely at ease.

"I knew the clutch wasn't perfect," he said, "and therefore it had to be a tactical race. I didn't want to push too much too soon. In fact, I was happy to run third, go easy on my fuel and tyres — and clutch."

By lap 13 he had decided to exert a little pressure, closing up on Boutsen, who, in turn edged closer to

1: The Williams crew tried to talk Mansell into the spare car but he stuck with the car he knew after the second re-start and was well clear in the lead when the tyre stops were done.

2: Senna had a race he could easily forget. He was saved by the first re-start when he broke a CV joint in the race car, then charging in the spare, Alboreto squeezed him off the road, costing him several placings.

3: Boutsen in the race of his life. He had Piquet and the lead in his sights when the gearshift began acting up.

4: We didn't mean it literally, Alex. The young Italian's car was one of two that didn't survive the carnage.

Piquet again. This trio had left Fabi a little, but the Italian was himself a comfortable 12 secs up on Patrese, who led Warwick and the rest. But hurtling up into the picture were the 'Pit Lane Flyers', Senna, Alboreto, Prost, who by now were close to point-scoring positions.

The man really worth watching was Michele, an absolute model of smooth aggression. Quite obviously he was being delayed a fraction by Senna and quite obviously — perhaps fired by his discussions with Balestre — he was in no mood to queue. On lap 15 red passed yellow into the Hella-Licht chicane, and only four laps later the Ferrari was by Patrese, and into fifth.

By now, sadly, Boutsen's aspirations had taken a dive. On lap 15 the Benetton was into the pits for attention to its gear linkage. "I changed down from sixth to fourth for the Rindtkurve," he said, "and the lever went slack..." By the time he rejoined, second had become 11th, and Thierry was highly disappointed. "I really felt I could take the lead from Piquet."

Mansell obviously felt the same way, and now was the time. Thierry's trip to the pits elevated Nigel to second, and immediately he began to close on Nelson. It was relentless, and presumably unsettling for Piquet, who had a huge moment at the Rindtkurve on lap 20, and very nearly put his car into the wall. Next time round, Mansell was into the lead, having audaciously jinked through as they lapped back-markers before the Boschkurve. And Piquet chose that moment to come in for tyres.

The Williams tyre stops took a little longer in Austria. After the race-losing incident in Hungary, it was decided to revert to pre-tyre changing practice, and fit wheel nut retaining clips. These had to be

removed, of course, before the wheels could come off, and that cost a couple of seconds or so. Time well spent, and Nelson was stationary for only 11 seconds.

Piquet's was the first of a flurry of tyre stops. Fabi came in, then Prost, then Mansell — who rejoined without losing his lead.

Nigel's first lap out of the pits was a full six secs faster than Nelson's equivalent lap, which is why, when the stops were all done, he had nearly an eight secs advantage over his team-mate. For a few laps the Brazilian gave vague chase, but then gave up. Mansell, indeed, pulled out from nine to 21 secs between laps 29 and 33!

So the battle for first place was over. But could Prost, now into third and gaining on Piquet, catch him before the end? It seemed most unlikely, but there was always hope. The world champion had dispensed with Alboreto and Senna but the Williams-Hondas were in another league, and that pit lane start had left him with too much to do.

Ayrton, meantime, was making strenuous efforts to separate Michele from fourth place. On lap 35 he took a run at the Ferrari into the Hella-Licht, and discovered, as have many before him, that Alboreto is as hard and as ruthless a racer as you will find. At the end of the lap, the Lotus was into the pits for new front wings...

"He weaved in front of me," Senna angrily said afterwards, "and then he hit the brakes. There was nothing I could do." The delay dropped him to ninth, but he resumed with as much vigour as before.

Lap 42, with only 10 to go, Alboreto was slowly in, boost gone. It was a sad end to a magnificent performance, the kind of thing Ferrari have too rarely allowed Michele to show.

And, at the same time, Prost was slowing, and slowing a lot. "From the start there had been some kind of electrical problem, because I'd been almost completely without instruments — fuel computer read-out, rev counter, and so on. Then I began to

lose power. Maybe it was the wastegate. I don't know. Perhaps even a turbo. They will find out at the factory."

"As for me," he went on, "I have to be realistic, and face the fact that I cannot any more compete for the championship this year — although I think we can still win races, maybe. But we have a lot of work to do . . ."

For the last 10 laps he struggled round, being overtaken by the Cosworths on the pit straight. Fabi passed him, then the resurgent Boutsen, then, on the last lap, Senna. That single point was hard-earned.

So, too, were Mansell's nine. Right to the end he kept the pace up, for that is how he likes to drive. And he said later that it had been a satisfying afternoon. Had the clutch played up in the race, after all? "Yes, it did. Never failed completely, but I could feel it going away. During the second half of the race, I used it only for changing down."

And the tooth? "Well, it hurts like hell — now! But I wasn't really aware of it in the race, even though it was bleeding quite a lot. Actually, I'm not too aware of it — because I bashed my head on a girder on the victory rostrum, and that hurts more at the moment . . ."

1: Happy 100th, Nigel. He celebrated his 100th grand prix the best way possible.

2: Mouth bleeding from a recent wisdom tooth operation and head aching from an argument with a girder on the way to the rostrum, Mansell puts his team-mate back in his place.

3: Away safely at last in the late afternoon, Piquet takes up the front running, with Mansell staying out of the picture in fifth, taking care of his clutch for later on.

AUSTRIAN GRAND PRIX

Round 10: August 16, 1987
Circuit: Osterreichring

Race data:	52 laps of 3.692 mile (5.94 km) circuit
Weather:	Warm, dry
Fastest lap:	Mansell, Williams FW11B, 1:28.318, 150.531mph
Existing record:	Berger, Benetton B186, 1:29.444, 148.457mph

ENTRIES

No	Driver (Nat)	Car/Chassis	Engine
1	Alain Prost (F)	McLaren MP4/3-4	TAG V6 Turbo
2	Stefan Johansson (S)	McLaren MP4/3-3*	TAG V6 Turbo
2T	Stefan Johansson (S)	McLaren MP4/3-2	TAG V6 Turbo
2T	Stefan Johansson (S)	McLaren MP4/3-1	TAG V6 Turbo
3	Jonathan Palmer (GB)	Tyrrell DG/016-6	Ford Cosworth V8
4	Philippe Streiff (F)	Tyrrell DG/016-5	Ford Cosworth V8
5	Nigel Mansell (GB)	Williams FW11B/3	Honda V6 Turbo
6	Nelson Piquet (BR)	Williams FW11B/4*	Honda V6 Turbo
6T	Nelson Piquet (BR)	Williams FW11B/1	Honda V6 Turbo
7	Riccardo Patrese (I)	Brabham BT56/4	BMW S4 Turbo
7T	Riccardo Patrese (I)	Brabham BT56/3*	BMW S4 Turbo
8	Andrea de Cesaris (I)	Brabham BT56/1	BMW S4 Turbo
9	Martin Brundle (GB)	Zakspeed 871/1*	Zakspeed S4 Turbo
9T	Martin Brundle (GB)	Zakspeed 871/3	Zakspeed S4 Turbo
10	Christian Danner (D)	Zakspeed 871/2	Zakspeed S4 Turbo
11	Satoru Nakajima (J)	Lotus 99T/5	Honda V6 Turbo
12	Ayrton Senna (BR)	Lotus 99T/6*	Honda V6 Turbo
12T	Ayrton Senna (BR)	Lotus 99T/3	Honda V6 Turbo
14	Pascal Fabre (F)	AGS JH22/02-032	Ford Cosworth V8
16	Ivan Capelli (I)	March 871/04	Ford Cosworth V8
17	Derek Warwick (GB)	Arrows A10/4	Megatron S4 Turbo
18	Eddie Cheever (USA)	Arrows A10/3	Megatron S4 Turbo
19	Teo Fabi (I)	Benetton B187-07	Ford V6 Turbo
20	Thierry Boutsen (B)	Benetton B187-06	Ford V6 Turbo
21	Alex Caffi (I)	Osella FA1H/86-03	Alfa Romeo V8 Turbo
23	Adrian Campos (E)	Minardi M186-02	Moderni V6 Turbo
24	Alessandro Nannini (I)	Minardi M186-03	Moderni V6 Turbo
25	Rene Arnoux (F)	Ligier JS29C-5	Megatron S4 Turbo
26	Piercarlo Ghinzani (I)	Ligier JS29C-4	Megatron S4 Turbo
27	Michele Alboreto (I)	Ferrari F187-100	Ferrari V6 Turbo
28	Gerhard Berger (A)	Ferrari F187-099	Ferrari V6 Turbo
28T	Gerhard Berger (A)	Ferrari F187-097*	Ferrari V6 Turbo
30	Philippe Alliot (F)	Lola LC87/02	Ford Cosworth V8

* Race car

QUALIFYING

FRIDAY: Dry, warm Driver		SATURDAY: Wet, drying Driver	
Piquet	1:23.357	Mansell	1:33.779
Mansell	1:23.459	Cheever	1:37.908
Berger	1:24.213	Berger	1:38.388
Boutsen	1:24.348	Senna	1:39.647
Fabi	1:25.054	Johansson	1:41.711
Alboreto	1:25.077	Brundle	1:42.383
Senna	1:25.492	Nakajima	1:43.002
Patrese	1:25.766	Prost	1:43.132
Prost	1:26.170	Alboreto	1:45.518
De Cesaris	1:27.672	Campos	1:47.128
Warwick	1:27.762	Boutsen	1:48.124
Cheever	1:28.370	Alliot	1:48.595
Nakajima	1:28.786	Danner	1:48.880
Johansson	1:29.003	Palmer	1:49.308
Nannini	1:29.435	Nannini	1:49.566
Arnoux	1:29.733	Piquet	1:49.991
Brundle	1:29.893	Caffi	1:50.273
Ghinzani	1:30.682	Streiff	1:51.624
Campos	1:30.797	Patrese	1:53.119
Danner	1:31.015	Capelli	1:54.807
Caffi	1:32.313	Fabre	1:57.236
Alliot	1:33.741		
Capelli	1:34.199		
Palmer	1:34.619		
Streiff	1:35.338		
Fabre	1:40.633		

STARTING GRID

No	Driver	Time
6	Piquet	1:23.357
5	Mansell	1:23.459
28	Berger	1:24.213
20	Boutsen	1:24.348
19	Fabi	1:25.054
27	Alboreto	1:25.077
12	Senna	1:25.492
7	Patrese	1:25.766
1	Prost	1:26.170
8	De Cesaris	1:27.672
17	Warwick	1:27.762
18	Cheever	1:28.370
11	Nakajima	1:28.786
2	Johansson	1:29.003
24	Nannini	1:29.435
25	Arnoux	1:29.733
9	Brundle	1:29.893
26	Ghinzani	1:30.682
23	Campos	1:30.797
10	Danner	1:31.015
21	Caffi	1:32.313
30	Alliot	1:33.741
16	Capelli	1:34.199
3	Palmer	1:34.619
4	Streiff	1:35.338
14	Fabre	1:40.633

RESULTS

Pos	No	Driver	Car	Laps	Time/Retirement
1	5	Mansell	Williams-Honda	52	1-18:44.898
2	6	Piquet	Williams-Honda	52	1-19:40.602
3	19	Fabi	Benetton-Ford	51	
4	20	Boutsen	Benetton-Ford	51	
5	12	Senna	Lotus-Honda	50	
6	1	Prost	McLaren-TAG	50	
7	2	Johansson	McLaren-TAG	50	
8	26	Ghinzani	Ligier-Megatron	50	
9	10	Danner	Zakspeed	49	
10	25	Arnoux	Ligier-Megatron	49	
11	16	Capelli	March-Cosworth	49	
12	30	Alliot	Lola-Cosworth	49	
13	11	Nakajima	Lotus-Honda	49	
14	3	Palmer	Tyrrell-Cosworth	47	
NC	14	Fabre	AGS-Cosworth	45	
R	7	Patrese	Brabham-BMW	43	Engine
R	27	Alboreto	Ferrari	42	Loss of turbo boost
R	8	De Cesaris	Brabham-BMW	35	Engine
R	17	Warwick	Arrows-Megatron	35	Engine
R	18	Cheever	Arrows-Megatron	31	Tyre failure
R	28	Berger	Ferrari	5	Turbo
R	23	Campos	Minardi-Moderni	3	Electrics
R	24	Nannini	Minardi-Moderni	1	Engine
DQ	9	Brundle	Zakspeed	48	
DNS	21	Caffi	Osella-Alfa Romeo		
DNS	4	Streiff	Tyrrell-Cosworth		

FASTEST LAP

Driver	
Mansell	1:28.318
Piquet	1:28.358
Senna	1:28.559
Boutsen	1:29.111
Johansson	1:29.238
Prost	1:29.291
Fabi	1:29.559
Alboreto	1:30.148
Berger	1:30.343
Patrese	1:30.629
Nakajima	1:31.585
Warwick	1:31.783
Cheever	1:31.814
De Cesaris	1:31.960
Danner	1:32.817
Ghinzani	1:34.372
Arnoux	1:34.785
Brundle	1:35.615
Capelli	1:35.616
Alliot	1:36.025
Campos	1:37.854
Palmer	1:38.245
Fabre	1:42.844
Nannini	2:06.843

CHAMPIONSHIP POSITIONS

DRIVERS			CONSTRUCTORS	
1	Piquet	54	1 Williams-Honda	93
2	Senna	43	2 McLaren-TAG	50
3	Mansell	39	3 Lotus-Honda	49
4	Prost	31	4 Ferrari	17
5	Johansson	19	5 Benetton-Ford	15
6	Berger	9	6 Tyrrell-Cosworth	8
7	Alboreto	8	7 Arrows-Megatron	7
	Boutsen	8	8 Brabham-BMW	6
9	Fabi	7	9 Zakspeed	2
10	Nakajima	6	10 Ligier-Megatron	1
11	Cheever	4	Lola-Cosworth	1
	De Cesaris	4	March-Cosworth	1
	Palmer	4		
	Streiff	4		
15	Warwick	3		
16	Brundle	2		
	Patrese	2		
18	Alliot	1		
	Arnoux	1		
	Capelli	1		

JIM CLARK CUP		COLIN CHAPMAN CUP	
1 Palmer	61	1 Tyrrell-Cosworth	106
2 Streiff	45	2 AGS-Cosworth	35
3 Fabre	35	3 Lola-Cosworth	25
4 Alliot	25	4 March-Cosworth	19
5 Capelli	19		

THE NEED TO WIN

Places were no good to him anymore. He had to win to protect his points lead and to do so embraced the latest technological breakthrough.

A testing session that went the distance of a grand prix gave Nelson Piquet no doubts. The 'active' suspension version of the Williams-Honda he had been testing secretly during the season, was now discernibly superior to the standard system. At Monza he had a conventional car as a spare, but there was never any indication that he would race it.

He put the new system on pole position — just — and led from the first lap to the time of his tyre stop. Among those who gave vain chase was Nigel Mansell, whose standard Williams was no match for it, and strangely not there in the engine compartment either. During the second half of the event Mansell's Honda V6 overheated drastically, forcing him to ease back into a distant third.

The man who made the race was Ayrton Senna in the Lotus. Sick of placings, the man who introduced the 'active' system to the winner's rostrum just months before, decided to make it through without a tyre stop. It was a close thing on wear, the tyre technicians warned, but it proved a worthy gamble as Senna hung onto the lead into the closing stages, with Piquet making hard work of the pursuit due to a blistered left rear.

Then eight laps from the end, deteriorating traction and a less than helpful backmarker caught Senna out at the Parabolica. He rejoined skilfully, somewhere in a sandstorm created by spinning wheels, but Piquet had gone two seconds up the road. Even an awesome attack on the lap record that was theoretically impossible on tyres past their life, couldn't salvage the situation for the younger Brazilian.

Was he sandbagging? That was the question everyone was asking about Nelson Piquet after the first qualifying day at Monza. In his debut of the 'active' Williams-Honda, the Brazilian was three-tenths slower than Nigel Mansell's 'standard' car.

No one was too surprised then when Piquet leapfrogged his team-mate on the Saturday. Following the Imola tests, a week earlier, Nelson had no doubts about the potential of the active car: it was, he reckoned, "a second a lap quicker than the normal FW11B."

The test results bore him out. At one stage he ran a full grand prix distance in the car — and his time for the 60 laps was *three minutes* faster than the time it took Mansell to win the race at Imola . . .

As usual, Piquet had a spare, conventional, Williams at his disposal for Monza, but he barely touched it. From the outset, he had no doubts that he wanted to run the active car. Well ahead in the world championship, he was, thanks to the best eleven scores rule, but he would have to start dropping points. And with no finish lower than second, those points would be lost in chunks of six.

1: Race leader Nelson Piquet hits the pits for his scheduled tyre stop, later than his rivals. But one rival, Ayrton Senna was still out there and showing no signs of wanting to stop.

2: Italian Nicola Larini and the new Coloni Cosworth made their GP debut, but only in qualifying as the local car didn't make the cut.

3: Another debutant at Monza was Swiss Franco Forini in a second Osella.

4: Boutsen laps Nannini as he likes on the way to challenging the status quo again. The Belgian had the Benetton into second on lap two and in Piquet's shadow after 10.

5: Forini was to get in 27 laps before the car failed. He could expect no more from the shoestring Osella.

Previous page: Piquet leaves his team-mate behind by embracing the next step in technology. This was the first race for the active system he had been studiously testing through the season.

What he needed was wins, and he believed the active car was a good place to start.

The debut of the active Williams was no less than sensational. It could run lower than the conventional car, and that in itself created a lot of downforce: ergo Piquet was able to run far less wing than Mansell, with his standard car. Monza — always, with its combination of long straights, fast corners and slow chicanes, what Nigel called "a compromise track" — was comparatively straightforward for Nelson. Less wing meant that the car was blindingly quick through the speed traps. During the final session Piquet was over the finish line at 210.963 mph, and by the trap before the first chicane he was up to 218.807 mph.

No one else was even close, and Mansell was nearly five mph away. There was no problem with a down-on-power engine or anything of the kind, Nigel said. Simply, for his car to be driveable, he had to run more wing than Nelson. For all that, he put up a hell of a fight. Fastest on the day, he was beaten by Piquet on Saturday, got the pole back, then lost it again. At the end of the session, needing to find only a tenth, he went out again, but stayed out a lap too long, and ran out of fuel.

Generally, he was pleased with the car, pleased to be so close to Piquet's time, although he suspected that, yes, Nelson *was* sandbagging, that we hadn't seen anything like the full potential of the active car. "He's got a big advantage on empty tanks," he said, "so in the race I just hope we're closer on full tanks."

Another worry loomed larger in his mind: "For the first time this year I've got what seems to be a fairly major fuel consumption problem. And that really bothers me, because Piquet and Senna are all right on fuel . . ."

The words hung in the air. After Honda's announcement on Friday that it was dropping Williams, there was all manner of Machiavellian speculation in the air. At the Honda press conference on Friday, the question had been asked: could the company confirm that, for the rest of this season, Mansell would have equipment on a par with Piquet's?

Mr Sakurai, Managing Director of Honda F1, was cautious in his reply: "Engine settings are exactly the same," he said, "but because there are some differences in driving styles, Mansell, Piquet, and also Senna, we change a little bit the settings. But basically the performance/economy balance is the same . . ."

There seemed to be a contradiction within that answer — particularly since Ayrton Senna's technique is known to be heavier on fuel than Piquet's or Mansell's. And Ayrton had no consumption worries during practice at Monza.

Even the Italians, supremely versed in the polemics of motor racing, were stunned by the Japanese machinations at Monza. Suddenly the Old Man of Maranello seemed like a softie.

Ferrari had anticipated the 1987 Italian Grand Prix more keenly than for many a year, for the Williams pair alone out-qualified Gerhard Berger, and Michele Alboreto would almost certainly have joined him on row two had it not been for a lack of boost and poor throttle response in the final session.

Michele used the spare F187 throughout the second day, having shunted his own car against the barriers at Lesmo on Friday afternoon. Both he and Gerhard complained of a little too much understeer, but all told they were happy with their cars, optimistic for the race. And Berger's last-ditch descent into the 1:23s bracket was a guarantee of chaotic traffic on Sunday morning.

And Senna, of course, was at hand, albeit a full second from Berger, let alone the two Williams. As ever, Ayrton gave his all, but after the last session reckoned he had reached the Lotus's limit. Not absolutely satisfied with the balance of the active car, he reckoned he had probably tried a little too hard: "I was trying to brake as late as possible, and so the brakes overheated. Then I let them cool down — and I must have overdone it because then I found they were locking into the chicane." As ever, his qualifying laps were worth going a long way to see. And he was sure he would have been quicker in the qualifying spare car, which was sidelined with a broken gearbox.

For Alain Prost, the problem was a familiar one: lack of power. "We've got the car nicely balanced," Alain said, "but at the top end the engine is finished. Between the finish line and the first chicane we are losing a lot."

Indeed. At the line the world champion's McLaren was clocked at 206.8 mph, on a par with Honda and Ferrari. But by the next trap the TAG-powered car was only slightly up on Christian Danner's Zakspeed. Fifth fastest, Prost was looking for his first trouble-free race since Spa in May.

His top-end power problems were shared by Thierry Boutsen and Teo Fabi, sixth and seventh in the Benettons. Fourth fastest on the opening day, Thierry was understandably angry by Saturday afternoon. Despite his feeling that the Ford V6 was getting tired by the end of the first session, Cosworth decided against changing it for the second day. During the morning it went off altogether, and the subsequent engine change took up much of the last session. As well as that, it was inevitably a hurried job: a turbo blanking plate was left in place, massive overheating the consequence. Most of his session was spent in the T-car, and he was able to improve only slightly on Friday's time.

Riccardo Patrese and Andrea de Cesaris both made the top 10 with their Brabham-BMWs, and the Arrows of Derek Warwick and Eddie Cheever again performed creditably, despite poor straightline speeds.

Jonathan Palmer looked to the normally-aspirated race with enthusiasm: "I can see it being a slip-streamer all the way, because there's only three-tenths between me, Alliot, Streiff and Capelli. The only thing is, the turbos will break it up as they lap us."

Round they came, at precisely 2.30 pm, to form up for the most dramatic start of the season. The grid at Monza builds an atmosphere beyond compare — but at the last second yellow flags were waved, the start aborted: at the back of Patrese's Brabham a merry little fire was burning. In fact, it was nothing serious, merely fumes from a breather pipe igniting from proximity to the turbo. There was no damage, and after a few minutes they went off again for a further parade lap. There would now be 50 racing laps, one fewer than originally scheduled.

At the green Piquet hesitated momentarily, allowing Mansell briefly to get the jump on him. But by the

4.

5.

117

first chicane Nelson had hit the front, and was comfortably clear by the end of the opening lap. Nigel followed him through, and then we had Berger, Boutsen, Prost and Senna.

Lap two brought change, with Boutsen now up to second. Berger had tried to take advantage of a sideways movement by Mansell at the second chicane, and briefly the Williams and Ferrari laid claim to the same piece of road at the same time. They touched momentarily and, while sorting themselves out, were both passed by the Benetton.

It was a repeat of the opening stages in Austria: Piquet leading, a very resolute Boutsen chasing.

the early going. Patrese's hopes were directed towards a Williams drive; de Cesaris must have wondered if this had been his last Italian Grand Prix.

Alboreto's race lasted little longer. Early in the race, Michele had been over a kerb a little forcefully, which loosened the Ferrari's undertray. It flapped around so much that eventually the bodywork from the left sidepod was dislodged, fluttering away at 190 mph. It affected the car's pace but little — Alboreto was running right with Senna — but a small piece of fibreglass found its way into the turbo. After 14 laps there was an audible groan from the stands as No. 27 came in to stay.

From the start Nigel had been running minimum boost, hoping to forestall fuel problems late in the race so was doing well. The practice days had warned him to expect them, and the messages had been right. All things being equal, he knew he couldn't run with Piquet.

Johansson began the planned tyre stops on lap 19, followed by Fabi (20), Mansell (21), Boutsen and Berger (23) and last, Piquet (24).

After a comparatively leisurely start, Ayrton Senna was coming increasingly into the picture. As the others pitted for new Goodyears, indeed, he took over the lead, on lap 25. When would he be coming in? As the laps went by, the question changed: *would* he be coming in? After 30 laps he was still out there, leading Piquet by nine secs, and not in any apparent trouble.

"The plan was to change tyres, like everyone else," Ayrton said, "but I knew if I stopped, the race was lost. When they called me in to change tyres, I radioed back about the possibility of staying out..."

Peter Warr got the answer from Goodyear: probably Senna's tyres *could* go the distance, but it was marginal. Ayrton was given his answer, and made his decision at once: he would stay out. "I decided it was worth taking a chance — I wanted to win this one, or be nowhere." Clearly he had had his fill of distant, lapped, third places.

So we had a race, after all. There were 20 laps left, and Ayrton had less than 10 secs on Piquet, now charging on fresh tyres. And perhaps charging too hard? Was that a tell-tale mark on the Williams' left rear? Indeed so. The gap to the Lotus was coming down, but not as quickly as expected.

"When the tyre blistered," Nelson said, "a bad vibration started through the car, and of course it got worse all the time." Did he think he was going to catch Ayrton? A shrug said it all. Who knew? From the trackside, though, Senna looked the more likely to come through.

It was strictly a race between the two. Piquet's tyre stop had taken longer than Mansell's, and after the Brazilian rejoined he had found his mirrors full of No. 5. Just briefly a repeat of the duels at Ricard, Silverstone and Zeltweg seemed in prospect, but it was not to be. Nigel simply could not stay with his 'active' team-mate this time, and began to fall away.

"He had a blistered tyre, too," said Patrick Head, "and also a fairly drastic loss of power. A few laps after his stop his air temperature went up 10, then 15 degrees on what it should have been. We think he picked something up which went into the intake. When that happened, all he could do was back off."

Still, he was a comfortable third, ahead of Boutsen and Berger, who continued to run in close company, with the rev-limited Johansson in the last point-scoring position, and a lack-lustre Fabi not too far behind.

Lap 37: a new fastest lap announced for... Prost! The little man may have been four laps back, but continued to go hard, reminding everyone that Porsche and Bosch may have slid from contention, but the man lacks for nothing.

By lap 40 Senna's lead was down to 4.6 secs, but still Nelson seemed not to be gaining quickly enough. He was paring a fifth here, half a second there, but there were only 10 laps to the flag — and *passing* the Lotus would not be easily done. The two countrymen do not exactly constitute a mutual admiration society.

Everything changed on lap 43. Ayrton had Ghinzani's Ligier to lap as he came down to Parabolica. Out from behind the blue car he came, and suddenly it was obvious that the Lotus was off line, running wide.

"I had a lot of trouble with backmarkers through the race," was Senna's rueful comment afterwards. "There could have been many accidents before, and with Ghinzani it was just the same, except that it went wrong. I wanted to pass him under braking for Parabolica, but he was right in the middle of the road, not on the left. I just couldn't stop the car enough for the corner, and went straight on..."

The yellow car ploughed and bucked through the run-off sand trap, and skirted the tyre barrier beyond. But Ayrton's delicate touch saved him from a shunt, and he was able to make a dusty return to the circuit — now in second place behind Piquet, of course.

After the morning warm-up, Thierry had felt highly optimistic: on power he was good, if not Honda good, and balance and grip were excellent. He felt confident of disturbing the Establishment again, and he was doing it now. After 10 laps he was closer to Piquet than after five.

After 10 laps, too, Prost was into the pits. Earlier he had been displaced in fifth by Senna, and then Alboreto, Johansson and Fabi had followed through. "It was a problem with the potentiometer," Alain related afterwards. "In other words, the old problem — engine cutting out, cutting in, cutting out... And it was getting worse and worse, so I came in."

Off came the rear bodywork of the McLaren, and the mechanics set to the task of changing the ignition control box. With no sign of the fury he must have felt, the world champion calmly sat there, waiting for the signal to go. By the time it came, four laps had been lost. But Prost is the true professional, and proceeded to drive as if in the leading bunch — while the electronics allowed. The engine was better after the stop, he said, but the essential problem remained. And that elusive 28th victory was out of reach for another weekend in this catastrophic season for McLaren.

Johansson had a different problem — beyond that of having to find work for 1988. "Right from the start," he said, "I had the rev limiter cutting in early on every single straight. And it was strange, because the rev counter was showing 12,000 — which would have meant I was doing about 220 mph... It was an electronics problem somewhere. All I could do was put the boost down to minimum, and just sit there all afternoon, feeling like an idiot."

Still, both McLaren men were still running, if hobbled, which was more than could be said of the Brabham representatives, both of whom expired in

Berger, though, was still giving hope to the faithful, still running third. But there were signs now that Mansell was on the move. He closed on the Ferrari, passing it on lap 17, and needed only another couple of laps to deal with Boutsen's Benetton.

Top: Senna wanted to win this one, he was sick of placings. That's why he gambled on no tyre stop. It was a gamble that almost paid dividends, as he desperately hung onto the lead in the dying stages.

Above: A happier Alboreto. The Ferrari was proving more competitive but yet again he was to retire due to the car's deep seated unreliability problem.

That looked to be the end of it, for surely Senna —his tyres with 160 miles on them now — would be in no state to offer a challenge? "I wanted to win this one or be nowhere . . ."

Amazingly, he began to catch the Williams, and now Piquet was the man under pressure. Ayrton was simply going for it, throwing tyres, fuel, everything to the wind. It was a reminder, as with Prost, that the Williams drivers had had it relatively easy.

Mansell's wretchedly unsatisfying afternoon almost came to a sudden halt on lap 45, when Palmer's Tyrrell went off the road under braking for the first chicane, then bounced back on smack in front of

the Williams, which had momentarily to go off in avoidance. But all was well.

The crowd's attention, though, was focused solely on the South American battle for the Italian Grand Prix. It never quite came to a barnstorming finish, although Senna was less than two secs back as they started the last lap. On the 49th lap Piquet, blistered tyre and all, had set a new fastest lap — which lasted only until Senna flashed over the line. This was awesome, from a man who well knew that his tyre wear situation was 'marginal'. . .

The normally-aspirated battle had been closely fought throughout, led first by Alliot from Streiff,

Capelli and an oversteering Palmer. Contact between the two Frenchmen left Alliot in the sand at Parabolica, Streiff to take maximum Jim Clark Trophy points. But really, at a place as quick as this, and with so much else going on, the Cosworths were barely noticed.

No, this was the day when Piquet put a tighter lock on the world championship, when Senna provided heroism. The Brazilian flags waved frantically afterwards and for a long time. Even the inscrutable Japanese probably allowed themselves a smile: Honda-Honda-Honda.

ITALIAN GRAND PRIX

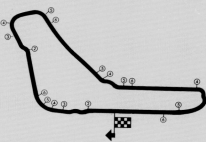

Round 11: September 6, 1987
Circuit: Monza

Race data:	50 laps of 3.603 mile (5.8 km) circuit
Weather:	Hot, dry
Fastest lap:	Senna, Lotus 99T, 1:26.796, 149.479mph
Existing record:	Fabi, Benetton B186, 1:28.099, 147.268mph

ENTRIES

No	Driver (Nat)	Car/Chassis	Engine
1	Alain Prost (F)	McLaren MP4/3-4	TAG V6 Turbo
1T	Alain Prost (F)	McLaren MP4/3-1	TAG V6 Turbo
2	Stefan Johansson (S)	McLaren MP4/3-5	TAG V6 Turbo
3	Jonathan Palmer (GB)	Tyrrell DG/016-6	Ford Cosworth V8
4	Philippe Streiff (F)	Tyrrell DG/016-7	Ford Cosworth V8
5	Nigel Mansell (GB)	Williams FW11B/3	Honda V6 Turbo
6	Nelson Piquet (BR)	Williams FW11B/5	Honda V6 Turbo**
6T	Nelson Piquet (BR)	Williams FW11B/4	Honda V6 Turbo
7	Riccardo Patrese (I)	Brabham BT56/4	BMW S4 Turbo
8	Andrea de Cesaris (I)	Brabham BT56/1	BMW S4 Turbo
9	Martin Brundle (GB)	Zakspeed 871/03	Zakspeed S4 Turbo
10	Christian Danner (D)	Zakspeed 871/02	Zakspeed S4 Turbo
11	Satoru Nakajima (J)	Lotus 99T/3	Honda V6 Turbo
12	Ayrton Senna (BR)	Lotus 99T/3	Honda V6 Turbo
14	Pascal Fabre (F)	AGS JH22/02-032	Ford Cosworth V8
16	Ivan Capelli (I)	March 871/2	Ford Cosworth V8
17	Derek Warwick (GB)	Arrows A10/4	Megatron S4 Turbo
18	Eddie Cheever (USA)	Arrows A10/2	Megatron S4 Turbo
19	Teo Fabi (I)	Benetton B187-04	Ford V6 Turbo
20	Thierry Boutsen (B)	Benetton B187-07	Ford V6 Turbo
21	Franco Forini (CH)	Osella FA1H/1	Alfa Romeo V8 Turbo
22	Alex Caffi (I)	Osella FAH/1	Alfa Romeo V8 Turbo
23	Adrian Campos (E)	Minardi M186/3	Moderni V6 Turbo
24	Alessandro Nannini (I)	Minardi M186/2	Moderni V6 Turbo
25	Rene Arnoux (F)	Ligier JS29C/05	Megatron S4 Turbo
26	Piercarlo Ghinzani (I)	Ligier JS29C/04	Megatron S4 Turbo
27	Michele Alboreto (I)	Ferrari F187/100	Ferrari V6 Turbo
28	Gerhard Berger (A)	Ferrari F187/099	Ferrari V6 Turbo
28T	Gerhard Berger (A)	Ferrari F187/097*	Ferrari V6 Turbo
30	Philippe Alliot (F)	Lola LC87/02	Ford Cosworth V8
32	Nicola Larini (I)	Coloni FC187/01	Ford Cosworth V8

* Race car   ** Active suspension

QUALIFYING

FRIDAY: Hot, dry Driver		SATURDAY: Hot, dry Driver	
Mansell	1:24.350	Piquet	1:23.460
Piquet	1:24.617	Mansell	1:23.559
Berger	1:25.211	Berger	1:23.933
Boutsen	1:25.250	Senna	1:24.907
Alboreto	1:25.290	Prost	1:24.946
Prost	1:25.340	Boutsen	1:25.004
Senna	1:25.535	Fabi	1:25.020
Patrese	1:26.453	Alboreto	1:25.247
Fabi	1:26.894	Patrese	1:25.525
Johansson	1:27.420	De Cesaris	1:26.802
Warwick	1:27.543	Johansson	1:27.031
Nakajima	1:28.463	Cheever	1:28.022
Arnoux	1:28.946	Warwick	1:28.083
Cheever	1:29.273	Nakajima	1:28.160
Nannini	1:29.738	Danner	1:29.465
Ghinzani	1:29.898	Brundle	1:29.725
Brundle	1:30.144	Campos	1:30.782
Danner	1:30.389	Caffi	1:31.029
Campos	1:31.094	Nannini	1:31.069
Caffi	1:32.768	Palmer	1:33.028
Capelli	1:34.205	Alliot	1:33.170
Palmer	1:34.218	Streiff	1:33.264
Forini	1:34.467	Capelli	1:33.311
Alliot	1:34.748	Forini	1:33.816
Streiff	1:34.760	Larini	1:35.721
Larini	1:38.460	Fabre	1:36.679
Fabre	1:39.393		
De Cesaris	1:40.285		

STARTING GRID

No	Driver	Time
6	Piquet	1:23.460
5	Mansell	1:23.559
28	Berger	1:23.933
12	Senna	1:24.907
1	Prost	1:24.946
20	Boutsen	1:25.004
19	Fabi	1:25.020
27	Alboreto	1:25.247
7	Patrese	1:25.525
8	De Cesaris	1:26.802
2	Johansson	1:27.031
17	Warwick	1:27.543
18	Cheever	1:28.022
11	Nakajima	1:28.160
25	Arnoux	1:28.946
10	Danner	1:29.465
9	Brundle	1:29.725
24	Nannini	1:29.738
26	Ghinzani	1:29.898
23	Campos	1:30.782
21	Caffi	1:31.029
3	Palmer	1:33.028
30	Alliot	1:33.170
4	Streiff	1:33.264
16	Capelli	1:33.311
22	Forini	1:33.816

RESULTS

Pos	No	Driver	Car	Laps	Time/Retirement
1	6	Piquet	Williams-Honda	50	1-14:47.707
2	12	Senna	Lotus-Honda	50	1-14:49.513
3	5	Mansell	Williams-Honda	50	1-15:36.743
4	28	Berger	Ferrari	50	1-15:45.686
5	20	Boutsen	Benetton-Ford	50	1-16:09.026
6	2	Johansson	McLaren-TAG	50	1-16:16.494
7	19	Fabi	Benetton-Ford	49	
8	26	Ghinzani	Ligier-Megatron	48	
9	10	Danner	Zakspeed	48	
10	25	Arnoux	Ligier-Megatron	48	
11	11	Nakajima	Lotus-Honda	47	
12	4	Streiff	Tyrrell-Cosworth	47	
13	16	Capelli	March-Cosworth	47	
14	3	Palmer	Tyrrell-Cosworth	47	
15	1	Prost	McLaren-TAG	46	
16	24	Nannini	Minardi-Moderni	45	
R	9	Brundle	Zakspeed	43	Gearbox
R	30	Alliot	Lola-Cosworth	37	Spun
R	23	Campos	Minardi-Moderni	34	Engine fire
R	18	Cheever	Arrows-Megatron	27	Driveshaft
R	22	Forini	Osella-Alfa Romeo	27	Turbo
R	21	Caffi	Osella-Alfa Romeo	16	Suspension
R	27	Alboreto	Ferrari	13	Turbo
R	17	Warwick	Arrows-Megatron	9	Metering unit
R	8	De Cesaris	Brabham-BMW	7	Broken upright
R	7	Patrese	Brabham-BMW	5	Engine

FASTEST LAP

Driver	
Senna	1:26.796
Piquet	1:26.858
Prost	1:26.882
Mansell	1:27.496
Johansson	1:28.468
Berger	1:28.519
Fabi	1:28.723
Boutsen	1:28.725
Alboreto	1:30.124
De Cesaris	1:31.279
Arnoux	1:31.335
Patrese	1:31.497
Danner	1:31.636
Nakajima	1:31.849
Ghinzani	1:32.488
Nannini	1:32.568
Brundle	1:32.663
Cheever	1:32.820
Warwick	1:33.180
Campos	1:33.629
Caffi	1:34.187
Streiff	1:34.722
Alliot	1:34.912
Palmer	1:35.154
Capelli	1:35.266
Forini	1:37.964

CHAMPIONSHIP POSITIONS

DRIVERS			CONSTRUCTORS	
1	Piquet	63	1 Williams-Honda	106
2	Senna	49	2 Lotus-Honda	54
3	Mansell	43	3 McLaren-TAG	51
4	Prost	31	4 Ferrari	20
5	Johansson	20	5 Benetton-Ford	17
6	Berger	12	6 Tyrrell-Cosworth	8
7	Boutsen	10	7 Arrows-Megatron	7
8	Alboreto	8	8 Brabham-BMW	6
9	Fabi	7	9 Zakspeed	2
10	Nakajima	6	10 Ligier-Megatron	1
11	Cheever	4	Lola-Cosworth	1
	De Cesaris	4	March-Cosworth	1
	Palmer	4		
	Streiff	4		
15	Warwick	3		
16	Brundle	2		
	Patrese	2		
18	Alliot	1		
	Arnoux	1		
	Capelli	1		

JIM CLARK CUP			COLIN CHAPMAN CUP	
1	Palmer	65	1 Tyrrell-Cosworth	119
2	Streiff	54	2 AGS-Cosworth	35
3	Fabre	35	3 Lola-Cosworth	25
4	Alliot	25	4 March-Cosworth	25
	Capelli	25		

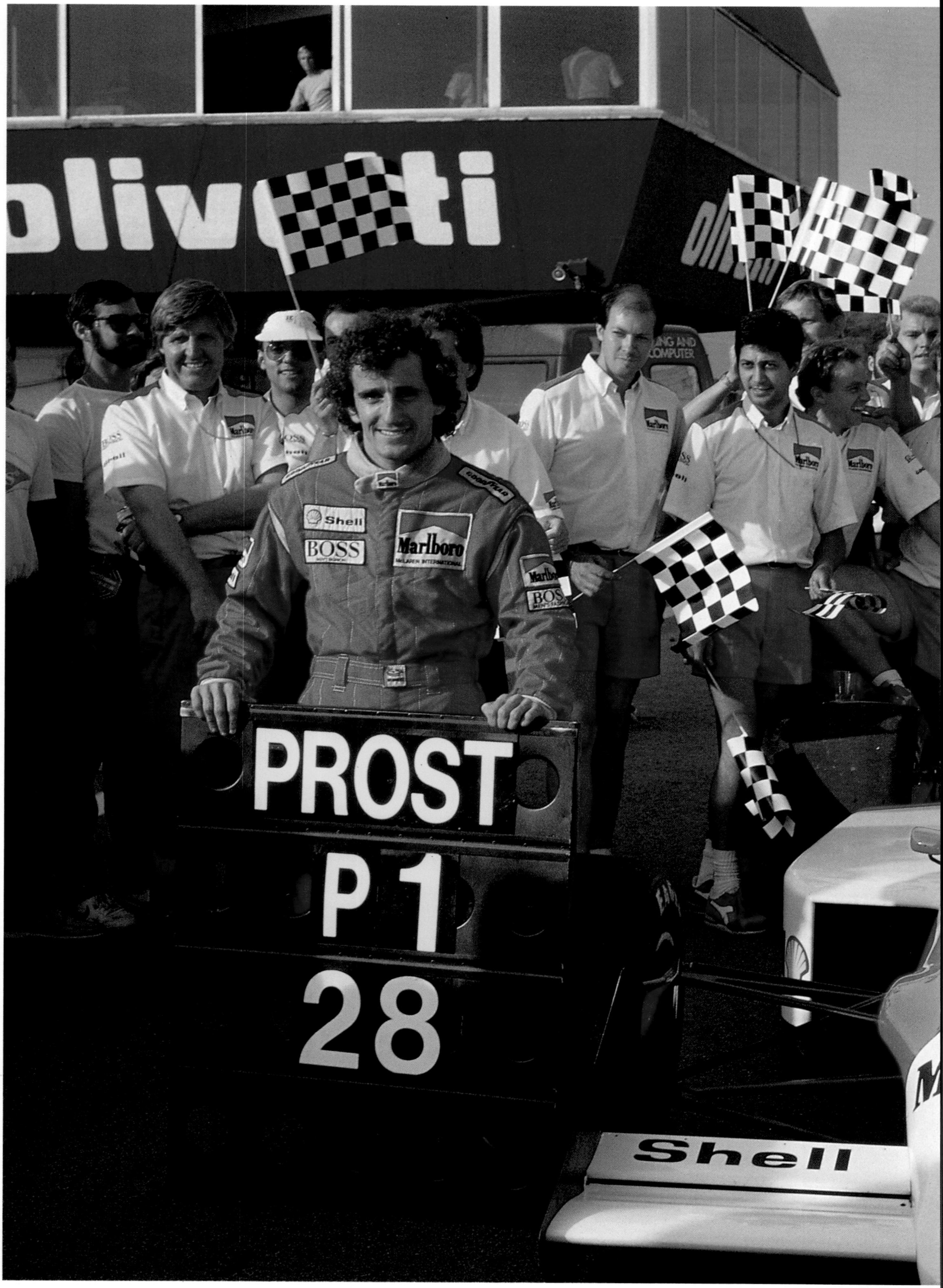
olivetti
PROST
P1
28
Shell
Marlboro
BOSS

Portugal

ROUND 12: September 20, 1987

TWENTY EIGHT TIMES

Through a myriad of electrical problems and endeavours to find more reliability, he waited, persisted. Then, after a drive of championship worth came the record that had refused to fall.

The world championship was gone. Alain Prost knew that. What he wanted most from the remnants of the season was that elusive record win, before the Porsche era at McLaren came to an end. And he wanted win No. 28 to be a good one, earned rather than inherited.

While he waited, the weekend was being stolen by the Ferrari of Gerhard Berger. He had, gasp, taken pole in a brave lap just before the rain, stopping a late challenge from Nigel Mansell. Then, with Mansell gone with a dead engine and Nelson Piquet stalled behind Prost after a slowish tyre stop and with the active Williams not working as it should, Berger took up the running, took control for the good of Formula One.

But it was Alain Prost behind, seeing win No. 28 a possibility as the race neared its end. Sustained pressure from the outgoing world champion pushed the young Austrian over the edge, with just three laps to go. The Ferrari, seemingly bound to consummate the long overdue Ferrari revival, was seen stationary, briefly, pointing the other way out of a cloud of dust. The tyres shot, it had got away from Berger and so too now had Prost, up the road and into the history books.

"I wasn't surprised to see it," the great Frenchman reported, "because I nearly did the same two or three times. It was the hardest drive of my life and I think maybe the best."

Berger and Prost, the new protagonists at the front had made the world championship situation almost incidental at this race. That byplay was behind them, Piquet hobbling to third, tightening his grip on the title.

Estoril was crunch time for Nigel Mansell and he knew it. To keep a realistic hope of beating Nelson Piquet to the championship, this was the one he had to win — one he had to keep Nelson from winning.

After Piquet's Monza victory — and following two days of testing at Brands Hatch — Nigel Mansell was in no real doubt that the 'active' Williams-Honda was what he needed from now on. The testing of early active systems at Lotus left Nigel with an abiding mistrust of the things, and throughout the season he has shown little inclination to become involved with the 'active' test programme. But the Brands Hatch test convinced him of the system's superiority — especially through slow corners — and the same was true at Estoril.

Williams, therefore, arrived with four cars for the first time in the season, each driver having one active, one conventional FW11B at his disposal. And on Friday Mansell set fastest time — in the standard car . . .

He had begun the day in the new one, but abandoned it during the morning session when a leak developed in the hydraulic system. Having put

1.

in more track time with the 'passive' car, he decided to stay with it for the afternoon's timed session.

There were sound reasons for so doing. Thursday had been dauntingly hot and muggy, the sky as good as cloudless. Friday, though, was merely grey and sweaty. There was a possible storm in the air, and the weekend forecast was not optimistic.

Time, then for the 'banker' lap, and Nigel took the standard Williams round in 1:17.9, the only man to beat 1:18. The 1986 pole time was 1:16.6, set by Senna in the Lotus-Renault, and, despite the absence of qualifying tyres and imposition of boost restriction in 1987, it had become the norm for 1986 lap times to be beaten, if not annihilated.

Not so at Estoril. For one thing, the track surface was filthy: if you got off line, it was like hitting a wet patch, and Piquet was not alone in comparing it with the somewhat freaky surface at the Hungaroring plus it was extremely difficult to find a clear lap. "I thought I could go quicker," Mansell said, "so we opted to keep with the regular car for the second set of tyres. But that was it: I'd had a clear lap on the first run and never got another . . ."

At the end of the session he went back out in the active car, and decided to stick with it for Saturday. "It has a *lot* more grip in the slow corners, and if it goes well tomorrow I feel I have to race it. The main problem is that I'm not really familiar with it, and it feels totally different from the normal car. I don't have quite as much confidence in it yet, but it's definitely better."

On Friday, another factor, too, worked against Nigel's active FW11B: it had a lousy engine, he said, whereas the one in the standard car felt great.

On Saturday, as expected, he concentrated on the active car, but was livid to find that the Japanese had not changed the engine overnight. The speed trap figures confirmed his complaint: on the second day speeds were up for all the leading runners — except Mansell. In the standard car he registered 204.3 on Friday, decimal points short of Gerhard Berger's Ferrari, which was quickest of all. The following day — in the active car — he was eighth fastest, slower than Thierry Boutsen's Benetton.

For all that, he set the third best time of the session, which said a lot for the grip of the active car. But which would he race? It rather depended on the engine situation on Sunday morning.

Starting first was Berger. A Ferrari on the pole! Even a Honda man, covering the badges on his shirt and glancing over his shoulder as he spoke, said he was happy with that. He liked the red cars, liked to see them doing well, thought it good for Formula One.

The first half of the final session was dry — but the odd spit of rain was always there, and with 25 minutes left there was a shower. Gerhard, fifth on the opening day, had a lucky break in that he got out on his second set of tyres before the rain came, but that is not to diminish his achievement. He always looked like a contender, and his was the only lap to beat Mansell's Friday time.

"One corner was getting wet when I set my best time," he commented. "Actually my fastest lap should have been the one before, when it was completely dry. But I made a mistake, got sideways and lost time. The first lap on new tyres is always the best for grip, so they weren't so good after that. Also, fourth gear was jumping out, and I had to drive the first corner with one hand, holding the lever with the other. Wasn't too much of a problem, but not perfect, you know?"

1: Mansell had long gone missing and Berger and Prost had left him in his wake, so championship leader, Piquet, troubled by a bout of oversteer and an unaccountably bumpy ride in the active Williams, aimed for a safe third to consolidate his title chances.
2: Danner stalks around helplessly as his crippled Zakspeed is hauled away. He was one of four to be caught up in the first lap melee and would not be there at the re-start.
3: Warwick spins off in the Arrows minutes after the start to avoid Piquet and Alboreto. It was the cue for those behind to drive into each other and off the road.
4: Arnoux sees to the damage on his Ligier, another casualty of the first lap carnage. He would be there for the re-start in the spare but it was also destined to stop.
Previous page: The great moment is noted officially. Alain Prost's long overdue 28th grand prix broke Jackie Stewart's record.

Michele Alboreto — who didn't get to use his second set before the rains came down — was content with sixth. "It's been a continuous development programme, this season," Michele smiled. "If you think about it, at Rio we were four seconds slower than the Hondas in qualifying, so there's been good progress, both with the engine and the chassis. What we need now is some reliability . . ."

Alain Prost would also settle for that. "What I would really like from 1987 now," he said on Friday, "is to get my 28th win — to do it before the end of the Porsche era. I think that would be nice."

He told a familiar story: chassis good, balance fine, power so-so, electronics occasionally maddening. Which is how the season had been for McLaren. But Prost's own personal commitment was as strong as ever: on Saturday morning, he even had a spin while experimenting with different bump-rubbers. In the afternoon he was beaten only by Berger and that was good for third overall.

Team-mate Stefan Johansson looked like joining him at the good looking end of the grid, but missed nearly all the dry part of the last sessions: "Bloody coil lead . . ." he said, through clenched teeth.

World championship leader, Piquet never bothered with his standard Williams. It was the active car throughout, and on Friday he was second fastest to his team-mate's standard machine. The car was fine, he said, traffic the only problem.

During Saturday morning, though, a vibration developed, and at first the gearbox was suspected. Later, though, the problem was traced to the clutch, the replacing of which takes almost as long as an engine change. The mechanics were not done by the start of the last session, but Nelson declined to take out his standard car. By the time the work was finished, so, too, was the dry weather. The Brazilian ran a single slow lap, and came in. Friday's time now

work in the race, starting from the third row, because passing is difficult here," he said, "but I think we've got the race set-up quite good."

They were the contenders. Riccardo Patrese did a typically fine job to qualify seventh in the Brabham-BMW — but how long would it last? And the Benettons, very much starring players since being allowed sensible boost through their Ford motors, slipped back at Estoril, with Boutsen ninth, Teo Fabi 10th. Both complained of too much oversteer, and in the last session Thierry had pop-off valve problems, and Teo spun, let the engine die.

There was a time when you expected Prost and McLaren to come right on race day. Prost was fastest indeed, for a change, fastest in the warm-up, followed by Berger, Mansell, Alboreto, Johansson and Boutsen. It was a reasonable image of qualifying — save that Piquet and Senna were down in seventh and eighth. That was strange, for Ayrton was fastest through the traps . . .

Mansell remained dissatisfied with his horsepower. Honda had changed the engine in his active car overnight, but Nigel said it felt no better, and the trap speeds bore him out. Nevertheless, he said wearily, he was going to stick with the car. But he could see himself getting picked off on the long Estoril straights.

He got away well from the grid, seizing the lead as Berger's wheels spun on the dirty right-hand side of the road. But it benefitted him nothing, for the 'race' was to last less than couple of minutes.

When Nigel and Gerhard got through the first turn in good shape, behind there was carnage. Piquet and Alboreto laid claim to the same piece of road at the same time, leaving the Ferrari off the road, the Williams-Honda limping with a punctured front tyre. Needless to say, each blamed the other.

Derek Warwick spun in the melee, and Satoru Nakajima, perhaps overreacting to the rotating

So it was a new race, full distance, with refuelling allowed. And Piquet, whose day had looked shot, was in with another chance. The undertray of Nelson's car was damaged during his punctured lap to the pits, but that was repaired in time for the restart. The Williams was also given a new nose, and this, the Brazilian would say later, gave him more oversteer than he would have liked.

T-cars were pressed into service for Brundle, Alliot, Arnoux and, most significantly, Alboreto. And the luckless Danner was left to spectate. Forty minutes after the shunt, the green light flashed for the second time — and again it was Mansell who made the most of it.

His lead, though, was short-lived. As they crossed the line at the end of the opening lap, Berger jinked out from the Williams' tow, and calmly drove by — just as Nigel had anticipated. It was unusual, to say the least, to see a Williams-Honda thus humbled.

Senna's third-placed Lotus had quite a queue behind it, led by a frustrated Piquet, and this allowed the leading duo to break away. In point of fact, Nigel was beginning to close on the Ferrari again when, on lap 14, his engine simply died.

This time there were no angry words: "I'm just very disappointed," he said. "Let's leave it at that, shall we? I was driving well within myself, feeling very comfortable, starting to catch Gerhard a bit, then . . ."

When the Williams-Honda was brought back to the pits after the race, its engine fired up and revved lustily. But by then its driver was long gone.

Piquet's, though, were in excellent shape. For 10 laps Nelson swarmed over Senna's Lotus wherever the road turned, but it was evident on the straights that the Honda in Ayrton's car had comfortably the legs of his fellow-countryman's. On lap 11, however, Piquet almost found a way by, and almost imme-

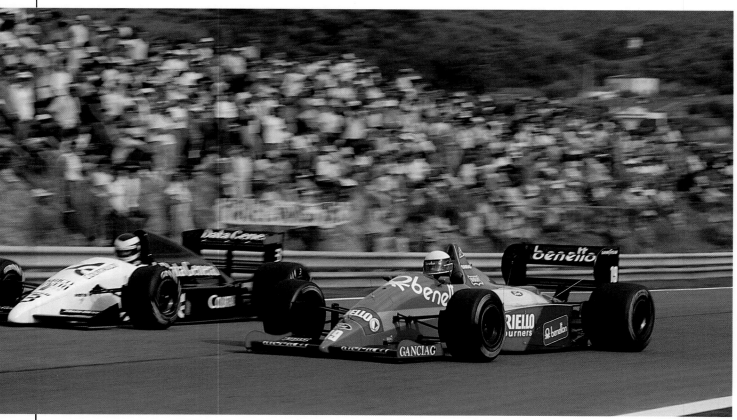

put him fourth on the grid, one place up on his Monza protagonist Ayrton Senna.

Ayrton did not have the happiest of qualifying days in Portugal, spinning twice — once to avoid a rotating Philippe Alliot — on Friday afternoon, and suffering an engine bay fire of some magnitude in the final session, caused by a hydraulic fluid leak onto the exhaust. That meant going to the spare, but the rain took care of any more quick times.

Senna wasn't too concerned. "It will mean harder

Arrows, squeezed Martin Brundle off the road and into the guardrail.

When the dust had settled, the cars of Philippe Alliot, Rene Arnoux, Christian Danner and Adrian Campos were also seen to be involved, and the track was virtually blocked. Scandalously, the red flag to halt the race was not shown until the field had blasted up to the accident, threaded its way through, somehow without further incident. Only after two laps was the race stopped.

Above: Palmer goes a lap down on Fabi. The Italian chose to stay out on one set and held second place mid-race, before ending the race in a dogged fourth.

Right: Prost's persistence was ominous, but his true form was not to be seen until after the pit stop which cured a tyre vibration problem and got him ahead of a calculating Piquet.

diately Senna began to fall back, being quickly swallowed up by Alboreto, Prost, Boutsen and Fabi. After 14 laps, the yellow car was into the pits.

The engine had died, caught, died again, and the problem was traced to a faulty throttle sensor. By the time he returned to the race, Ayrton had lost two laps, and was down in 22nd spot. He then produced a mesmeric drive, which by the end would bring him up to seventh, just four secs away from a championship point.

Fifteen laps into the race, then, and two of the leading lights — Mansell and Senna — were out of contention. Ferrari, with Berger still in front and Alboreto third, were looking very fine, and there seemed even a chance that Honda might be about to lose a race. Piquet, although now established in a comfortable second place, was 10 secs adrift of the leader, and not pushing hard.

"Because of the new nose, I had too much oversteer," he said later, "but I managed to run quite

well. The biggest problem I had during the race, though, was that the suspension just got too hard — I don't know what happened to it. I've driven the active car a lot of testing miles, you know, and this had never happened before. It was very uncomfortable to be bounced around like that. Reminded me of the ground effect days . . ."

Traffic too, was a problem, as always at Estoril. On lap 27, indeed, Alboreto was able to catch and nip by the Williams, but soon afterwards Michele was

Below: Hail the man who has won more grands prix than anybody else. He is flanked by the man who helped make him wait so long, and the man whose great years were ahead.

Bottom: Berger has it won and the Ferrari slump was about to end. Except that Prost was starting to apply the pressure, three secs behind.

trapped behind Nakajima's Lotus, and Nelson took back his second place.

He came in for tyres on lap 30, the first of the front runners to do so. Next time around it was Prost's turn, and now the Frenchman's race took on new impetus. "I had a very quick stop, which put me in front of Nelson," Alain said, "but more important was that the car felt much better than before. On my first set of tyres I had a lot of vibration for some reason, but after my stop it was OK.

"Apart from the electronics unreliability," he went on, "the big problem with my car this year has been that it loses too much downforce when I am behind other cars. That makes it difficult to keep right behind, and maybe I have had to use the tyres a bit more than I should. Also, I was not very quick on the straight, so it was difficult to overtake Michele or Nelson. But in the second part of the race I really wanted to push hard. I was good on fuel during the first half, and on the new tyres the car was perfect —especially when I was running alone.

"After all this time, I really wanted to *win*, you know! I put the boost up a bit, and after that I was marginal on fuel. Also marginal on tyres, brakes and driver . . . but I didn't want to settle for second or third."

Berger made his tyre stop on lap 33, which let team-mate Alboreto briefly into the lead, until he came in three laps later. The reshuffled order was: Berger, 16 secs up on Fabi (who was to run the whole race without changing Goodyears), then Prost, Piquet and Alboreto. But soon afterwards Michele was out with a broken gearbox, and now Maranello hopes and prayers rested with Gerhard.

Still, the Austrian looked strong. Prost and Piquet dealt swiftly with Fabi, but were more than a quarter of a minute adrift of the Ferrari. Thirty laps remained. For a time Nelson more or less hung on to Alain, but the McLaren's new lease of life on fresh tyres, as well as Nelson's increasingly bumpy ride, soon persuaded the Williams man that discretion was his best plan. And as Prost began to charge, Piquet fell away.

Until lap 50 Berger looked under no genuine threat. Prost would take half a second there, a tenth here, but Gerhard seemed able to respond, appeared to be controlling the race. But as they went into the final 20 laps, the gap began to reduce significantly: 11.4, 10.8, 8.1, 6.34, 5.1 and Alain was setting new fastest laps virtually every time around.

So he kicked again, and it seemed to be working. By lap 61 Prost was within three secs of the Ferrari, but thereafter Berger pulled out a little more, and all looked lost for McLaren. The two men were now trading new fastest laps, and really there was little to choose.

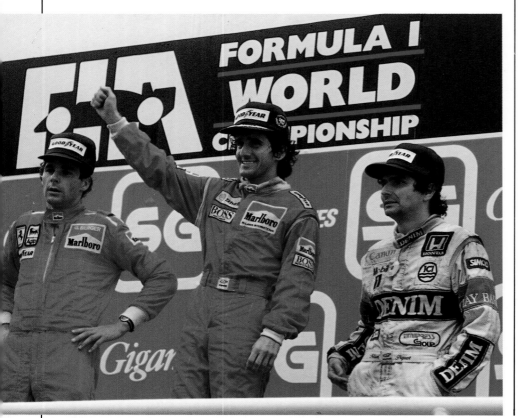

Until lap 68. Suddenly there was a cloud of tyre smoke at a downhill right-hander, and when it cleared there was the red car, facing the wrong way. Berger had spun, and Prost was already through, past No. 28 on the way to No. 28.

"I felt that if I could go into the last two laps with a three secs advantage, I would be OK," Gerhard shrugged afterwards. "I was driving every lap as hard as possible, and I tried to do a real quick one to make my position safe. But my tyres were completely finished, and ... and I just took too much risk. I could not control it. That's life."

At the rostrum there was sympathy for Berger, joy for Prost and Jackie Stewart, winner of 27. "People might not believe me," smiled Stewart, "but I'm glad to see Alain take my record — I'm glad it's *he* who has done it, because he's the one who deserves it. There's no doubt in my mind that he's the best race driver of the generation."

The record his, Alain grinned at the next goal. "Maybe the championship is possible after all, huh. No, it's not very realistic, is it? I just know this: there are four races left this year. And I'm going to try to win them all ..."

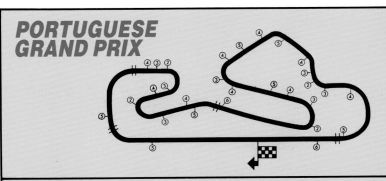

PORTUGUESE GRAND PRIX

Round 12:
September 20, 1987
Circuit: Estoril

70 laps of 2.703 mile (4.35 km) circuit

Weather: Hot, dry
Fastest lap: Berger, Ferrari F187, 1:19.282, 122.734mph
Existing record: Mansell, Williams FW11, 1:20.943, 120.215mph

ENTRIES

No	Driver (Nat)	Car/Chassis	Engine
1	Alain Prost (F)	McLaren MP4/3-4	TAG V6 Turbo
2	Stefan Johansson (S)	McLaren MP4/3-5	TAG V6 Turbo
2T	Stefan Johansson (S)	McLaren MP4/3-1	TAG V6 Turbo
3	Jonathan Palmer (GB)	Tyrrell DG/016-6	Ford Cosworth V8
4	Philippe Streiff (F)	Tyrrell DG/016-3	Ford Cosworth V8
4T	Philippe Streiff (F)	Tyrrell DG/016-7	Ford Cosworth V8
5	Nigel Mansell (GB)	Williams FW11B/6	Honda V6 Turbo
5T	Nigel Mansell (GB)	Williams FW11B/3	Honda V6 Turbo
6	Nelson Piquet (BR)	Williams FW11B/5	Honda V6 Turbo
6T	Nelson Piquet (BR)	Williams FW11B/4	Honda V6 Turbo
7	Riccardo Patrese (I)	Brabham BT56/4	BMW S4 Turbo
8	Andrea de Cesaris (I)	Brabham BT56/3	BMW S4 Turbo
9	Martin Brundle (GB)	Zakspeed 871/03	Zakspeed S4 Turbo
9T	Martin Brundle (GB)	Zakspeed 871/01*	Zakspeed S4 Turbo
10	Christian Danner (D)	Zakspeed 871/02	Zakspeed S4 Turbo
11	Satoru Nakajima (J)	Lotus 99T/3	Honda V6 Turbo
12	Ayrton Senna (BR)	Lotus 99T/3	Honda V6 Turbo
14	Pascal Fabre (F)	AGS JH22/02-032	Ford Cosworth V8
16	Ivan Capelli (I)	March 871/2	Ford Cosworth V8
17	Derek Warwick (GB)	Arrows A10/4	Megatron S4 Turbo
18	Eddie Cheever (USA)	Arrows A10/2	Megatron S4 Turbo
18T	Eddie Cheever (USA)	Arrows A10/3*	Megatron S4 Turbo
19	Teo Fabi (I)	Benetton B187-08	Ford V6 Turbo
20	Thierry Boutsen (B)	Benetton B187-06	Ford V6 Turbo
20T	Thierry Boutsen (B)	Benetton B187-07	Ford V6 Turbo
21	Alex Caffi (I)	Osella FA1H/1	Alfa Romeo V8 Turbo
22	Franco Forini (CH)	Osella FA1H/3	Alfa Romeo V8 Turbo
23	Adrian Campos (E)	Minardi M186/1	Moderni V6 Turbo
24	Alessandro Nannini (I)	Minardi M186/3	Moderni V6 Turbo
25	Rene Arnoux (F)	Ligier JS29C/05	Megatron S4 Turbo
25T	Rene Arnoux (F)	Ligier JS29C/03*	Megatron S4 Turbo
26	Piercarlo Ghinzani (I)	Ligier JS29C/04	Megatron S4 Turbo
27	Michele Alboreto (I)	Ferrari F187/100	Ferrari V6 Turbo
27T	Michele Alboreto (I)	Ferrari F187/097*	Ferrari V6 Turbo
28	Gerhard Berger (A)	Ferrari F187/098	Ferrari V6 Turbo
30	Philippe Alliot (F)	Lola LC87/03	Ford Cosworth V8
30T	Philippe Alliot (F)	Lola LC87/02*	Ford Cosworth V8

* Race car

QUALIFYING

FRIDAY: Overcast, dry		SATURDAY: Dry then wet	
Driver		Driver	
Mansell	1:17.951	Berger	1:17.620
Piquet	1:18.164	Prost	1:17.994
Senna	1:18.382	Mansell	1:18.235
Prost	1:18.404	Senna	1:18.354
Berger	1:18.448	Alboreto	1:18.540
Alboreto	1:20.069	Patrese	1:19.965
Johansson	1:20.134	Johansson	1:20.227
Boutsen	1:20.305	Fabi	1:20.548
Fabi	1:20.483	Boutsen	1:20.558
Cheever	1:21.324	Cheever	1:21.207
Warwick	1:21.397	Warwick	1:21.587
Patrese	1:21.506	De Cesaris	1:21.725
Nannini	1:21.784	Nannini	1:22.128
De Cesaris	1:22.060	Danner	1:22.350
Nakajima	1:22.222	Brundle	1:22.794
Brundle	1:22.400	Arnoux	1:23.237
Danner	1:22.424	Alliot	1:23.580
Arnoux	1:23.637	Campos	1:23.591
Streiff	1:23.810	Capelli	1:23.905
Ghinzani	1:24.105	Palmer	1:24.217
Alliot	1:24.181	Streiff	1:24.436
Palmer	1:24.392	Ghinzani	1:24.979
Capelli	1:24.533	Caffi	1:25.232
Caffi	1:24.792	Forini	1:26.635
Campos	1:24.822	Fabre	1:26.946
Forini	1:27.219		
Fabre	1:28.756		

STARTING GRID

No	Driver	Time
28	Berger	1:17.620
5	Mansell	1:17.951
1	Prost	1:17.994
6	Piquet	1:18.164
12	Senna	1:18.354
27	Alboreto	1:18.540
7	Patrese	1:19.965
2	Johansson	1:20.134
20	Boutsen	1:20.305
19	Fabi	1:20.483
18	Cheever	1:21.324
17	Warwick	1:21.377
8	De Cesaris	1:21.725
24	Nannini	1:21.784
11	Nakajima	1:22.222
10	Danner	1:22.358
9	Brundle	1:22.400
25	Arnoux	1:23.237
30	Alliot	1:23.580
23	Campos	1:23.591
4	Streiff	1:23.810
16	Capelli	1:23.905
26	Ghinzani	1:24.105
3	Palmer	1:24.217
21	Caffi	1:24.792
22	Forini	1:26.635

RESULTS

Pos	No	Driver	Car	Laps	Time/Retirement
1	1	Prost	McLaren-TAG	70	1-37:03.906
2	28	Berger	Ferrari	70	1-37:24.399
3	6	Piquet	Williams-Honda	70	1-38:07.201
4	19	Fabi	Benetton-Ford	69	
5	2	Johansson	McLaren-TAG	69	
6	18	Cheever	Arrows-Megatron	68	
7	12	Senna	Lotus-Honda	68	
8	11	Nakajima	Lotus-Honda	68	
9	16	Capelli	March-Ford	67	
10	3	Palmer	Tyrrell-Cosworth	67	
11	24	Nannini	Minardi-Moderni	66	Out of fuel
12	4	Streiff	Tyrrell-Cosworth	66	
13	17	Warwick	Arrows-Megatron	66	
14	20	Boutsen	Benetton-Ford	64	
R	8	De Cesaris	Brabham-BMW	54	Broken injection pipe
R	27	Alboreto	Ferrari	38	Gearbox
R	9	Brundle	Zakspeed	35	Gearbox
R	22	Forini	Osella-Alfa Romeo	32	Rear wheel bearing
R	30	Alliot	Lola-Cosworth	31	Electrics
R	25	Arnoux	Ligier-Alfa Romeo	29	Holed radiator
R	21	Caffi	Osella-Alfa Romeo	27	Turbo
R	26	Ghinzani	Ligier-Megatron	24	Electrics
R	23	Campos	Minardi-Moderni	24	Accident
R	5	Mansell	Williams-Honda	13	Electrics
R	7	Patrese	Brabham-BMW	13	Engine
DNS	10	Danner	Zakspeed		Eliminated in first race

FASTEST LAP

Driver	
Berger	1:19.282
Prost	1:19.509
Senna	1:20.217
Piquet	1:21.191
Boutsen	1:21.535
Fabi	1:21.821
De Cesaris	1:22.504
Cheever	1:22.682
Johansson	1:22.807
Mansell	1:22.834
Alboreto	1:22.989
Warwick	1:23.259
Nakajima	1:23.828
Patrese	1:24.433
Nannini	1:24.626
Palmer	1:24.652
Streiff	1:25.003
Capelli	1:25.012
Brundle	1:25.760
Arnoux	1:26.131
Caffi	1:26.811
Ghinzani	1:26.811
Campos	1:26.892
Alliot	1:27.020
Forini	1:29.223

CHAMPIONSHIP POSITIONS

	DRIVERS			CONSTRUCTORS	
1	Piquet	67	1	Williams-Honda	110
2	Senna	49	2	McLaren-TAG	62
3	Mansell	43	3	Lotus-Honda	54
4	Prost	40	4	Ferrari	26
5	Johansson	22	5	Benetton-Ford	20
6	Berger	18	6	Arrows-Megatron	8
7	Boutsen	10		Tyrrell-Cosworth	8
	Fabi	10	8	Brabham-BMW	6
9	Alboreto	8	9	Zakspeed	2
10	Nakajima	6	10	Ligier-Megatron	1
11	Cheever	5		Lola-Cosworth	1
12	De Cesaris	4		March-Cosworth	1
	Palmer	4			
	Streiff	4			
15	Warwick	3			
16	Brundle	2			
	Patrese	2			
18	Alliot	1			
	Arnoux	1			
	Capelli	1			

	JIM CLARK CUP			COLIN CHAPMAN CUP	
1	Palmer	71	1	Tyrrell-Cosworth	129
2	Streiff	58	2	AGS-Cosworth	35
3	Fabre	35	3	March-Cosworth	34
4	Capelli	34	4	Lola-Cosworth	25
5	Alliot	25			

GETTING A FAIR CHANCE

Fuming at his team-mate's sudden speed late in qualifying, he had it out with his team management. On race day he had no complaints and wondered where the competition went.

On a track where you could only dream of not being held up, Ayrton Senna was Nigel Mansell's unwitting ally. The yellow Lotus-Honda, blindingly fast in a straight line, tardy in turns, beat all but the Williams pair to the first corner. The pattern of the race was set, the yellow car heading a long, sometimes unruly, star-studded crocodile for most of the afternoon.

After botching his tyre stop in a race that abounded with errors on his part, Nelson Piquet too was ensnared. He joined Alain Prost, Thierry Boutsen and the Ferrari pair in efforts to get by. They all failed, stopped for tyres, started all over, hoped that the road would clear and they would make up time on fresh rubber. Unfortunately for them Senna stayed out and it was back in the queue.

Then with nine laps left, and Mansell in a race of his own, the failing grip on Senna's Goodyears no longer made it possible to hold back the flood of those who had gone the distance. They passed on all sides in a scramble for the minors.

Blissfully aware of this race within a race, Mansell had driven aggressively at the start to prevail over his team-mate. More audacious in the traffic, he won seconds and after that he had nothing to concern him.

The win and Piquet's fourth place still gave the Englishman a mathematical chance of winning the title, but he didn't want to think too much about that, preferring to concentrate on each race and ensure he had a car equal to his team-mate's. "All I ask is for a reliable car and a fair chance," he stated pointedly. "Win or lose, I'll be happy with that."

A certain amount of status quo was restored to the proceedings in Jerez insofar as there was a Williams-Honda front row. Nigel Mansell set the pace on the opening day and Nelson Piquet in the 'active' FW11B found a little extra in the final session.

Although Nelson and Nigel each had an active and a standard Williams in Spain, Piquet once more showed no real interest in his passive car. He was familiar and comfortable with the active version. Mansell, by contrast, remained wary of it, although he conceded its inherent superiority, particularly in slow corners. At present he reckoned he drove the regular car better, knew it thoroughly and had absolute confidence in it.

Therefore, the Englishman was not too upset on Friday morning when a hydraulic leak and then clutch problems temporarily sidelined his active car. The standard one, he said, felt terrific. In the afternoon he set fastest time with it, a hair quicker than Gerhard Berger's Ferrari but six-tenths inside Piquet's best active time.

He would probably try his own active car again on Saturday morning, he added, but his mind was pretty well made up: all things being equal, he would

Previous page: Mansell had heated words with his team management on Saturday and the following day he was entirely happy. He was back on the winner's list and still in with a chance for the championship.

Above: Prost's record-breaking win in Portugal gave the McLaren team new hope to continue to the end of the season on a high note. This time Mansell got in the way.

Right: The Williams front row clear away from the Ferrari second row and the fast-starting Senna. In a few minutes Mansell would fly by Piquet for a race on his own.

stick with what he knew best, race the conventional Williams.

All seemed well with his world: "I've got a few traction problems — quite bad wheel-spin out of the slow corners," Nigel smiled, "but other than traffic — this is a very difficult place for getting a clear lap — I've no complaints. And I'm quite sure we can improve tomorrow."

It didn't work out that way, and the elements played a hand. Threatening black clouds did not interrupt the qualifying session, but an hour later there was a downpour. And on Friday evening a massive storm left the *Circuito de Jerez* a little ravaged. The rain dampened down the surrounding sand, which was welcome, but washed away the rubber which had been put down on Friday. Most drivers commented that a lot of the grip had gone.

Staying in the standard Williams, Mansell was having trouble getting near his Friday time, but there seemed no reason to fret. Berger, nearest rival the day before, was marooned in the pits, awaiting completion of an engine change.

Perhaps Piquet was a threat, though. Indeed, yes. On this first flying lap, Nelson was down to 1:23.4

—quicker than he had managed on the opening day. Yet the track was reckoned to be slower . . .

Piquet's next few hot laps were not quite so fleet, and it was Mansell who set the new mark for the session, albeit a couple of tenths off his previous best. The car felt good, and he was pushing even harder than before. That settled it for him: the track definitely was slower. Berger came out, and so did Alboreto, but neither could approach the times of Friday.

And then Nelson showed his hand, just as he had in Italy. Suddenly his name blinked to the top of the monitor screens, and his time — 1:22.4 — shook everyone, not least Nigel. "I got a clear lap," Piquet said later, "and I just closed my eyes a little bit, and went for it. No way I could have gone any quicker . . ."

Mansell was not impressed with the news. Into pit lane he came, ignoring both red light and yellow flag indicating that his car had been randomly selected for a weight check. An official blocked his path, and the Williams was pushed back onto the weighbridge — though now without its driver, who had alighted with some speed, and was making his hurried way to the pits, there to take out his own active car.

Less than 10 mins remained, and Nigel's best was

1:23.9. On a final banzai lap he found Martin Brundle's slithery Zakspeed in the way, and that was that. In he came, off with the belts, away. "I'm getting out of here," he said as he strode towards the car park, "because if I stay I'm going to fall out with everyone . . ."

Which car did he reckon to race? "You'd better ask the team. I'm just a driver," he growled.

Two hours later, showered, changed and composed, he was back. "I didn't want to start rowing with people," he said, "so I thought it best to get out of the circuit for a while, calm down and then come back to talk it all through. And that's what I'm doing now."

So why had he been so upset? "Look," he said, "I know I'm a reasonably quick driver, and I was fastest yesterday. Today there was less grip, for sure, and it was hot. I was busting a gut to get near my time from yesterday. And suddenly — in these conditions — Piquet improves by a *clear second!* I'm not thrilled with my straightline speeds, and I got blocked on my last quick lap and . . ."

Probably he realised he had been duped by all Piquet's qualifying times prior to the pole lap. All along, the active car had been quicker.

1.

When he came back to the circuit, too, he learned that the weighbridge incident had cost him a $3000 fine and the loss of all his final session times. "I don't blame FISA or the stewards for that," he said. "I deserved it. Now I'm going to talk to the team about tomorrow."

Piquet-Mansell, then, followed by Berger-Alboreto. And Ferrari also had a busy day. In the morning Michele destroyed his car at a fifth gear right-hander: "My fault — I was pushing too hard…" That put him into the *muletta* for the balance of the weekend —which meant that Berger, whose own car was undergoing an engine change, had to sit out more than half the final session.

Gerhard plucked out a tremendous lap on Friday afternoon. Almost a second faster than any of his others, it was only a tenth away from Mansell. But in the last session he had finally to go out in a second, brand-new, T-car, and not surprisingly was off his earlier pace.

Still, Ferrari were right there again, with row two to themselves. "Not a bad place to be," Michele smilingly murmured. "And maybe the *best* place to be at the first corner, with Piquet and Mansell ahead…"

Immediately *behind* Alboreto was Ayrton Senna.

He had a troubled couple of days with the Lotus-Honda, among the twitchiest of cars through the quick right behind the paddock. The engine of the qualifying car cut out on the opening lap of the first timed session, which put him into the race chassis, and the following morning he damaged the undertray on one of the high kerbs in which Jerez abounds. But in the afternoon he pounded round and round, whittling at his times and eventually qualifying fifth.

Teo Fabi vaulted into the reckoning on Saturday afternoon, qualifying sixth despite encountering traffic, he said, on every single quick lap. There was a

1: The three-litre Coloni gets a start, but Larini was to have just eight laps before the engine failed.

2: The first lap and already Mansell is clearing out on his team-mate and the Williams men are clearing out from the pack queued behind an obstinate Senna.

3: Woes continued for Brabham. De Cesaris ended his race on lap 26 with a gearbox breakage. Patrese finished, but in 13th.

4: The queue starts here. Senna's Lotus-Honda was like lightning in a straight line but hopeless when the road turned on this twisty circuit.

3.

4.

2.

little more oversteer from the Benetton than he would have liked, but all in all the car pleased him —and there was little of which to complain in the horsepower department.

Thierry Boutsen, invariably the quicker of the Benetton men, was less happy by far. On Saturday he was delighted with the car, but in the afternoon was mystified suddenly to find it very difficult to drive. The set-up hadn't been touched between the sessions, yet Thierry was six-tenths away from his best in the morning.

After his victory in Portugal Alain Prost was also disappointed. "Here we seem to have the same problem as in Hungary," he said. "For the first hour of Friday morning — when the track got better — we start to lose grip at the back . . ."

Was that why the world champion spun in the afternoon?

"No, I spun because the engine cut — our electrical problems again. I started to run wide, out onto the marbles, and decided to spin the car, rather than try to take the corner and maybe go off. You know what? For the whole race at Estoril I never had an engine problem at all — and we have no idea why! But here it seems to be back.

But the Friday night storm took care of that. Alain was down in seventh, and not too hopeful: "Here you are in trouble if you don't start from the first two rows."

Prost predicted correctly. A resolute Mansell put a

133

pass on team-mate Piquet on the opening lap, and simply drove away into the sunset. Behind him was the race. Into the first turn, Senna was ahead of all but the Williams pair, and swiftly a queue formed behind him. "Like a bottle," Alain Prost said, "with Senna as the cork . . ."

The cork stayed in place for an hour and a half. When finally it popped, only nine laps remained, and Mansell was far out of reach. Prost, Piquet, Boutsen, Alboreto, Berger . . . all reckoned they could have run with Nigel, had it not been for Senna and his yellow chicane.

You couldn't blame Ayrton. The active Lotus-Honda had behaved badly throughout the qualifying days: the only high cards in his hand were horsepower and his own talent. It was decided to run the car with as little wing as possible, go with straightline speed and maybe a single set of tyres.

Senna stuck to his work, intimidated by no one. And the ploy almost came off. In the end, though, all Ayrton did was to hand Mansell an easy time. Nigel had a few problems with third gear and cramp, but otherwise sailed plain, wondering where the rest had gone.

Prost, in the meantime, was putting his grey cells to work. Useless to sit at the back of this line, he reasoned. "The biggest problem with this year's car — apart from the misfiring, of course! — is that it doesn't work very well when you are close up behind another car. You lose downforce, you get bad understeer, you hurt the front tyres. So I decided to stop early for tyres, to try to overtake everyone with a good pit stop, like I did with Piquet in Estoril."

It was a good plan, and, as Alain pointed out, he had little to lose by it. When he resumed on his new set, he found the McLaren working perfectly. Soon he was setting fastest laps, and quickly he reeled in the crocodile group again — none of whose members had yet changed Goodyears.

Still, it was frustrating, for everyone's lap times were restricted by the necessarily obstinate Senna. Running alone, Prost's car may have been the fastest in the race, but it was penned in with the rest. Indeed, Alain felt that he might have worried Mansell, had he been able to get by the Lotus.

As it was, though, Nigel's position was increasingly serene. Considerably more audacious than Piquet in the traffic, he pulled out a further 10 secs in four laps when they started lapping the rabbits. And now the scheduled tyre stops were beginning.

Prost had been in on lap 27, and then came Boutsen (33), Johansson (35) and Mansell (42). By the time of Nigel's stop, his lead was such that he didn't lose it in the pits. Piquet came in on lap 45: up went the Williams on the jacks — and Nelson forgot to put his foot on the middle pedal. "Brakes!" they screamed at him several times, and eventually he responded, allowing the wheel change to be properly carried out. But the Williams was stationary for 20 secs, so that Piquet now found himself in fourth place, in the line behind Senna . . .

Ferrari, for their part, blew it by stopping too late. Berger on lap 47, Alboreto on 52. Both fought through again, but now the primary pressure group behind the Lotus was made up of Prost and Piquet. On lap 47 Nelson put the hammer down, closed on the McLaren down the pit straight, tried to pass it into the first turn — and spun. That dropped him to sixth.

In 1986 Senna won the Spanish Grand Prix by fourteen-hundredths of a second, and he was the only leading driver to run the race without a stop. At mid-race Peter Warr considered a tyre stop, then discounted it. "I knew," Ayrton said, "that if I came in the best I could hope for was maybe fourth or fifth. I only had a real problem in the slow corners — in the quick ones I was OK, and there was no problem on the straights. So I decided to stay out, fight, and hope that the tyres would last."

But now Prost was pushing him very hard. "I was glad to see Nelson disappear for a while," he grinned, "but it was his own fault, I didn't block him, and I never weaved. I simply stayed out on my line."

He nevertheless stayed stuck behind Senna and soon he had the pressure to face from Boutsen, really storming in the Benetton. The Belgian went past the world champion on lap 55, and next time round the resurgent Piquet was also ahead of the McLaren. Berger, too, was coming back into the

picture, following his tyre stop, but was shortly to quit with engine failure. Alboreto's would also blow, spectacularly, only four laps from the flag.

Boutsen briefly harrassed Senna, feinted left and right in the hope that Ayrton would make a mistake, run wide somewhere, let him through. But then the Benetton's brakes began to go away.

"I really thought I was going to pass Senna,"

Below: Hello, Alain. Where have you been today? Mansell didn't catch a glimpse of his opponents again after the flag dropped.

oil dropped by Berger's Ferrari. Nelson said he simply lost it. Whatever, the Williams was off the road for some considerable distance, and now Prost was into second place. At the end of lap 68 Piquet was into the pits briefly to have grass and debris removed from the radiators. His team seemed to think he would have done better to stay out: it dropped him to fourth, behind Johansson.

Stefan's had been a relatively uneventful race: "I lost a load of time in the early stages, stuck behind de Cesaris and Cheever. Then I caught up, made my tyre stop — and had to deal with the traffic again. My

Thierry remarked later, "and I thought I would then be able to back off, save my brakes for the rest of the race. But it didn't work out that way: one time I just brushed the brake pedal and the car snapped sideways . . ."

And spun. The green and red car finished up in deep sand at the side of the track, and there it stayed. Fabi had retired earlier, engine temperature off the clock.

Four laps later Piquet finally forced his way past Senna. Ayrton's tyres were completely shot, and there was a no-holds-barred battle for second place.

At the very next turn Piquet went off, perhaps on

car was like Alain's, good on its own, understeering like crazy behind someone else. But overall it wasn't a bad race for me."

Not bad, either, for Mansell. "Everything worked very well, really, except that it was difficult to change down to third. That was the only mechanical problem of any kind. Otherwise, I had a new seat in the car today, which moved around too much. I think I may have trapped a nerve in my back or something, because my left leg was hurting for the last part of the race."

Physically, Jerez is a demanding track, with no straight worth the name, no opportunity to relax even momentarily. Nigel looked a tired man afterwards, more so by far than Prost or Johansson.

"That was fun, really," Alain said of The Scrap, "but I wouldn't want it every Sunday . . . You know these kind of races, where no one can overtake: I suppose they're exciting for the spectators, but for a driver they're very frustrating because you are lapping maybe two secs slower than you could. A lot of people were weaving and blocking today — well, you know, anyone can do that, but it's not really racing, *hein?* But I can understand Ayrton . . . you know, when you are racing for the championship."

Piquet admitted afterwards that this had not been one of his better races: "I think I made more mistakes today than in the rest of the season. But at least now I have a low score to drop."

He had a better afternoon than most. Rene Arnoux had a blitz of a race, clouting Derek Warwick at the first corner, punting Jonathan Palmer out towards the end of the race, and incurring the wrath of pretty well everyone in between times. "He's just a total bloody idiot," Derek said afterwards. "Always was, always will be."

It was especially unfortunate for Jonathan, who had led the normally-aspirated class — just — from Philippe Alliot's Lola right from the start. He had been trying to *lap* Arnoux's Ligier at the time: "He just drove into the side of me, and that was that."

Martin Brundle finished 11th with the Zakspeed, a full lap behind Alliot's Cosworth car. "Actually, I feel very pleased with myself today," he said, "I can honestly say that I drove flat out the whole way. The steering on that thing's unbelievably heavy, and I'm absolutely spent. But I finished nowhere, so who's going to notice?"

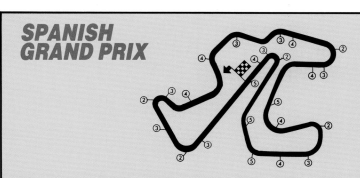

SPANISH GRAND PRIX

Round 13: September 27, 1987
Circuit: Jerez

Race data:	72 laps of 2.621 mile (4.22 km) circuit
Weather:	Hot, dry
Fastest lap:	Berger, Ferrari F187, 1:26.986, 108.489mph
Existing record:	Mansell, Williams FW11, 1:27.176, 108.252mph

ENTRIES

No	Driver (Nat)	Car/Chassis	Engine
1	Alain Prost (F)	McLaren MP4/3-4	TAG V6 Turbo
1T	Alain Prost (F)	McLaren MP4/3-1	TAG V6 Turbo
2	Stefan Johansson (S)	McLaren MP4/3-5	TAG V6 Turbo
3	Jonathan Palmer (GB)	Tyrrell DG/016-6	Ford Cosworth V8
4	Philippe Streiff (F)	Tyrrell DG/016-3	Ford Cosworth V8
5	Nigel Mansell (GB)	Williams FW11B/8	Honda V6 Turbo
5T	Nigel Mansell (GB)	Williams FW11B/3	Honda V6 Turbo
6	Nelson Piquet (BR)	Williams FW11B/5**	Honda V6 Turbo
6T	Nelson Piquet (BR)	Williams FW11B/3	Honda V6 Turbo
7	Riccardo Patrese (I)	Brabham BT56/4	BMW S4 Turbo
8	Andrea de Cesaris (I)	Brabham BT56/3	BMW S4 Turbo
9	Martin Brundle (GB)	Zakspeed 871/03	Zakspeed S4 Turbo
10	Christian Danner (D)	Zakspeed 871/02	Zakspeed S4 Turbo
11	Satoru Nakajima (J)	Lotus 99T/3	Honda V6 Turbo
12	Ayrton Senna (BR)	Lotus 99T/4	Honda V6 Turbo
14	Pascal Fabre (F)	AGS JH22/02-032	Ford Cosworth V8
16	Ivan Capelli (I)	March 871/2	Ford Cosworth V8
17	Derek Warwick (GB)	Arrows A10/4	Megatron S4 Turbo
18	Eddie Cheever (USA)	Arrows A10/2	Megatron S4 Turbo
19	Teo Fabi (I)	Benetton B187-08	Ford V6 Turbo
20	Thierry Boutsen (B)	Benetton B187-06	Ford V6 Turbo
21	Alex Caffi (I)	Osella FA1H/1	Alfa Romeo V8 Turbo
22	Franco Forini (CH)	Osella FA1H/3	Alfa Romeo V8 Turbo
23	Adrian Campos (E)	Minardi M186/1	Moderni V6 Turbo
24	Alessandro Nannini (I)	Minardi M186/3	Moderni V6 Turbo
25	Rene Arnoux (F)	Ligier JS29C/06	Megatron S4 Turbo
26	Piercarlo Ghinzani (I)	Ligier JS29C/04	Megatron S4 Turbo
27	Michele Alboreto (I)	Ferrari F187/100	Ferrari V6 Turbo
27T	Michele Alboreto (I)	Ferrari F187/097*	Ferrari V6 Turbo
28	Gerhard Berger (A)	Ferrari F187/098	Ferrari V6 Turbo
28T	Gerhard Berger (A)	Ferrari F187/095	Ferrari V6 Turbo
30	Philippe Alliot (F)	Lola LC87/02	Ford Cosworth V8
32	Nicola Larini (I)	Coloni FC187/01	Ford Cosworth V8

* Race car   ** Active suspension

QUALIFYING

FRIDAY: Overcast, dry		SATURDAY: Overcast, dry	
Driver		Driver	
Mansell	1:23.081	Piquet	1:22.461
Berger	1:23.164	Mansell	1:23.281
Piquet	1:23.621	Senna	1:24.320
Alboreto	1:24.192	Fabi	1:24.513
Prost	1:24.596	Alboreto	1:24.832
Senna	1:25.162	Prost	1:24.905
Fabi	1:25.263	Berger	1:25.250
Johansson	1:26.147	Boutsen	1:25.295
Boutsen	1:26.372	Patrese	1:25.335
Patrese	1:26.639	De Cesaris	1:25.811
Warwick	1:26.728	Johansson	1:26.147
Cheever	1:27.062	Warwick	1:26.882
Arnoux	1:28.241	Cheever	1:27.970
Palmer	1:28.353	Streiff	1:28.330
Capelli	1:28.477	Alliot	1:28.361
Nakajima	1:28.776	Arnoux	1:28.362
Nannini	1:28.823	Nakajima	1:28.367
Brundle	1:28.876	Palmer	1:28.426
Streiff	1:28.970	Brundle	1:28.597
Alliot	1:29.147	Nannini	1:28.602
Campos	1:29.538	Danner	1:28.667
Ghinzani	1:29.663	Capelli	1:28.694
Danner	1:30.325	Ghinzani	1:29.066
Caffi	1:31.284	Campos	1:30.204
Larini	1:31.319	Fabre	1:30.694
De Cesaris	1:31.981	Larini	1:30.982
Fabre	1:32.490	Caffi	1:31.069
Forini	1:34.723	Forini	1:35.572

STARTING GRID

No	Driver	Time
6	Piquet	1:22.461
5	Mansell	1:23.081
28	Berger	1:23.164
27	Alboreto	1:24.192
12	Senna	1:24.320
19	Fabi	1:24.523
1	Prost	1:24.596
20	Boutsen	1:25.295
7	Patrese	1:25.335
8	De Cesaris	1:25.811
2	Johansson	1:26.147
17	Warwick	1:26.728
18	Cheever	1:27.062
25	Arnoux	1:28.241
4	Streiff	1:28.330
3	Palmer	1:28.353
30	Alliot	1:28.361
11	Nakajima	1:28.367
16	Capelli	1:28.477
9	Brundle	1:28.597
24	Nannini	1:28.602
10	Danner	1:28.667
26	Ghinzani	1:29.066
23	Campos	1:29.538
14	Fabre	1:30.694
32	Larini	1:30.982

RESULTS

Pos	No	Driver	Car	Laps	Time/Retirement
1	5	Mansell	Williams-Honda	72	1-49:12.692
2	1	Prost	McLaren-TAG	72	1-49:34.917
3	2	Johansson	McLaren-TAG	72	1-49:43.510
4	6	Piquet	Williams-Honda	72	1-49:44.142
5	12	Senna	Lotus-Honda	72	1-50:26.199
6	30	Alliot	Lola-Cosworth	71	
7	4	Streiff	Tyrrell-Cosworth	71	
8	18	Cheever	Arrows-Megatron	70	Out of fuel
9	11	Nakajima	Lotus-Honda	70	
10	17	Warwick	Arrows-Megatron	70	
11	9	Brundle	Zakspeed	70	
12	16	Capelli	March-Cosworth	70	
13	7	Patrese	Brabham-BMW	68	
14	23	Campos	Minardi-Moderni	68	
R	27	Alboreto	Ferrari	67	Engine
R	20	Boutsen	Benetton-Ford	66	Spun off
R	28	Berger	Ferrari	62	Engine
R	3	Palmer	Tyrrell-Cosworth	55	Accident
R	25	Arnoux	Ligier-Megatron	55	Engine
NC	10	Danner	Zakspeed	50	
R	24	Nannini	Minardi-Moderni	45	Turbo
R	19	Fabi	Benetton-Ford	40	Engine
R	8	De Cesaris	Brabham-BMW	26	Gearbox
R	26	Ghinzani	Ligier-Megatron	24	Ignition
R	14	Fabre	AGS-Cosworth	10	Engine
R	32	Larini	Coloni-Cosworth	8	Engine

FASTEST LAP

Driver	
Berger	1:26.986
Piquet	1:27.108
Patrese	1:27.150
Prost	1:27.459
Alboreto	1:27.738
Johansson	1:28.133
Boutsen	1:28.299
Mansell	1:28.444
Fabi	1:29.319
Cheever	1:29.934
Senna	1:30.008
Alliot	1:30.365
Capelli	1:30.407
Palmer	1:30.514
De Cesaris	1:30.670
Nannini	1:30.722
Warwick	1:31.105
Nakajima	1:31.228
Streiff	1:31.279
Brundle	1:31.373
Danner	1:32.074
Ghinzani	1:32.604
Arnoux	1:32.650
Larini	1:33.108
Campos	1:33.503
Fabre	1:35.672

CHAMPIONSHIP POSITIONS

DRIVERS			CONSTRUCTORS	
1	Piquet	70	1 Williams-Honda	122
2	Mansell	52	2 McLaren-TAG	72
3	Senna	51	3 Lotus-Honda	56
4	Prost	46	4 Ferrari	26
5	Johansson	26	5 Benetton-Ford	20
6	Berger	18	6 Arrows-Megatron	8
7	Boutsen	10	Tyrrell-Cosworth	8
	Fabi	10	8 Brabham-BMW	6
9	Alboreto	8	9 Lola-Cosworth	2
10	Nakajima	6	Zakspeed	2
11	Cheever	5	11 Ligier-Megatron	1
12	De Cesaris	4	March-Cosworth	1
	Palmer	4		
	Streiff	4		
15	Warwick	3		
16	Alliot	2		
	Brundle	2		
	Patrese	2		
19	Arnoux	1		
	Capelli	1		

JIM CLARK CUP			COLIN CHAPMAN CUP	
1	Palmer	71	1 Tyrrell-Cosworth	135
2	Streiff	64	2 March-Cosworth	38
3	Capelli	38	3 AGS-Cosworth	35
4	Fabre	35	4 Lola-Cosworth	34
5	Alliot	34		

Mexico
ROUND 14: October 18, 1987

TWICE AS MANY

The rivalry between the two team-mates festered anew, spilt into the public arena. You did, accused one. I didn't, refuted the other.

The sixth win meant six to three and Nigel Mansell was still in the world championship. He had survived a chaotic weekend on this loudly condemned, bumpy track, and had been central to the chaos with two big accidents during the qualifying days.

He had never been optimistic, the grip of the Williams-Honda on such a circuit no match for the stability of Ferrari or Benetton. But still he took pole. The race confirmed his views: Thierry Boutsen and Gerhard Berger disappeared into the heat haze, had a race of their own. Neither lasted long and it was Nigel who was clear of the rest, having only to keep clear of team-mate, Nelson Piquet, to keep the world championship dangling still, just out of reach of the Brazilian.

No problems there. While Piquet was into a stormer of a drive, he was no threat in fourth. This was the response to being last on the first lap following a coming together with Alain Prost. Piquet spun, stalled and got a controversial push-start. Prost exited from the world championship, steering askew in the McLaren.

The chaos at Mexico continued with the race becoming a two-parter, the organisers overreacting to Derek Warwick's big crash. So Mansell had to do it over and contend with a team-mate still pumped up from the first part.

A thrust at the lead in the second part was met with a snarl from Piquet, so badly wanting to wrap up the title at this race. Mansell therefore wisely settled for a safe second. He had no need to fret, his advantage from the first part of was more than enough to bring overall victory.

Above: Take that ya . . .! Piquet douses sparring partner Mansell. Although they shared wins in the two-part race, Mansell took his sixth win on aggregate.
Left: What have I got to do to wrap up the championship? Piquet had planned to end the issue in Mexico, a favourite venue for him.
Previous page: Thierry Boutsen leads a grand prix for the first time. A win was on the cards, he felt. Then the car began to misfire.

Nelson Piquet was all smiles before the start of the qualifying, in confident frame of mind. The key to his third world championship was already in the lock, and victory here would turn it. Also, he liked Mexico, which gave him a psychological advantage. And he even had nice things to say about the circuit. One of his favourites he said.

Almost all the drivers agreed that this is a very satisfying Formula One circuit. At the end of the preceding straight the drivers snick down to fifth, then — according to skill, bravery, and the efficiency of their cars — they are back on the power throughout this turn, which goes on and on, finally leading into the pit straight. Just beyond is the start/finish line, which the quick fellows were crossing at close to 190 mph. And before braking for the next turn, the fast men are nudging 210.

If the drivers relished the layout of the track, they vociferously hated its condition. On Friday it was in a decidedly dirty state, and everyone spoke of the lack of grip. Parts of it were actually vacuumed before the first qualifying session, and one wondered why it hadn't been done on Thursday.

More important by far, though, was the actual track surface. When Formula One returned to Mexico in 1986 after an absence of 16 years, there were complaints aplenty about the bumps. A deal of resurfacing work was requested. There was no sign that this had been done. Some of the bumps, though, had apparently been shaved, and it was hoped that the problems would be alleviated.

Not so. "I actually think it's worse than last year," commented Derek Warwick. Alain Prost felt the same way: "A complete joke — but what can you do?" "They've done absolutely nothing," added Nigel Mansell. "It makes Detroit look like Silverstone," offered Jonathan Palmer.

Jean-Marie Balestre — treated like a Head of State in Mexico — reacted vigorously: this was a great circuit, he said, and the only problem was the dust. The organisers had spent millions of dollars on improving the track, and all the requested work had been done. Indeed, the drivers ought to thank the Mexicans, who were losing money by staging a grand prix.

"So the bumps are no problem, huh?" responded Eddie Cheever. "Well, he'd know, wouldn't he? What did he use to inspect it — a Cadillac?"

The bumps — particularly through the banked turn 16 — were indeed vicious. Cheever caught one wrong on Friday afternoon, got briefly airborne: "I couldn't see the road any more — I was just looking for some place to land . . ."

Gerhard Berger, who won in 1986, was fastest on the first day, but admitted that his quick lap had not been altogether pleasurable. "Even on the straights the bumps are so bad that you're jumping up and down, getting wheelspin in sixth gear, which is very hard on the car. But through that last corner, when you hit the bumps, you lose downforce. All you can do is take a big risk, close your eyes and go flat out over them. If you're lucky, you don't spin out — and if you're not, you have what Nigel had . . ."

What Nigel had was a mighty fortunate escape. Commitment as awesome as ever, he had gone into the turn faster than before, trying to separate Berger from the pole. And he almost made it through. But at the end of the corner the Williams hit a bump, flicked sideways, and began to run wide. At the exit it hit the kerbing, and swapped ends, proceeding down the road backwards at around 170 mph, and clipping the end of the pit barrier before coming to a stop. Mansell had bruises, nothing more.

The car, too, survived without serious damage, but Nigel was not too optimistic about his chances for the race — one he had to win to keep alive any championship hopes. "To be honest, I just don't think we're truly competitive here — not with Ferrari or Benetton or McLaren. The car's hopeless in the slow corners, and not that brilliant in the fast ones. We're just very short of grip."

For all that, he was third fastest on the opening day. And everyone was complaining of little or no grip. Ayrton Senna's 1986 pole position — a little over 1m16s — never looked like being approached. Which rather vindicated the drivers' opinions of the condition of the circuit.

On the second day Mansell took pole position

—and had another shunt, this time at the fast left preceding the banking. "Something broke in the right front suspension — the tie-rod, I think. I turned in, everything OK, and then the right front dropped. I just went straight off, into the kerb, then the wall. It's flat in fifth there . . ."

Both right-hand corners were rooted, of course, and it looked like the T-car for Nigel on race day. "And to cap it all," he said, "I've burned my bloody fingers. The car was in a dangerous place, so I was trying to get it off the circuit. Put my hand on the wheel, and we're not running brake cooling here . . ."

Still, there was the satisfaction of pole position —and Mansell's 15th consecutive front row start, a record.

All the FW11Bs in Mexico, to Piquet's chagrin, were standard cars, the team having decided to put aside the active ones for the balance of the season. Nelson was fourth on the opening day, third on Saturday.

Times in the final session were incredibly even and close, the two Williams separated by only eight-hundredths — with Berger's Ferrari between them. In the closing minutes Piquet made a final effort to take the pole, but a swift spin took him off the road and over a high kerb, so that was that. Everything, said Nelson, pointed to an unusually close race. And he really did want to clinch the title here.

Over the finish line Piquet was fastest at 188.991 mph. Mansell (fifth) at 183.695. At the trap before the first corner Nelson (second to Senna) went through at 209.046, Nigel (13th!) at 200.262. In the circumstances the Englishman's pole position was quite an achievement . . .

As was Berger's second spot, for the Ferrari failed even to reach 200. Gerhard was fabulous throughout the qualifying, really getting his teeth into this circuit in a supremely well-balanced and stable car.

For his team-mate, Saturday brought good and bad news. In the morning Michele Alboreto learned that his wife had given birth to their first child; in the afternoon his grid position slipped from sixth to 10th. "I blew up another engine," he explained. "One in each session today. Then I took the spare, got traffic, everything. I'm really upset, because the car is good, you know, but I think I've fixed the race set-up. We're going to try to run the whole distance on one set only . . ."

Tyres were a major consideration. In 1986, Berger ran non-stop to victory on Pirellis, while the Goodyear runners needed at least one change. This track is hard on rubber, and so for once Goodyear changed their previously rigid 1987 game plan — every car was allotted 15 sets, rather than the usual 10, these made up of 10 sets of soft Cs (as used in Estoril and Jerez) and five of harder Bs (Monza/Zeltweg compound). For the first time, therefore, tyre choice came into the equation.

Williams spoke of trying to get through with only a single change, Ferrari not even that. "We'll make a final decision," Michele said, "after running full tanks in the race day warm-up."

As expected, the Benetton-Fords — especially Thierry Boutsen's — were right in with a shout. Through the slower turns, indeed, the Belgian looked faster than anyone, his car beautifully balanced, needing less road than most, putting its power down well. Thierry had thoughts of the pole on Saturday, but traffic problems on his first set of tyres hampered his efforts, and on the second set he found a considerable increase in understeer. Teo Fabi, sixth, was only three-tenths slower.

In the Benetton sandwich was Prost, and it was the usual McLaren-TAG story: handling and top speed good, acceleration less so. Alain was a model of smooth throttle control through the long banked turn, but he and Stefan Johansson had their worries for Sunday: during the qualifying days, they lost no fewer than five engines.

Nor was it a 'chip' problem, the world champion sighed: each engine had failed for a different reason. The luckless Stefan had two go on Saturday, one in each session. In the T-car he failed to improve in the final hour, dropping from ninth to 15th.

Senna, the pole man of 1986, reported the 'active' Lotus-Honda was good over the bumps, but terribly low on grip. As in Portugal and Spain, the car's straightline speed was prodigious, but still the Brazilian's best efforts could get the yellow car no higher than seventh on Friday. And Saturday afternoon was something else.

There were signs that Ayrton was trying to find that elusive second within himself. He had done it before, and it had worked, but not this time. In the dying moments of the final session, only two or three mins after a spin, the Lotus hit a bump at . . . the last turn. The car came down hard. "Then the wheels came off the ground," Senna later said, "and the car slid sideways." It hit the tyre wall very hard. Practice was immediately stopped.

It was some time before Senna stumbled from the car, and when he did he immediately slumped against the tyres, obviously in some pain and disorientation. At the track hospital he was checked over, and there was nothing seriously awry. But the impact had given his neck a jolt.

As usual, both Brabhams were fleet in qualifying, Riccardo Patrese and Andrea de Cesaris both making the top 10. And, as usual Derek Warwick and Eddie Cheever were right behind, the Arrows looking especially wayward over the bumps.

The makings were there of an unusually dangerous race. "I'll bet there are at least a couple of suspension failures," one driver forecast gloomily. "Full tanks, and those bumps . . ." Another perilous factor was the speed differential between the top turbos and the Cosworths extenuated by the high altitude, which robbed the normally-aspirated cars of nearly one quarter of their power.

Sunday was like the days before: perfect. Sky cloudless, sun hot, humidity negligible. So here was something to enjoy about Mexico.

Mansell badly needed the half-hour warm-up session, for he was driving effectively a brand new FW11B, built up by the mechanics overnight to replace the one damaged in the last qualifying session. There seemed little wrong with it, for he was quickest — until Boutsen and Berger leapfrogged him at the end. Perhaps his fears about Benetton and Ferrari were justified.

After the warm-up came tyre decisions, and everyone was aiming for a non-stop run — on the softer Cs, surprisingly enough. Apart from Piquet, that is, who opted for Bs.

Nelson's decision had quite an effect on the opening lap. Berger and Boutsen took off at the front, followed by Piquet, Prost and Mansell who had got away with too much wheelspin. And halfway round that opening lap there was the scarcely believable sight of the world champion being involved in a shunt.

Into a tight right-hander the McLaren dived for the inside of Piquet's Williams. The two cars touched, putting Prost out on the spot, with damaged steering. Piquet, undamaged, was in the middle of the road,

stalled. After frantic signals from the Brazilian, track workers applied muscle and got him on his way again, a solid last.

Push starts are not allowed, of course, unless the car is adjudged to be in a 'dangerous place.' As in Portugal, where the race was stopped after his first corner accident with Alboreto, luck was riding with Piquet again.

"Prost tried to pass me at a place where there was only room for one car," was Nelson's version.

"Piquet was on hard tyres," Alain commented, "and was so unbelievably early on the brakes that I had to go to one side or the other to avoid running into him. I wasn't trying to pass! Then I got on the dirt and locked up. He chopped across, and that was that. Just one of those things."

After that drama Berger and Boutsen were beginning to go away in a private race. Mansell followed in third place, and then came Alboreto, Fabi and Senna.

There was more trouble before lap two was very old. Going into the first turn, Satoru Nakajima appeared to forget about braking and cannoned into the back of Warwick. Johansson spun his McLaren while trying to slot through, but came to

Philippe Streiff could be excused for riding the kerbs on his way to eighth behind Tyrrell team-mate Palmer. The drivers chorused their complaints about the bumps on the track surface.

rest without hurt — until Christian Danner arrived. The two cars were both written off, and a furious Stefan stalked back to the pits.

Warwick came in for new undertray and rear wing, the Arrows mechanics also giving the car a quick check over. Derek then rejoined, a move he was later to regret . . .

In the course of lap two Boutsen got by Berger, and for the first time Thierry was leading a grand prix. Doing it confidently, too, and opening out a cushion to the Ferrari for a while. "If felt good," he said. "At that stage the car was perfect, and I had no problem at all in holding him off . . ."

Rarely do race drivers think alike. "I let him through," was Gerhard's version. "We had a long race ahead, and I felt I could handle him. He certainly had better engine response than I did, but there were two places where I was quicker."

After only four laps the two of them were more than 11 secs clear of Mansell, who was himself well ahead of Senna, now up to fourth. But the man really on the move was de Cesaris, who was moving onto Ayrton's tail after dispensing with both Patrese and Fabi.

By lap 12 Berger was closer to Boutsen once more: the Benetton was starting to misfire. "At first it wasn't too serious," said Thierry, "but then it cut out completely, and Gerhard passed me."

This was lap 15, and at the end of the 16th the Benetton was into the pits for good. Later, after the mechanics had changed the engine management control box, it fired up and ran sweetly. But that was of no use to Boutsen, who spent the balance of the afternoon commentating for TV.

Berger now looked set to repeat his win of 1986 but the Ferrari lasted little longer than the Benetton; at the end of lap 21 it was smokily into the pits with

turbo failure. Team-mate Alboreto was already out with a blown engine.

A lap later de Cesaris, too, was gone, and a fine drive was over. For a long time he had really threatened Senna, but now the Brabham was off on the grass. A familiar sight, this, but Andrea was angry afterwards: "Senna missed a gear, and when I got alongside him he just drove me off the road."

So now Mansell was into the lead, and for once it

was inherited. With a 32 secs advantage over Senna, he was comfortably fixed, but that man Piquet was moving into a serious points position. After his first lap delay, Nelson had stormed through the field, and, further aided by the lamentable attrition rate, was now up to fourth, ahead of Cheever and Fabi.

Teo caused a brief flurry of speculation about tyres by stopping, as early as lap 15. Did this mean the Goodyear Cs were not man enough for the job after all? Had Nelson, uniquely on Bs, made the right decision? But it was a Fabi problem, not a Goodyear one. He had blistered his tyres, and would do the same with his second set.

For quite a while it got a little tedious. Complacency, though, is out of place in Formula One: at the end of the long banked turn before the pits Warwick's Arrows was running wide . . .

The car never looked remotely like making this corner — indeed seemed as if on ice. It hit the tyre wall with colossal force, at something more than 170 mph and came to rest with left hand wheels gone.

Derek's head was upright in the cockpit, but it was some time before he gathered his senses and began to move. Then he took off the steering wheel, and began levering himself out. "I'm quite certain that something broke, as a result of the bash I got from Nakajima on the second lap," he said. "During that last third of the corner it just went away and away, and I couldn't do a thing about it."

To roars of approval from the stands, Warwick ran across the road to the pits. And a crane set to work on removing the wrecked Arrows from the trackside. It had already been winched into the air when, to general astonishment, the red flag was suddenly waved, followed by a black one. The race was being stopped.

Slowly they made their way back to the start/finish area, forming up on the grid in race order. So what we had now was a two-part race, the first since Jonathan Palmer's shunt stopped the 1984 British GP at Brands Hatch. In these circumstances tyre changes are not normally permitted, but in light of the track surface problems in Mexico, the rule was waived. This time Fabi, like Piquet, chose Bs, the rest Cs.

Fifteen cars took part in the second heat, but Arnoux's Ligier failed to survive the formation lap . . .

At the green Piquet got away superbly from his fourth slot, and down to the first turn the two Williams-Hondas were absolutely side by side, Mansell in the inside line. It looked as if Nigel must claim the corner, but at the last second Nelson darted across into the lead. If he were to win this race, the Brazilian had to make nine secs on Patrese, 15 on Senna, 45 on Mansell. This last was obviously out of the question, but second place was a realistic hope, and quite obviously Piquet had every intention of going for it.

The total race distance had been reduced from 68 to 63 laps, following the stoppage, which meant that Nelson had 33 more with which to work. And Nigel was not going to make it easy for him. As the two Williams-Hondas circulated in close order, it was obvious he was looking to go by.

On one occasion Mansell seemed to have done enough, but into the first turn Piquet closed the door.

After that, Nigel relaxed a bit, let Nelson go. With a time advantage such as his, there was little point in risking everything. But he wasn't amused. "No, I can't say I enjoyed the second part of the race much," he said. "My team-mate tried to push me off the road twice, which I don't think was very professional."

"*Bullshit!*" responded Piquet angrily. "I'm very professional — if I want to take someone off, I do without any problems. I didn't try to take anyone off . . ."

On time, Nelson moved ahead of Patrese into third place on lap 33, and five laps later moved by Senna for second. With Mansell still 40 secs ahead overall he might have left it there, sat back, settled for six points, instead he continued to charge.

Elsewhere Cheever and Patrese, whose relationship is about as warm as that shared by the Williams drivers, circulated together — Eddie ahead — right to the flag. But Riccardo knew he had only to keep the Arrows in sight, having finished well ahead in the first 'heat'.

Top: The bumpy circuit brought Ferrari and Benetton alive, and also the Brabhams. Riccardo Patrese ended the day third overall. It had been a long time between visiting the rostrum.

Above: Cheever disposes of Brundle. The American's fourth in the Arrows was his best performance since Belgium.

Right: Berger is readied to shine out. He surrendered his early lead to Boutsen — by choice, he said. Turbo failure soon after put paid to plans of grabbing it back.

"It was kind of a strange race for me," Cheever said of his 100th grand prix. "In the first part I was so down on boost that the car was using hardly any fuel! So it was like driving on full tanks all the time. But later the engine started working well. I enjoyed the second half."

Senna didn't. He had lost his clutch, and while trying to change down without it, locked his brakes and spun. With no clutch to disengage, there was no way to avoid stalling, and he beseeched marshals to come and give him a shove. This they failed to do to his satisfaction, and, after stepping from the hobbled Lotus, he slugged one of them. Or was it two? Well, whatever, it cost him a $15,000 fine from the stewards.

So this race, so full of promise and potential a couple of hours earlier, ground to its conclusion, with Mansell taking a well-deserved sixth victory of the season — exactly twice as many as the man who preceded him in the world championship.

"I'm pleased to have won," said Nigel, "but someone else seems to be having an awful lot of luck. I remember the days when you got disqualified for a push start, so long as you weren't in the way, but there you are . . ."

The gap between them, with two races left, was now just 12 points.

MEXICAN GRAND PRIX

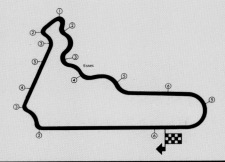

Round 14: October 18, 1987
Circuit: Autodromo Hermanos Rodriguez

Race data: 63 laps of 2.747 mile (4.42 km) circuit
Weather: Very hot, dry
Fastest lap: Piquet, Williams FW11B, 1:19.132, 124.980mph
Existing record: Piquet, Williams FW11, 1:19.360, 124.596mph

ENTRIES

No	Driver (Nat)	Car/Chassis	Engine
1	Alain Prost (F)	McLaren MP4/3-4	TAG V6 Turbo
1T	Alain Prost (F)	McLaren MP4/3-3	TAG V6 Turbo
2	Stefan Johansson (S)	McLaren MP4/3-5	TAG V6 Turbo
3	Jonathan Palmer (GB)	Tyrrell DG/016-5	Ford Cosworth V8
4	Philippe Streiff (F)	Tyrrell DG/016-2	Ford Cosworth V8
4T	Philippe Streiff (F)	Tyrrell DG/016-7	Ford Cosworth V8
5	Nigel Mansell (GB)	Williams FW11B/1	Honda V6 Turbo
5T	Nigel Mansell (GB)	Williams FW11B/3	Honda V6 Turbo
6	Nelson Piquet (BR)	Williams FW11B/6	Honda V6 Turbo
6T	Nelson Piquet (BR)	Williams FW11B/4	Honda V6 Turbo
7	Riccardo Patrese (I)	Brabham BT56/4	BMW S4 Turbo
8	Andrea de Cesaris (I)	Brabham BT56/2	BMW S4 Turbo
8T	Andrea de Cesaris (I)	Brabham BT56/3	BMW S4 Turbo
9	Martin Brundle (GB)	Zakspeed 871/03	Zakspeed S4 Turbo
10	Christian Danner (D)	Zakspeed 871/02	Zakspeed S4 Turbo
11	Satoru Nakajima (J)	Lotus 99T/3	Honda V6 Turbo
12	Ayrton Senna (BR)	Lotus 99T/4	Honda V6 Turbo
12T	Ayrton Senna (BR)	Lotus 99T/6*	Honda V6 Turbo
14	Pascal Fabre (F)	AGS JH22/02-032	Ford Cosworth V8
16	Ivan Capelli (I)	March 871/1	Ford Cosworth V8
16T	Ivan Capelli (I)	March 871/2	Ford Cosworth V8
17	Derek Warwick (GB)	Arrows A10/4	Megatron S4 Turbo
18	Eddie Cheever (USA)	Arrows A10/2	Megatron S4 Turbo
18T	Eddie Cheever (USA)	Arrows A10/3	Megatron S4 Turbo
19	Teo Fabi (I)	Benetton B187-08	Ford V6 Turbo
20	Thierry Boutsen (B)	Benetton B187-09	Ford V6 Turbo
21	Alex Caffi (I)	Osella FA1H/1	Alfa Romeo V8 Turbo
23	Adrian Campos (E)	Minardi M186/3	Moderni V6 Turbo
24	Alessandro Nannini (I)	Minardi M186/4	Moderni V6 Turbo
25	Rene Arnoux (F)	Ligier JS29C/06	Megatron S4 Turbo
26	Piercarlo Ghinzani (I)	Ligier JS29C/04	Megatron S4 Turbo
27	Michele Alboreto (I)	Ferrari F187/101	Ferrari V6 Turbo
28	Gerhard Berger (A)	Ferrari F187/098	Ferrari V6 Turbo
28T	Gerhard Berger (A)	Ferrari F187/097*	Ferrari V6 Turbo
29	Yannick Dalmas (F)	Lola LC87/02	Ford Cosworth V8
30	Philippe Alliot (F)	Lola LC87/03	Ford Cosworth V8

* Race car

QUALIFYING

FRIDAY: Hot, dry Driver		SATURDAY: Hot, dry Driver	
Berger	1:19.992	Mansell	1:18.383
Prost	1:20.572	Berger	1:18.426
Mansell	1:20.696	Piquet	1:18.463
Piquet	1:20.701	Boutsen	1:18.691
Boutsen	1:20.766	Prost	1:18.742
Alboreto	1:21.290	Fabi	1:18.992
Senna	1:21.361	Senna	1:19.089
Patrese	1:21.720	Patrese	1:19.889
Johansson	1:22.185	Alboreto	1:19.967
Fabi	1:22.666	De Cesaris	1:20.141
De Cesaris	1:22.930	Warwick	1:21.664
Warwick	1:23.347	Cheever	1:21.705
Nakajima	1:23.750	Brundle	1:21.711
Danner	1:23.992	Nannini	1:22.035
Arnoux	1:24.299	Nakajima	1:22.214
Cheever	1:24.445	Johansson	1:22.382
Brundle	1:25.184	Danner	1:22.593
Nannini	1:26.055	Arnoux	1:23.053
Streiff	1:27.011	Campos	1:23.955
Ghinzani	1:27.059	Capelli	1:24.404
Capelli	1:27.161	Ghinzani	1:24.553
Alliot	1:27.184	Palmer	1:24.723
Palmer	1:27.306	Dalmas	1:24.745
Caffi	1:27.670	Alliot	1:25.096
Campos	1:27.798	Streiff	1:26.305
Dalmas	1:28.156	Fabre	1:28.655
Fabre	1:30.285	Caffi	1:30.010

STARTING GRID

No	Driver	Time
5	Mansell	1:18.383
28	Berger	1:18.426
6	Piquet	1:18.463
20	Boutsen	1:18.691
1	Prost	1:18.742
19	Fabi	1:18.992
12	Senna	1:19.089
7	Patrese	1:19.889
27	Alboreto	1:19.967
8	De Cesaris	1:20.141
17	Warwick	1:21.664
18	Cheever	1:21.705
9	Brundle	1:21.711
24	Nannini	1:22.035
2	Johansson	1:22.185
11	Nakajima	1:22.214
10	Danner	1:22.593
25	Arnoux	1:23.053
23	Campos	1:23.955
16	Capelli	1:24.404
26	Ghinzani	1:24.553
3	Palmer	1:24.723
29	Dalmas	1:24.745
30	Alliot	1:25.096
4	Streiff	1:26.305
21	Caffi	1:27.670

RESULTS

Pos	No	Driver	Car	Laps	Time/Retirement
1.	5	Mansell	Williams-Honda	63	1-26.24.207
2.	6	Piquet	Williams-Honda	63	1-26.50.383
3.	7	Patrese	Brabham-BMW	63	1-27.51.086
4.	18	Cheever	Arrows-Megatron	63	1-28.05.559
5.	19	Fabi	Benetton-Ford	61	
6.	30	Alliot	Lola-Cosworth	60	
7.	3	Palmer	Tyrrell-Cosworth	60	
8.	4	Streiff	Tyrrell-Cosworth	60	
9.	29	Dalmas	Lola-Cosworth	59	
R.	12	Senna	Lotus-Honda	54	Spun off
R.	16	Capelli	March-Cosworth	51	Engine
R.	21	Caffi	Osella-Alfa Romeo	50	Engine
R.	26	Ghinzani	Ligier-Megatron	43	Engine
R.	23	Campos	Minardi-Moderni	32	Engine
R.	25	Arnoux	Ligier-Megatron	29	Ignition
R.	17	Warwick	Arrows-Megatron	26	Accident
R.	8	De Cesaris	Brabham-BMW	22	Spun off
R.	28	Berger	Ferrari	20	Turbo
R.	20	Boutsen	Benetton-Ford	15	Electrics
R.	24	Nannini	Minardi-Moderni	13	Turbo
R.	27	Alboreto	Ferrari	12	Engine
R.	9	Brundle	Zakspeed	3	Turbo
R.	2	Johansson	McLaren-TAG	1	Accident
R.	11	Nakajima	Lotus-Honda	1	Accident
R.	10	Danner	Zakspeed	1	Accident
R.	1	Prost	McLaren-TAG	0	Accident

FASTEST LAP

Driver	
Piquet	1:19.132
Mansell	1:19.527
Senna	1:20.586
Fabi	1:20.829
Cheever	1:20.934
Patrese	1:21.057
Berger	1:21.520
Boutsen	1:22.170
De Cesaris	1:22.535
Warwick	1:23.124
Alboreto	1:23.273
Caffi	1:23.628
Ghinzani	1:23.659
Arnoux	1:23.887
Capelli	1:24.274
Alliot	1:24.320
Dalmas	1:24.405
Palmer	1:24.657
Nannini	1:24.668
Campos	1:25.734
Streiff	1:26.039
Brundle	1:28.816
Johansson	1:43.361
Nakajima	1:43.533
Danner	1:44.266
Prost	No time

CHAMPIONSHIP POSITIONS

	DRIVERS			CONSTRUCTORS	
1	Piquet	73	1	Williams-Honda	137
2	Mansell	61	2	McLaren-TAG	72
3	Senna	51	3	Lotus-Honda	56
4	Prost	46	4	Ferrari	26
5	Johansson	26	5	Benetton-Ford	22
6	Berger	18	6	Arrows-Megatron	11
7	Fabi	12	7	Brabham-BMW	8
8	Boutsen	10	8	Tyrrell-Cosworth	8
9	Alboreto	8	9	Lola-Cosworth	3
	Cheever	8	10	Zakspeed	2
11	Nakajima	6	11	Ligier-Megatron	1
	Patrese	6		March-Cosworth	1
13	De Cesaris	4			
	Palmer	4			
	Streiff	4			
16	Warwick	3			
	Alliot	3			
18	Brundle	2			
19	Arnoux	1			
	Capelli	1			

JIM CLARK CUP			COLIN CHAPMAN CUP		
1	Palmer	77	1	Tyrrell-Cosworth	145
2	Streiff	68	2	Lola-Cosworth	46
3	Alliot	43	3	March-Cosworth	38
4	Capelli	38	4	AGS-Cosworth	34
5	Fabre	35			
6	Dalmas	3			

OVER BEFORE IT STARTED

The title was decided before the protagonists raced, when the one who was chasing, tried too hard, too early. The pressure off, a new era was ushered in prematurely.

At about the same time as Gerhard Berger was a scarlet blur under the chequered flag in Japan, Nigel Mansell's aeroplane was landing at home on the Isle of Man with a grimace of pain from the Englishman. The championship was over, two races before it could have been, Mansell's dramatic accident on Friday had settled it in his team-mate's favour.

The pressure was off and Berger knowing it, admitting it, exploited Mansell's absence, Nelson Piquet's smugness, and began a new phase in Formula One, before he should have. From a convincing pole he resolutely and gleefully embarrassed the remaining Honda-powered cars on the track the Japanese car company owned. How ironic. And he ended the longest drought in the great team's history.

Ferrari hit back after two years of despair. And hit back hard. In the paddock afterwards the result was immensely popular, for no one there with any feeling for the sport liked to see Ferrari out of the game for so long. The second half of the season had been building to this. And in truth, few wept to see the Honda machine humbled for once.

In fact a Honda was never in it at the beginning, and Ayrton Senna's second place in the Lotus-Honda came through attrition. For the early laps it had been Alain Prost's McLaren TAG, performing the best it had all season, and Thierry Boutsen's Benetton-Ford, which offered opposition, if only temporarily.

Prost, knowing the championship was gone, wanted to win the last two races of the season. Lap two and a puncture saw to that. In a charge back up the field from last to seventh, he unlapped himself from Senna and Piquet, setting the fastest lap as he did it. He was no longer the world champion, but he was still the world's best.

The man who took his crown celebrated by sitting behind Senna for most of the race, and with Mansell's absence concentrated all his venom on the other driver he disliked. While he stewed, Senna's rubber dust built up in the Williams' radiator intakes. It would upset the finishing record that won him the world championship.

At 1.21 pm on Friday, October 30, the 1987 World Championship was decided, in Nelson Piquet's favour. The Brazilian and his Williams-Honda team-mate, Nigel Mansell, are anything but close friends, as everyone knew and all were hoping to see the two of them fight for the title to the last lap in Adelaide.

By Friday evening that was out of the question. Mansell, following a huge accident in the first qualifying session at Suzuka, was in hospital. He wasn't in bad shape, the medical reports said, but he was hurting, and there were further tests to be done.

"There's nothing seriously wrong, apparently," Frank Williams said. "They've X-rayed him, and there are no fractures. But he's got a lot of pain in his back, for some reason, and they're keeping him in to run some more checks. I suppose he might be OK to drive on Sunday, but tomorrow is out of the question."

Practice to that point, had been typical of Mansell. On Thursday, a free session for acclimatisation to a circuit new to most of the Formula One drivers, he had set fastest in the unofficial session, and looked set to stay that way in the afternoon.

Only five minutes into the qualifying, Nigel had lapped in 1:43.06. Slow lap to cool the tyres, then another hot one: 1:42.61. After that he was in the pits, staying in the car, watching the portable TV monitor above his steering wheel, keeping an eye on the others. Seventeen minutes into the session, Piquet set a new mark of 1:42.42.

At this point Mansell went out again, but it was not,

as many assumed, in response to Piquet's quick lap. Nigel had always intended to use his second set of tyres for his final effort: this was simply a recce, a look at how the track surface was developing, whether or not it was picking up speed.

The Williams crashed at the fast S-section behind the paddock. Coming out of a right-hander, the car ran a little wide, clipping a kerb on the exit. Off the normal line, the track was dirty there, and there was a kick of dust as the Williams began to slide, then spin.

Nigel had the brakes on hard before the car went off the road, but even so hit a tyre barrier backwards with a force that seemed to multiply as the car bounced off it. The Williams was high into the air, and looking set to somersault, but eventually came down four square on its wheels. Extremely hard. Not as quickly as it should have been, the session was stopped.

Mansell, in the meantime, was still in the car. In considerable pain from his back and right leg, he was unable to get himself out, and it was some time before track workers and doctors could release him to be stretchered away, first to the track's medical centre, then, by helicopter, to hospital in Nagoya.

At first all sorts of stories were circulating, but happily they proved to be the usual exaggerations. By Saturday morning the official word was that Nigel was badly knocked about, certainly, but there was nothing seriously wrong. More on the mind, almost certainly, than his pain was the thought that, perhaps a single small mistake — made by every driver many

better, but the night had been sleepless, and he looked a weary man. "I don't feel great," he admitted in the afternoon, "but the car was good today. After the session was restarted, I went out again, but made a mistake on my quick lap and didn't go so quick."

Many were surprised, in fact, that the surviving Williams made a second run, but there were challenges from other than Mansell. Both Ferrari drivers, for example, and Prost.

Berger it was who finished up with second fastest time, despite complaints of a 'long' brake pedal and a down-on-power engine — despite the fact that the red cars were fastest of all down the back straight, Gerhard's 197.7 mph beaten only by Michele Alboreto's 198.8!

The Ferrari drivers were happy with their car's balance and grip, but both spoke of poor throttle response at Suzuka — a complaint made also by Prost of his McLaren-TAG, fourth fastest.

The world champion was nearing the end of his reign — for now — but it made little difference to his resolution: "Yes, the title is gone now, I know that. But there are two races left, and I want both of them!" Alain was content with his chassis, but never got a clear lap in the timed session on this, a track where slow traffic is a major problem — as team-mate Stefan Johansson confirmed.

"I've been coming here for a long time," Stefan said, "and it is a great circuit — although not as challenging as it was before the modifications. But for traffic, it's disastrous because it's narrow."

The Swede was fastest of all for much of the

crews pursuing him everywhere. The advertising hoardings for the race did nothing to relax him, either: they showed Lotus No. 11 leading Piquet and Prost!

Nakajima was 13th, behind Riccardo Patrese's Brabham-BMW and the Arrows-Megatrons of Derek Warwick and Eddie Cheever. "I know this track better than anyone else, I suppose," the Japanese said, "and I hoped to be quicker. But they've changed Suzuka a lot. It seems almost like a new circuit."

Second day. By Saturday morning it was made known that Nigel Mansell would be taking no further part in the Japanese Grand Prix — perhaps in the rest of the season. He had spent a good night in the hospital in Nagoya, but early the following morning a visit by Professor Watkins, FISA's permanent Formula One doctor, confirmed everyone's suspicions: Mansell was not medically fit to drive. All he wanted, he said, was to get back home to the Isle of Man as quickly as possible, however painful the journey.

So that was that: Nelson Piquet, with only three wins in 1987, was world champion; Nigel Mansell with six, was not. And now the Brazilian was the lone Williams-Honda driver for the weekend, hoping to defend his Friday pole position. Honda hoped for that, too, for Nelson represented very obviously its only hope of starting from the front. The Lotus-Hondas were clearly not contenders.

On Saturday afternoon Piquet improved his time — and dropped from first to fifth! Ahead were two

times in a grand prix season — had wiped away his last hopes of the 1987 World Championship.

All hoped he would be back on Sunday. But if so, what kind of shape would he have been in for 191 miles around a place as tough as this? It is indeed a tough place — and an impressive one. A driver's circuit in the best sense of the word. "I think it's fantastic," Gerhard Berger commented. "Until I came here, Brands Hatch was my favourite circuit. Not any more . . ."

And many other drivers echoed his words. A bit narrow in places, a bit short of run-off in others, maybe. But as a challenge — a track to give you pleasure in your car and your ability.

Piquet finished the first day on pole position, his early quick lap remaining unbeaten. It was not at all where he had expected to be. Having survived the joys of Mexico without a tremor, Nelson was suffering badly with a stomach upset on Thursday, and did not run many laps. By Friday morning he felt a little

morning, but in the afternoon his perennial poor luck returned: blown turbo on the first run, tightening engine on the second.

Both the Benetton-Fords made the top seven on Friday, Thierry Boutsen a little quicker than Teo Fabi once again. More complaints of poor throttle response, and Thierry also complained of a lack of grip. Teo had more oversteer than he would have liked. For all that, on the track they looked very stable.

So, too, did the Lotus-Hondas, although Ayrton Senna wouldn't agree. No balance, he said, and no grip. Also, the traction was poor out of the slow corners — and there are many at Suzuka, including a new, fatuously tight, first gear chicane near the end of the lap, which looks for all the world like a pit lane entry road.

In the afternoon Ayrton had to stop out on the circuit with a broken driveshaft, and there was no way back to the pits in time to take out the other 99T. On straightline speed the Lotus-Hondas had little to fear, being beaten through the back straight speed trap only by the Ferraris. Satoru Nakajima, in fact, was third quickest here — ahead of Senna — so Honda must have been giving him good stuff at home, for he certainly wasn't coming off the previous corner as quickly as Ayrton . . .

Japan's only grand prix driver had a relatively uneventful day in the car on Friday (apart from the slight shock of his cockpit fire extinguisher going off during the morning session!), but out of the car the pressure on him was tremendous, with local film

Ferraris, a McLaren and a Benetton. At this, far and away the most important race of their season, Honda had its worst qualifying session of 1987. Only in Portugal had they missed the pole; at every race they had started from the front row.

But not here, at Suzuka, where it really mattered. The man who took the pole was the man who stole it at Estoril: Gerhard Berger.

Pole position changed hands several times in the final session, and, in truth, Piquet was never a serious contender. Within 10 mins of the start, Nelson's Friday time had been beaten by Gerhard — who was himself removed from the pole by Boutsen's Benetton.

The Belgian looked set to stay there — for the first time in his Formula One career — but with little more than five minutes of the session left Berger put in a stunning lap, nearly a full second faster than Thierry, and no one was going to better that.

Prost, however, gave it his best shot, in the dying seconds of the session the McLaren went round in 1m40.6s, half a second away from Berger, but quicker than Boutsen.

Alboreto, too, improved significantly, the fourth and last of the elite group to beat 1:41. As time ticked away Piquet, now down fifth, embarked on a desperate series of laps, no thought given to cooling tyres once in a while. Nelson put in three stormers on the trot, each looking like a possible pole lap. But the times simply weren't there: when it was all over, the Williams — the first Honda — was only three-

1.

2.

tenths quicker than before. And more than a second from Berger.

"I think it's kind of funny," Gerhard said afterwards, "that Honda should dominate this year, then come to Japan and qualify fifth!" The local interpreter smiled bravely, then sought a tactful way of turning it into her own language . . .

Had the pole lap been perfect? "No, not really," Berger answered. "Fabi held me up a little. He was going very slowly, and kept out of the way, but you never really know in these circumstances, and I lifted a fraction. Then, on a sixth gear corner later in the lap, I put two wheels on the grass. It was a hard moment, but I lifted off, and the car came back on

the track. A perfect lap, I think, would have been 1:39.8, but I'm quite happy."

Piquet, new world champion, was predictably far less so. "We made a lot of mistakes today. I ran full tanks this morning, and for the afternoon they didn't soften the settings again for qualifying. They also took off some of the brake ducting, so that I couldn't brake very deeply, and kept locking up the rears."

Would he have been quicker, someone asked, if Nigel had been in the race? Nelson said no. Without Nigel in the race, he thought, his chances were excellent. "If Mansell had been here, I would have had to think only in terms of beating him, finishing ahead of him, for the sake of the championship.

Now I can plan my race without any thoughts like that.

"Here," Piquet went on, "fuel consumption is going to be critical. I can see this being a race where there are a lot of changes in the last few laps. Tyres? No problem — only one stop."

Berger was less confident about his: "This place is very hard on tyres. We'll certainly make one stop, maybe two . . ."

In Japan Goodyear were back to its policy of 'one tyre for all'. There was no choice of compound, such as in the freak conditions of Mexico. Here everyone was given the softer Cs, and told to get on with it.

All told, it looked the most open race for a long time. Prost was happy with second, his best grid position of the season. "This is a good track, but a narrow one, considering how quick it is," he said. "In qualifying I've been taking care with the traffic — perhaps too much care. But there's no point in risking your car in practice. The balance is fine, just as I like it, but I never found a clear lap when my tyres were at their best — in fact, my quickest lap, right at the end, was on my second run on the second set of tyres. I was surprised there was so much grip left in them.

"Now that Nigel is out," Alain added, "the season has turned into a bit of an anti-climax, hasn't it? Today I am no longer world champion. OK. What I want next is to be the first to win 30 grands prix . . ."

The troubles of Ayrton Senna continued on the second day. In the morning he had again to park out on the circuit, this time because the Lotus-Honda's on-board fire extinguisher went off, just as Nakajima's had done the previous day. Ayrton parked hurriedly to avoid risk of the cold 'burns' which the gases can cause.

The afternoon brought disappointment, too. At one stage a spin by Senna brought the session temporarily to a halt. "I was just trying too hard, I suppose," he commented. "We just couldn't find enough grip. The track got faster as the session went on — but then I ran out of fuel . . ."

In the end Ayrton was less than a second faster than Nakajima, who did a fine job on his home territory, qualifying 11th, only three-tenths slower than Johansson's McLaren, and ahead of the Arrows pair.

Fastest of the normally-aspirated brigade was Philippe Alliot's Lola, followed by Jonathan Palmer's Tyrrell and Ivan Capelli's March. Jonathan, like most of his colleagues, thought the circuit wonderful: "It's so satisfying, and what I really like about it is that your times improve as you try harder. At some tracks it's the other way round. But here you can see some reward for effort. I think it's great."

With Mansell gone from the scene, only 26 cars remained — which meant that the AGS qualified. On this occasion it was driven by Roberto Moreno, rather than Pascal Fabre, which meant that it was moved at unaccustomed speed. The Brazilian did well to qualify only half a second adrift from Streiff's Tyrrell, but the wayward French car had no business in grand prix racing, and no one looked forward to lapping it on Sunday. Not on a track as quick — and narrow — as this.

So Japan prepared for its first grand prix in 10 years, and the country's taste for Formula One was beyond doubt. Access to the Suzuka circuit was poor, and the organisers decided to limit the paying spectators to 100,000. Why, you had to take part in a lottery before you could think about buying a ticket! Success in the first allowed you to apply for the second. In places like Jerez, Zeltweg and Paul Ricard, they dream of such things. Japan has the track for the job, and the support for it. What was needed now, for Sunday, was decent weather. The qualifying days had been overcast, dul, sometimes chilly. And there was rain in the air.

It continued cloudy on race morning, but the forecasters promised a dry race. It also remained cool, which soothed the drivers' worries about excessive tyre wear. This was a very grippy track.

The morning warm-up times slightly reshuffled the pack. Pole man Berger ran both his own and the spare Ferrari, finishing up with precisely the same time — to the thousandth — as Piquet. Ahead of them was Alboreto and, ominously of all, the

At the front of the field, though, they had got away cleanly, Berger confidently leading into the first turn, from Prost, Boutsen, Senna, Piquet and Fabi. Apart from Alboreto, therefore, all the right people were in the right place. You thought of Berger's determination the afternoon before, of Prost's confidence after the warm-up, of Piquet again beaten away by Senna, and reckoned something good was in prospect here — but not for long. As Prost chased Berger into lap two, he felt the McLaren sit down slightly as it went through the first turn, and a glance in his mirror revealed that the left rear tyre was deforming. Puncture. For as long as he reasonably could, Alain

3.

second lap the Austrian already had more than six secs over Boutsen, who was himself pulling comfortably clear of those two 'friendly' Brazilians.

Before qualifying began, Senna expressed the belief that Mansell was going to win the world championship. This was certainly his hope. While Ayrton had his well-documented run-ins with Nigel, they were nothing compared with the animosity which exists between himself and Piquet. Over the previous season he had tired of Nelson's referring to him as "the Sao Paulo taxi driver," and the two of them made no secret of their intense mutual dislike. Even at his press conference to celebrate the world

4.

McLaren of Prost. "Everything is good," Alain said. "The only worries here, I would say, are fuel consumption and tyre wear." In every way, clearly, he felt he had everyone handled.

Senna, though, had his troubles. The 'active' system malfunction warning light came on, and attempts to solve the problem failed, which meant Ayrton in the spare Lotus for the race.

The start was mildly chaotic. On the grid Alboreto found his clutch going 'solid', and finally the Ferrari stalled, obliging those behind to seek a hazardous path. All went well until Rene Arnoux cut to Michele's left, and collected Alliot's Lola, which was out on the spot. Rene went on his way, bent steering arm and all.

held off Senna and the rest, but halfway round the lap they swamped him. "After that, the tyre began to break up badly. I had to take it very easy back to the pits . . ."

The McLaren arrived back at the pits on three tyres and a rim. New tyres, a quick check over, and Alain was back out, well over a lap behind. Last. He was about to start one of his greatest drives, despite the absolute hopelessness of his position. Even running at the limit, he would not catch and pass Moreno's AGS until lap 23, but there was never a though of cruising.

So, effectively we were robbed of our race within the first couple of minutes, for no one else looked like offering a challenge to Berger. By the end of the

1: A race begins without Nigel Mansell and with the championship decided before the lights flashed green.

2: Not a Honda engine to be seen as poleman Berger charges away in the Ferrari during the first Japanese Grand Prix in 10 years.

3: It's early in practice and the Japanese would soon crowd the circuit to watch the Honda engines at work.

4: Boutsen rejoined the pursuit of Berger in Japan, but this time he was hampered by no clutch from the start and a fuel readout that was far from smiling. He started backing off.

Below: Yes, this had to be Japan. But the brand of technical wizardry that created the Honda grand prix engine was about to be shown up at the most impolite time.

Below: Yes, this had to be Japan. But the brand of technical wizardry that created the Honda grand prix engine was about to be shown up at the most impolite time.

of Senna and Piquet — who themselves had now been joined by Johansson and Fabi. Then there was Patrese, being caught by the highly motivated Nakajima, and Cheever.

Capelli's March recorded a first on lap 14, by shunting hard into the guardrail — on the pit lane! At the hairpin Capelli had attempted to pass Arnoux, never a move to be undertaken lightly. Jonathan

championship, Piquet couldn't resist a snipe: "Senna hasn't been able to get the car as he would like it this year," he murmured. "Maybe next year he'll do better . . . with help from Prost."

So there was a particular bite to any battle between these two especially now that Nelson was hogging the headlines in Brazil. Already the Lotus and Williams were tied together, and if Nelson was going to do anything about winning this thing, he had to get by quickly, set off after Boutsen and, more particularly, Berger, who was pulling away by the lap.

Piquet, it turned out, was even more angry with Senna than usual. "I am going to call him 'handbrake' now. At the start he went off the circuit, over the white line, and when he came back he just pushed his way in. I had to back off to avoid being hit by him . . ."

Ayrton, as you might imagine, saw it rather differently: "I had to go around Piquet at the start because he was so slow getting away. I went to the right of him because if I'd gone left there might have been an accident. Alboreto was stalled there — what else could I do?"

The Brazilian Two-Step was therefore the focal point of the race, the one battle in progress. Except that it didn't really look that way. Upset Nelson may have been, but he never channelled his anger into true aggression: and way along, you felt that it would take a mistake by Ayrton for his compatriot to get by. Later in the day he would take a single really determined run at the Lotus, but was firmly rebuffed.

Ferrari hearts skipped a beat at the end of lap six, when Berger seemed to be fumbling in search of a gear as he went up through the 'box out of the final corner. He found one eventually and went on his way, but next time round it happened again. After that the problem recurred.

At 10 laps Gerhard led by as many seconds and more, and Boutsen was falling back into the clutches

Palmer had a fine view of the action: "I saw him try it, and thought 'no way . . . not with Arnoux . . .' The Ligier just chopped across, and they hit."

Ivan was coming into the pits for attention to his battered nosecone, but this unfortunately wedged itself beneath the car, lifting the front wheels off the deck. Which meant that when the pit entry road turned, the March didn't. Capelli was cross, and justifiably so. Arnoux, as you might expect, said that Ivan had run into him . . .

Briefly the March blocked the pit lane, but the marshals moved it swiftly, and it was good they did because not long afterwards Cheever arrived for tyres. Five seconds later Warwick followed him in, so now we had both Arrows pitting at the same time!

"The lap before," said Derek, on his way to an 'interview' with Eddie, "I got a pit signal telling me to come in for tyres. I get there — and find he's nicked them! So I had to go out again, then come back a couple of laps later." He didn't seem too angry, though. By the end of the race, too many other things had gone wrong: only third and fifth gears were in operation for the later laps.

The first significant retirement came on lap 16, when Fabi cruised into pit lane, his Benetton's Ford V6 having detonated. The team's fortunes, once more so bright in the early stages, were again in decline: Boutsen without a clutch almost from the start, had nevertheless revelled in his car's handling, but had been passed by Senna, Piquet and Johansson, and was back to fifth.

"In the early laps I really thought I could win this race," Thierry said. So what had slowed him? "Only fuel. My read-out told me I was using way too much, so I had to turn the boost down and cruise for the rest of the race. In the straights I was having to lift off! It's a very boring way to race . . ."

The Ferraris had no consumption problems. Certainly Berger and Alboreto needed to keep a

weather eye on their gauges — but not to the extent of lifting on the straights.

Following his delayed start, Michele had come back splendidly, and by one-third distance was up to sixth. And Nakajima, to local delight and much waving of flags, had got by Patrese for seventh.

Johansson began the tyre stops, on lap 20. He had anyway been trapped behind the warring Brazilians for some time, and there was every sign that he was being held up. Better to come in, hope for a quick stop, maybe get ahead of them when they pitted. The ploy worked just as he had hoped.

Four laps later came the vital one: Berger. And the Ferrari mechanics, no doubt lifted by the Austrian's performance, did sensational work, the car stationary for precisely 6.97 secs. And Gerhard never truly lost the lead, for next time round Senna — and Piquet! — both came in for the new Goodyears.

For both crews, the pressure was on: a mistake here could end the Brazilian battle. It was inevitable, though, that the Williams stop would take longer than the Lotus one: since Mansell's debacle in Hungary (when his car shed a wheel in the late stages, losing him the race), the team had religiously fitted retaining pins outside the wheel-nuts and these took time to remove.

So Ayrton and Nelson resumed the race in the same order — but both were now behind Johansson, who was discernibly closing on the leading Berger.

But not really. "I'd had a big lead before the stops," said Gerhard, "and afterwards I went a little bit asleep. Suddenly I saw Stefan in my mirrors and the next thing was that he was nearly under my wing! Then I really had to push again."

At the end of lap 30 the gap was down to 2.6 secs, but the McLaren would get no closer than that. Johansson had the same problem as Boutsen: "I was on the wrong side on fuel, that was all. Otherwise the car was perfect — I've never felt so frustrated in a race, just having to turn the boost down, watch him disappear into the distance again . . ."

So Ferrari was safe, under no threat — except from its own reliability, which for the season had been lamentable. "When I got here first," Berger commented later, "I didn't really like the circuit — or, rather, I liked the circuit, but it seemed to have a combination of corners which our engine wouldn't like. But we worked hard on the car, improved it, and in the race it was about perfect, like in Hungary. But there, of course, we didn't last . . ."

Once he had the hammer down again, Gerhard drew swiftly away from Stefan, who was now having to tread softly, of course. For some time he drew away by a second a lap, sometimes more.

But he wasn't going as quickly as Prost. No one was. After being delayed for a while by Alboreto — who was a lap ahead but probably didn't realise it — Alain reeled in Piquet and Senna as if they were backmarkers. Nelson knew of the McLaren's situation, and waved it through, but Ayrton was less co-operative, keeping Prost back for three laps. Once past, Alain left them behind.

"I think today the car was maybe the best I have had all season," he smiled afterwards, disappointed by the result, exhilarated by the drive. "And, you know I think that puncture cost me a very easy win." You didn't doubt him. There had been no problems with tyres, none with fuel consumption — although Prost, of course, knew he would run one lap less than the full distance.

Into the late stages. At the end of lap 46 the yellow of Senna swept into sight, without the white of Piquet at his tail. After a few seconds the Williams appeared, making its oily way to the pit lane. Nelson had followed Ayrton for so long that his car's radiator ducts had become clogged with rubber. The Honda V6 overheated, then expired hugely. Car No. 6 had finally retired a grand prix, and Piquet must have wished he had forced a way past the Lotus and into clean air.

There were no wholesale retirements in the late stages: Alex Caffi and Cheever ran out of fuel, and Patrese and Yannick Dalmas were both creeping around with major engine ailments. Both Ligiers ran dry. Warwick stammered round with his two selectable gears.

[FUJI TELEVISION]
JAPAN GRAND PRIX
SUZUKA, 1987

And on the last lap Johansson, hobbled still by his high mpg and consequently low boost, lost second place to Senna. "I didn't know he was that close," Stefan grimaced. "They didn't tell me on the radio." Ron Dennis retorted that he should have looked at his pit signals. Whatever, he deserved six points, rather than four.

No doubt, though, about the man who deserved nine. Berger had started from the front, and led all the way in superb style. "It's sometimes much easier to win than to finish, maybe, sixth," he grinned. "But I had no real pressure today — Alain had his puncture right at the start. And, of course, Nigel wasn't in the race at all. So I think I was lucky really."

Victory in the normally-aspirated class clinched the Jim Clark Trophy for Jonathan Palmer, who also finished the race in eighth place overall. It was an uneventful afternoon for the Tyrrell man, whose main opposition — Alliot and Capelli — were eliminated by Arnoux.

Team-mate Philippe Streiff, a distant second in class, finished second in the cup standings.

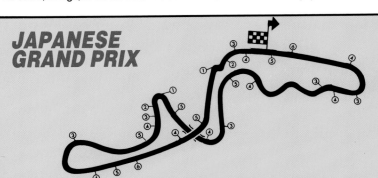

JAPANESE GRAND PRIX

Round 15: November 1, 1987
Circuit: Suzuka

Race data: 51 laps of 3.640 mile (5.86 km) circuit
Weather: Overcast, dry
Fastest lap: Prost, McLaren MP4, Average speed: 1:43.844, 126.210mph

ENTRIES

No	Driver (Nat)	Car/Chassis	Engine
1	Alain Prost (F)	McLaren MP4/3-4	TAG V6 Turbo
1T	Alain Prost (F)	McLaren MP4/3-1	TAG V6 Turbo
2	Stefan Johansson (S)	McLaren MP4/3-5	TAG V6 Turbo
3	Jonathan Palmer (GB)	Tyrrell DG/016-5	Ford Cosworth V8
4	Philippe Streiff (F)	Tyrrell DG/016-2	Ford Cosworth V8
5	Nigel Mansell (GB)	Williams FW11B/1	Honda V6 Turbo
6	Nelson Piquet (BR)	Williams FW11B/6	Honda V6 Turbo
6T	Nelson Piquet (BR)	Williams FW11B/4	Honda V6 Turbo
7	Riccardo Patrese (I)	Brabham BT56/4	BMW S4 Turbo
7T	Riccardo Patrese (I)	Brabham BT56/3	BMW S4 Turbo
8	Andrea de Cesaris (I)	Brabham BT56/2	BMW S4 Turbo
9	Martin Brundle (GB)	Zakspeed 871/03	Zakspeed S4 Turbo
9T	Martin Brundle (GB)	Zakspeed 871/01	Zakspeed S4 Turbo
10	Christian Danner (D)	Zakspeed 871/02	Zakspeed S4 Turbo
11	Satoru Nakajima (J)	Lotus 99T/3	Honda V6 Turbo
12	Ayrton Senna (BR)	Lotus 99T/4	Honda V6 Turbo
12T	Ayrton Senna (BR)	Lotus 99T/6*	Honda V6 Turbo
14	Roberto Moreno (BR)	AGS JH22/02-032	Ford Cosworth V8
16	Ivan Capelli (I)	March 871/1	Ford Cosworth V8
16T	Ivan Capelli (I)	March 871/2	Ford Cosworth V8
17	Derek Warwick (GB)	Arrows A10/4	Megatron S4 Turbo
18	Eddie Cheever (USA)	Arrows A10/2	Megatron S4 Turbo
18T	Eddie Cheever (USA)	Arrows A10/3	Megatron S4 Turbo
19	Teo Fabi (I)	Benetton B187-04	Ford V6 Turbo
20	Thierry Boutsen (B)	Benetton B187-09	Ford V6 Turbo
20T	Thierry Boutsen (B)	Benetton B187-07	Ford V6 Turbo
21	Alex Caffi (I)	Osella FA1H/1	Alfa Romeo V8 Turbo
23	Adrian Campos (E)	Minardi M186/3	Moderni V6 Turbo
24	Alessandro Nannini (I)	Minardi M186/4	Moderni V6 Turbo
25	Rene Arnoux (F)	Ligier JS29C/06	Megatron S4 Turbo
26	Piercarlo Ghinzani (I)	Ligier JS29C/04	Megatron S4 Turbo
26T	Piercarlo Ghinzani (I)	Ligier JS29C/03	Megatron S4 Turbo
27	Michele Alboreto (I)	Ferrari F187/101	Ferrari V6 Turbo
28	Gerhard Berger (A)	Ferrari F187/098	Ferrari V6 Turbo
28T	Gerhard Berger (A)	Ferrari F187/097*	Ferrari V6 Turbo
29	Yannick Dalmas (F)	Lola LC87/02	Ford Cosworth V8
30	Philippe Alliot (F)	Lola LC87/03	Ford Cosworth V8

* Race car

QUALIFYING

FRIDAY: Overcast, dry

Driver	
Piquet	1:41.423
Berger	1:42.160
Alboreto	1:42.416
Prost	1:42.469
Mansell	1:42.616
Boutsen	1:43.130
Fabi	1:43.351
Johansson	1:43.612
Senna	1:44.026
Patrese	1:44.767
Warwick	1:44.768
Cheever	1:45.427
Nakajima	1:45.898
De Cesaris	1:46.399
Brundle	1:46.715
Palmer	1:48.902
Nannini	1:48.948
Caffi	1:49.017
Danner	1:49.337
Alliot	1:49.470
Capelli	1:49.814
Arnoux	1:50.542
Streiff	1:50.896
Dalmas	1:51.230
Campos	1:51.554
Moreno	1:51.835
Campos	1:53.455

SATURDAY: Overcast, dry

Driver	
Berger	1:40.042
Prost	1:40.652
Boutsen	1:40.850
Alboreto	1:40.984
Piquet	1:41.144
Fabi	1:41.679
Senna	1:42.723
Patrese	1:43.304
Johansson	1:43.371
De Cesaris	1:43.618
Nakajima	1:43.385
Cheever	1:44.277
Warwick	1:44.626
Nannini	1:45.612
Brundle	1:46.023
Danner	1:46.116
Arnoux	1:46.200
Alliot	1:47.395
Palmer	1:47.775
Capelli	1:48.212
Campos	1:48.337
Dalmas	1:48.887
Ghinzani	1:49.641
Streiff	1:49.741
Moreno	1:50.212
Caffi	1:50.902

STARTING GRID

No	Driver	Time
28	Berger	1:40.042
1	Prost	1:40.652
20	Boutsen	1:40.850
27	Alboreto	1:40.984
6	Piquet	1:41.144
19	Fabi	1:41.679
12	Senna	1:42.723
7	Patrese	1:43.304
2	Johansson	1:43.371
8	De Cesaris	1:43.618
11	Nakajima	1:43.685
18	Cheever	1:44.277
17	Warwick	1:44.626
24	Nannini	1:45.612
9	Brundle	1:46.023
10	Danner	1:46.116
25	Arnoux	1:46.200
30	Alliot	1:47.395
3	Palmer	1:47.775
16	Capelli	1:48.212
23	Campos	1:48.337
29	Dalmas	1:48.887
21	Caffi	1:49.017
26	Ghinzani	1:49.641
4	Streiff	1.49.741
14	Moreno	1:50.212

RESULTS

Pos	No	Driver	Car	Laps	Time/Retirement
1	28	Berger	Ferrari	51	1-32:50.072
2	12	Senna	Lotus-Honda	51	1-33:15.416
3	2	Johansson	McLaren-TAG	51	1-33:15.766
4	27	Alboreto	Ferrari	51	1-34:18.513
5	20	Boutsen	Benetton-Ford	51	1-34:23.648
6	11	Nakajima	Lotus-Honda	51	1-34:34.551
7	1	Prost	McLaren-TAG	50	
8	3	Palmer	Tyrrell-Cosworth	50	
R	18	Cheever	Arrows-Megatron	50	Out of fuel
10	17	Warwick	Arrows-Megatron	54	
11	7	Patrese	Brabham-BMW	49	
12	4	Streiff	Tyrrell-Cosworth	49	
R	26	Ghinzani	Ligier-Megatron	48	Out of fuel
R	29	Dalmas	Lola-Cosworth	47	Engine
R	6	Piquet	Williams-Honda	46	
R	25	Arnoux	Ligier-Megatron	44	Out of fuel
R	21	Caffi	Osella-Alfa Romeo	43	Out of fuel
R	14	Moreno	AGS-Cosworth	38	Engine
R	24	Nannini	Minardi-Moderni	35	Engine
R	9	Brundle	Zakspeed	32	
R	8	De Cesaris	Brabham-BMW	26	Turbo
R	19	Fabi	Benetton-Ford	16	Engine
R	10	Danner	Zakspeed	13	Accident
R	16	Capelli	March-Cosworth	13	Accident
R	23	Campos	Minardi-Moderni	2	Engine
R	30	Alliot	Lola-Cosworth	0	Accident

FASTEST LAP

Driver	
Prost	1:43.844
Senna	1:45.540
Berger	1:45.805
Johansson	1:46.323
Alboreto	1:46.534
Piquet	1:46.706
Boutsen	1:47.182
Cheever	1:47.421
Nakajima	1:48.206
Patrese	1:48.581
Fabi	1:49.170
Warwick	1:49.221
Arnoux	1:49.384
Ghinzani	1:49.915
Palmer	1:50.111
Brundle	1:50.367
De Cesaris	1:50.422
Streiff	1:51.236
Nannini	1:51.848
Caffi	1:51.917
Dalmas	1:52.080
Capelli	1:52.213
Danner	1:52.813
Moreno	1:54.015
Campos	1:59.121

CHAMPIONSHIP POSITIONS

DRIVERS

1	Piquet	73
2	Mansell	61
3	Senna	57
4	Prost	46
5	Johansson	30
6	Berger	27
7	Boutsen	12
	Fabi	12
9	Alboreto	11
10	Cheever	8
11	Nakajima	7
12	Patrese	6
13	De Cesaris	4
	Palmer	4
	Streiff	4
16	Alliot	3
	Warwick	3
18	Brundle	2
19	Arnoux	1
	Capelli	1

CONSTRUCTORS

1	Williams-Honda	137
2	McLaren-TAG	76
3	Lotus-Honda	63
4	Ferrari	38
5	Benetton-Ford	24
6	Arrows-Megatron	11
7	Brabham-BMW	10
8	Tyrrell-Cosworth	8
9	Lola-Cosworth	3
10	Zakspeed	2
11	Ligier-Megatron	1
	March-Cosworth	1

JIM CLARK CUP

1	Palmer	86
2	Streiff	74
3	Alliot	43
4	Capelli	38
5	Fabre	35
6	Dalmas	7

COLIN CHAPMAN CUP

1	Tyrrell-Cosworth	160
2	Lola-Cosworth	50
3	March-Cosworth	38
4	AGS-Cosworth	34

Australia

ROUND 16: November 15, 1987

A REVIVAL CONFIRMED

The drought had turned into a flood. It swept away those who had profited from the famous team's unprecedented dry spell and gave new interest to a series prematurely resolved.

This was strictly a one-man show. It was Gerhard Berger, the new superstar, on pole by a chunk in the resurgent Ferrari. It was Berger who led all the way, but for the first minute, Berger who took the fastest lap.

This proved to be an easy win, his third, in the most difficult of circumstances. It was hot and the vigorous Austrian driver felt not so hot. The thermometer had said he didn't have a temperature, a virus-infested Berger wheezed, but he was sure he did.

This was an idiosyncrasy of a new superstar to get used to. Like some other great drivers, including Nigel Mansell, he seemed to be one of those susceptible to any malady on the market. They speak of how lousy they feel, then climb into a race car and disappear from the healthy.

The healthy were involved in the other part of the race, in a fierce scrap for the minors. That involved Nelson Piquet, Alain Prost, Ayrton Senna and Michele Alboreto and gave some indication of the Austrian's achievement in Australia. When Piquet fell back with his tyre stop, then fell out, when Alain Prost spun lightly and harmlessly into retirement with spent brakes and when Alboreto's Ferrari didn't work as well as his team-mate's, that left Senna's Lotus as the only hope to halt the Berger roll.

In the late stages, Senna pressed hard, started to close in, but this was just momentary drama. The tyres no longer responded to the Brazilian's will. In any case Berger had kicked, knowing his fuel was OK. It wouldn't have matter however, if Senna was able to make it a race to the flag. At mid-evening the second-placed Lotus was disqualified for a brake ducting infringement, a symptom of the problems most teams had been experiencing with brakes from the first day.

The significance of this was that Alboreto was promoted to second place. Ferrari had a one-two.

After Japan most of the drivers rushed off to the Barrier Reef in search of serious sun. In the paddock there were some very expensive tans. The Italians, in their droves, went for Hamilton Island. Prost stayed around Cairns, played a couple of rounds of golf each day. Others, including Nelson Piquet and Derek Warwick, came straight from Tokyo to Adelaide.

This place has taken on that lovely end-of-term feeling which used to be the hallmark of Watkins Glen. If the Australian Grand Prix's position in the calendar were changed, everyone agreed, the race just wouldn't be the same.

A month before we were in Mexico for a weekend which somehow combined officiousness and dis-organisation. Here was a relaxed ambience, hand in hand with attention to detail. Could this continent truly be on the same planet as Latin America?

Another layer was perhaps added to the laid-back atmosphere by the fact that this time nothing was at stake. The championships were all settled, and this would be a race for the sake of it.

From Blighty had come the news that Nigel Mansell's injuries were apparently serious enough to keep him from running. Who would replace him in the No. 5 Williams-Honda? They had talked about Alan Jones, but Alan's Toyota sports car connections were enough to rule that out. Ortwin Podlech, Keke

1.

Rosberg's business partner and former manager, suspected that Keke might have thought about a one-off here, but said he hadn't been asked.

However, Bernie Ecclestone had told Frank Williams he was prepared to release Riccardo Patrese ahead of time, and so Riccardo changed jobs a little earlier than expected. Formula 3000 champ Stefano Modena was drafted in by Brabham, which meant that for almost certainly the last time in his Formula One career Andrea de Cesaris found himself as team leader.

The weather in South Australia was blissfully hot on Friday, hotter the following day. For race day, the forecasters warned, bring a hat and plenty of zinc cream.

For all that, the track was quicker than before. There was more grip than in previous years, but only on the line. Move off it just a few inches, they all said, and you were gone. There were more spins during the practice than anyone could remember. Why, on Friday afternoon we had seen the sight of Prost's McLaren rotating — twice! Team-mate Stefan Johansson said he had made a note of it in his diary — it was good to remind himself that Alain occasionally made a mistake.

The following day Prost spun again and tweaked his back. Investigation showed him to have displaced vertebra. Prost being Prost he played the discomfort

2.

3.

4.

1: The end of term party begins under the Australian sun. This was a race for the sake of it, the championship being resolved.

2: Brakes were the big problem during qualifying. All the teams, including Lotus, tried to nut out the problem. Note the ducting peaking out from the inside of the front wheels on Senna's car. Its modification was to prove contentious on race day.

3: Boutsen's Benetton lays bare at the back. The problem for him in practice was at the other end: faulty shocker keeping him out of the battle for the front row.

4: The familiar red flags sprouted like wild flowers. It seemed everyone in Australia had one.

1.

3.

down. Would he race? someone asked. Are you mad? said Alain's expression: of course he would race. More of a worry in his mind were the brakes, which were not holding up too well around the street circuit.

Health problems seemed to abound in the paddock. Since his Suzuka victory, Gerhard Berger had picked up the sort of cold you get from long flights and air conditioning. He sneezed a lot, and complained of earache. He felt lousy, he said. And team-mate Alboreto, suffering drastically from hay fever, said that went for him, too.

These walking wounded were to figure strongly in qualifying, however. Berger won in Japan, and, without that puncture early in the race, Prost indubitably would have won. The story was the same. When qualifying was all done, Gerhard and Alain were the front row.

"We're in good shape," the Austrian sniffed afterwards. "Balance is quite nice, and we're OK on straightline speed. Also, the Ferrari is efficient on fuel . . ."

Very important, this last point. Adelaide is tough on mpg. Most teams thought they'd get by, but it was close.

Prost's major worry was brakes. McLaren had two thicknesses of disc from which to choose, but neither was ideal. In terms of stopping the car well enough for long enough, the narrower ones were marginal; and on the long straight at Dequetteville the others were getting over-cool. So that was the besetting problem.

On Friday, Berger, Piquet and Prost sparred over pole position, until Gerhard — runny nose and all — put the thing beyond dispute with an incredible lap in 1:17.267, more than a second inside Mansell's time — on qualifying tyres — a year before! This, despite the fact that the track was very much more crowded than before, thanks to the absence of the one-lap wonders.

No one could get close to the Ferrari. It was a typical Berger hot lap, all tip-toe stuff, using the kerbs, pitching into the corners. And he also said he was left-foot braking. It wasn't flowing in the Prost style, but mighty effective. In the race, though, you suspected that Alain might maintain a real pace with more ease than Gerhard.

The No. 28 Ferrari appeared only in the late stages of the Saturday afternoon session. The

1: Traffic jam at the start of the third Australian Formula One Grand Prix. Seconds later, Derek Warwick and Jonathan Palmer, just exiting the picture in front of the pack of backmarkers, would have a coming together when Derek tried a desperate move which didn't work.
2: The Adelaide street circuit was much faster than in previous years and that took its toll on both drivers and brakes.
3: Piquet had snatched the lead momentarily but Berger quickly took charge, leaving the new world champion to fall into the clutches of the most determined former world champion.
4: Roast beef? Tea & coffee? Is that Aussie tucker? The familiar names helped the foreign visitors make sense of the local lexicon in the sign.

temperature was up, and grip, by general consensus, correspondingly down. Berger was off his Friday pace, and so also was Piquet. But Prost worked away, staying out there, seeking a clear lap.

He began his 29th in just a few seconds before the chequered flag ended the session. By now most were back in the pits, and traffic was light. Typically, Alain saved his best till last, scraped into the 1:17

bracket, moved up to the front row. The chassis was fine, he said, and engine good. It was just those brakes . . .

Piquet, too, was in stopping trouble. "There was no point in coming out again at the end," he said, "because my brakes were completely gone. Also, I'd blistered my last set of tyres."

In Adelaide there was a reappearance of the 'active' Williams-Honda, but Lotus don't like that term to be used for a system far less sophisticated than their own, so it was described as 'hydropneumatic'.

Nelson's enthusiasm for the system has always been high, but through qualifying he preferred to concentrate on the conventional FW11B. The race, he said, might be a different matter: he would try both in the warm-up, then decide.

There was no such choice for Patrese, who had only a regular car for his Williams debut. In truth, he hardly shone on Friday, and admitted as much. "I didn't drive very well today. I spun on my second set which blistered the rears — not good for setting a quick time." And the car? "It's a nice car to drive, but I need more time to get used to it — especially the gear-change." The Honda V6 impressed Riccardo considerably. "A lot of power, and much smoother than the BMW."

Three places up on Patrese was Ayrton Senna, sharing row two with Piquet. Ayrton said he thought fuel consumption would be absolutely crucial in this race — that, and stopping. "I think a lot of people could be in trouble with brakes tomorrow," he said, "because the track is so much faster than last year."

Thierry Boutsen, less than a tenth slower in the Benetton-Ford, had high hopes despite a character-building final session. On his second set of tyres, and going for it, Thierry found the car suddenly pulling hard left under braking. The problem was with a front shock absorber, but he kept on with the quick lap, and was rewarded by fifth on the grid, ahead of Alboreto's Ferrari. The sister Benetton of Teo Fabi was, as usual, quite a lot slower.

The grid had almost a pre-programmed look about it, with everyone more or less where you expect to find them. De Cesaris made the top 10, just ahead of the Arrows duo, and Alessandro Nannini impressed with a smooth qualifying run, to 13th place. So, too, did the shy Mr. Modena, who finished up 1.5 secs from de Cesaris.

Philippe Alliot seemed to go off the road at least once on each of his laps, but when he put on together it took him less time than anyone else in the normally-aspirated class. Ligier, drastically short of engines as usual, had a dreadful time of it, and the unfortunate Alex Caffi failed to make the cut, one of his Osellas having burned to a crisp during the first morning.

So, while Adelaide went out to party, the teams considered what promised to be a day of attrition. It was going to be hard on brakes and fuel, that much was sure. And, with temperatures up in the nineties, it wasn't going to be easy on the men, either.

Sunday morning was not as overtly bright and sunny as the qualifying days but it was hotter than ever, despite the haze. As midday approached it was in the nineties, and the drivers prepared for probably the most sapping race of the season.

Berger said he felt better. His ear was still aching, but the cold symptoms had calmed. Still, he added, this was probably physically tougher than any other track on the world championship schedule, with an abnormal amount of gear changing. It was also, at going on two hours, about the longest of all grands prix.

The warm-up was curiously reminiscent of Japan: once again Gerhard had an engine problem in his race car, and opted to take the spare 097 chassis for the race.

Prost, second fastest, said he felt much better, too, that his back problem in qualifying had eased.

Third fastest was Alboreto, but thereafter the list went frequently haywire. Fourth and fifth, for example, were the Brabhams of de Cesaris and debutant Modena. Up in ninth spot was Piercarlo Ghinzani's Ligier, followed by Christian Danner's Zakspeed. And down near the foot was Patrese, whose Williams-Honda was locking its rear brakes to the point of rendering it undriveable. By race time, though, Riccardo was happy.

Team-mate Piquet had decided against using his 'active' FW11B. He got his regular car off the grid to perfection: revs and timing were absolutely right, and before the first turn Nelson was by both Prost and Berger, through into the lead. Was this to be a day when Piquet declared his right to the title of world champion?

Berger, though, was in no mood to mess around. Piquet was in front for less than half a minute. By the end of the first lap the Ferrari was comfortably established. The Williams ran second, but Senna had momentarily zapped Prost for third — a situation Alain rectified in the course of lap two.

Walking back already was the unfortunate Nannini, who had hit the wall avoiding a Derek Warwick moment in the course of which Derek also clipped Jonathan Palmer's Tyrrell. "The steering was a bit peculiar after that," Jonathan said, "but not a big problem. I think a steering arm must have been a bit bent. I found I had oversteer on right-handers, understeer on left-handers . . ."

A few laps later Palmer would pit for new tyres — a faulty valve was causing the left front slowly to deflate — and rejoined 23rd. An extremely fine drive thereafter would bring him another normally-aspirated class win.

After three laps Berger was more than four secs up on Piquet, and Prost was showing interest in getting by the Williams. Alboreto, too, was moving along, passing Senna for fourth on lap five, then closing on Prost. This was stoking up nicely, and there was the thought that Berger just might be pressing his hand on full power.

No tyre changes were planned, Goodyear assuring everyone that, unless maltreated, one set would go the 192 miles. But fuel was an important considera-tion, and so, to a greater degree, were brakes. Tyres, after all, you can change if you have to. So perhaps the others were taking it easy behind Berger, reckoning that the real race would start in the closing laps, when the fast man would be he who could stop . . ."

McLaren had opted, finally, for its thicker brake discs, with suitably modified cooling ducts. "It's the only thing to do," Prost had said after the warm-up. "I still don't have as much brakes as I would like, but at least these might last the race. The other ones . . . no way. I have to be very careful on full tanks, I think."

Well, yes, up to a point. But being careful and staying ahead of such as Alboreto are difficult ambitions to combine. Alain seemed to find a way, but could not get by Piquet.

So there was Berger, six or seven secs clear of the Piquet-Prost-Alboreto combo, then a short breathing space to another close group: Senna, Patrese and Johansson.

A tyre stop by de Cesaris on lap 14 caused a flurry of speculation about wear rates. The Brabham's rear tyres were badly blistered — was this a portent of trouble for everyone? Not so, it was simply Andrea driving with his usual light touch. Over the next hour or so, he would stop for three more sets . . .

Actually, that was less than charitable. Fabi needed more Goodyears soon afterwards, and so did Modena. In fact, the young Italian gave Berger an edgy moment immediately after rejoining. At the left-right after the pits he drove his BT56 right over the kerbs to give the Ferrari an uninterrupted line through — and got sideways in front of it as he came back on the track. But Gerhard made it by without problem.

By lap 20 he was seriously involved in lapping backmarkers, and perhaps Piquet had better luck with the traffic, for the gap came down a little. At the same time Prost had detached himself from the attentions of Alboreto, and was closing again on Piquet. Michele, in fact, was being reeled slowly in by Senna. And on lap 20 Patrese spun, under pressure from Johansson, which let the second McLaren into sixth place. So it was busy out there.

Boutsen, next up, should have played a prominent part in it, but had been in severe brake trouble almost from the start despite Benetton's decision to run cast iron discs. "The pedal went to the floor after only two laps or so," Thierry disconsolately reported afterwards, "and I just had to live with it. A pity, because the car was perfect otherwise . . ."

Later in the race he would encounter another problem — in the shape of his petulant team-mate, whom he was trying to lap. Teo Fabi had not responded well to being blown away by Boutsen or

to the team's decision to show him the door. And when Thierry came up to lap him, the Italian resolutely held him back, despite angry signals from his pit. "What were you doing — weaving like that?" Boutsen indignantly asked after the race. "Two or three times you had me on the grass . . ."

"That pays you back for Portugal," Fabi retorted. "You held me up there. Anyway," he added childishly, "come back and talk to me when you've got three pole positions . . ."

In a similar manner Philippe Alliot held up Prost, as the McLaren tried to lap the Lola. Philippe was perhaps preoccupied with trying to get ahead of eager young Yannick Dalmas. Whatever, Alain lost a lot of time to Piquet, and, at the first corner, most uncharacteristically went off the road, and over the kerbs.

Fortunately, the car was undamaged by the incident, but this was the first real indication that Prost's brake problems in practice had not been solved. The car had gone off because its driver couldn't get it stopped properly.

This put Alboreto back on Alain's tail, but after a cautious lap to check that all was well with the McLaren, the Frenchman began to pull away once more — indeed, close again on Piquet.

As it turned out, however, Prost had no need to pass the Williams, for on lap 35 Nelson was into the pits for tyres. On the way out he very nearly collected half the Brabham mechanics, who were pushing Modena's car back into its pits. Stefano, whose Formula One debut could hardly have come in more taxing circumstances, was totally exhausted after three-quarters of an hour in this heat.

The tyre stop dropped Piquet to sixth, and he was never to be a serious factor again. Ahead of him, by some way now, were Berger, 16 secs clear of Prost, then Alboreto, Senna and Johansson. Patrese, his tyres scarcely improved by the spin earlier, also came in for new ones, on lap 36. Riccardo's Williams debut was proving less than distinguished.

In three laps Prost took three secs from Berger, then lost it all — and more — as he came up on backmarkers, including the inevitable Rene Arnoux. In no time at all Alain's advantage over Alboreto and Senna was gone. And the start of lap 41 produced one of those moments you don't believe you've seen . . .

Down the pit straight towards the first turn Alain was blocked in — and right behind him now were Michele and Ayrton. Prost seemed to have the Ferrari covered, but it was going to be busy into the corner — and suddenly Senna had closed his eyes and gone for the inside! In a flash the Lotus was up from fourth to second, and Alboreto, too scrambled by.

Lap 49 saw the end of Johansson's fifth place, the McLaren parked against a tyre barrier. But Stefan had not goofed: the left front carbon disc had simply disintegrated, and soon afterwards Prost, too, spun off into retirement for the very same reason.

"As I said in Japan," Alain shrugged, "this has not been my season . . . Actually, it was a pity about the brakes because everything else about the car was great today."

Both McLarens gone, then, in the space of five laps. And that left us with Berger, 12 secs up on Senna, then Alboreto, a failing Piquet, a brakeless Boutsen, a smokey Patrese.

Briefly, it seemed, there now existed a real threat to the leading Ferrari, for steadily, stealthily, Ayrton

Left: Jonathan Palmer had already won the Jim Clark Trophy for drivers of the atmospheric cars. The pressure in this race came from driving the Tyrrell with bent front suspension after the early race incident with Warwick.
Below left: The most experienced grand prix driver — Riccardo Patrese — joins Williams one race early. He found it difficult to fill Mansell's shoes after a season at the wheel of the inferior Brabham-BMW.
Below: Just hot air between Senna and Berger now as the Brazilian, after disposing of Alboreto and Prost, closes on the Austrian.

Top: *Boutsen was never able to get off the leash. His brakes were all but finished in the first few laps. Third at Senna's disqualification was a reward for pure bravery.*
Inset: *Patrese's career gets a lift. The Italian was well placed early but a spin and finally an increasing amount of smoke out of the exhaust spelt doom. He tried to switch off before the engine self-destructed, only to lose control in the process and spin into the tyres.*
Below: *Troubled by faulty brakes, Alboreto had to play second fiddle again to Berger and pace himself in Senna's wake.*

began to catch Gerhard. Usually you were talking tenths, maybe fifths, but the gap was unquestionably coming down: 12.1, 11.7, 11.4, 10.9 . . . And there were 25 laps to the flag.

Piquet's race ended about now. He came into the pits for attention to the gear linkage, and the mechanics of course set about a routine tyre change. But when they removed the left front, a lot of fragments fell to the ground. What remained of the car's carbon brake disc was about the size of a saucer.

All eyes were now on Berger and Senna, and the diminishing gap between them. "I gave it everything," Ayrton said, and it looked that way. The interval came down to seven secs on lap 64, then began to open out again. "Nothing I could do — my tyres were finished . . ."

And, in fact, Berger kicked again. It was remarkable, really. Here was a man feeling less than great, on a set of tyres now elderly, yet on lap 67 he produced a new fastest lap, which he further improved on the 72nd. "I had decided at half-distance not to come in

for tyres," he reported later, "and they were really not too bad — I was surprised how well they stood up. On fuel I had no problem at all; I was always on the right side with that. Brakes? No, they were perfect all the way."

Gerhard didn't pretend, however, that his race was other than very hard work. "Without any doubt, this track takes more out of you physically, than any other. And today was very hot. I was careful to go easy on the fuel, but I drove the car on the limit all the way. By the end I felt very tired, I must say."

For the last 20-odd laps only three cars were on the lead lap, and Alboreto was a long way behind Berger and Senna. "My rear brakes gave me trouble most of the way — maybe there was an air lock in there somewhere. The pedal went 'hard' a few times. Otherwise, no problems."

Patrese, fourth, looked like salvaging something from a disappointing weekend for Williams, but that smoke was getting thicker with every gearchange. Past the pits, on lap 77, it was billowing, and Riccardo tried to switch off at the first turn, spinning lightly into the tyre barrier, as he did so. Boutsen was now up to fourth, Palmer to fifth, the impressive Dalmas to sixth.

Berger, though, stayed where he had always been, first. As he took the flag, he was ore than 30 secs clear of Senna, and the Ferrari banners in the stands were ecstatically waved.

Later, much later, came news of the Benetton protest against Lotus: the brake ducting on the 99T, it was claimed, was wider than regulations permitted. And in the middle of the evening there was FISA's confirmation that the Lotus was out. New results sheets were issued, with amended world championship points.

Nigel Mansell, doubtless watching in Port Erin, knew in any case that his second place in the championship was safe. But perhaps he pondered on this: Piquet had finished in neither of the races he had missed. If Nigel had finished second to Berger — forget about wins — in Suzuka and Adelaide, he would have scored 12 points, equalling Nelson's final score. And Mansell, with six wins to Piquet's three, would have got the nod. He would have won the world championship . . .

AUSTRALIAN GRAND PRIX

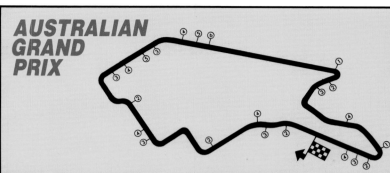

Round 16: November 15, 1987
Circuit: Adelaide

Race data:	82 laps of 2.348 mile (3.78 km) circuit
Weather:	Very hot
Fastest lap:	Berger, Ferrari F187, 1:20.416, 105.120mph
Existing record:	Piquet, Williams FW11, 1:20.787, 104.637mph

ENTRIES

No	Driver (Nat)	Car/Chassis	Engine
1	Alain Prost (F)	McLaren MP4/3-4	TAG V6 Turbo
1T	Alain Prost (F)	McLaren MP4/3-1	TAG V6 Turbo
2	Stefan Johansson (S)	McLaren MP4/3-5	TAG V6 Turbo
3	Jonathan Palmer (GB)	Tyrrell DG/016-2	Ford Cosworth V8
4	Philippe Streiff (F)	Tyrrell DG/016-7	Ford Cosworth V8
5	Riccardo Patrese (I)	Williams FW11B/1	Honda V6 Turbo
6	Nelson Piquet (BR)	Williams FW11B/8**	Honda V6 Turbo
6T	Nelson Piquet (BR)	Williams FW11B/4*	Honda V6 Turbo
7	Stefano Modena (I)	Brabham BT56/4	BMW S4 Turbo
8	Andrea de Cesaris (I)	Brabham BT56/2	BMW S4 Turbo
8T	Andrea de Cesaris (I)	Brabham BT56/3	BMW S4 Turbo
9	Martin Brundle (GB)	Zakspeed 871/03	Zakspeed S4 Turbo
9T	Martin Brundle (GB)	Zakspeed 871/01	Zakspeed S4 Turbo
10	Christian Danner (D)	Zakspeed 871/02	Zakspeed S4 Turbo
11	Satoru Nakajima (J)	Lotus 99T/3	Honda V6 Turbo
12	Ayrton Senna (BR)	Lotus 99T/4	Honda V6 Turbo
12T	Ayrton Senna (BR)	Lotus 99T/6	Honda V6 Turbo
14	Roberto Moreno (BR)	AGS JH22/02-032	Ford Cosworth V8
16	Ivan Capelli (I)	March 871/1	Ford Cosworth V8
16T	Ivan Capelli (I)	March 871/2	Ford Cosworth V8
17	Derek Warwick (GB)	Arrows A10/5	Megatron S4 Turbo
18	Eddie Cheever (USA)	Arrows A10/2	Megatron S4 Turbo
19	Teo Fabi (I)	Benetton B187-04	Ford V6 Turbo
19T	Teo Fabi (I)	Benetton B187-07*	Ford V6 Turbo
20	Thierry Boutsen (B)	Benetton B187-09	Ford V6 Turbo
21	Alex Caffi (I)	Osella FA1H/1	Alfa Romeo V8 Turbo
23	Adrian Campos (E)	Minardi M186/02	Moderni V6 Turbo
24	Alessandro Nannini (I)	Minardi M186/04	Moderni V6 Turbo
25	Rene Arnoux (F)	Ligier JS29C/06	Megatron S4 Turbo
26	Piercarlo Ghinzani (I)	Ligier JS29C/04	Megatron S4 Turbo
27	Michele Alboreto (I)	Ferrari F187/101	Ferrari V6 Turbo
28	Gerhard Berger (A)	Ferrari F187/098	Ferrari V6 Turbo
28T	Gerhard Berger (A)	Ferrari F187/097*	Ferrari V6 Turbo
29	Yannick Dalmas (F)	Lola LC87/02	Ford Cosworth V8
30	Philippe Alliot (F)	Lola LC87/03	Ford Cosworth V8

* Race car   ** Active

QUALIFYING

FRIDAY: Very hot		SATURDAY: Very hot	
Driver		Driver	
Berger	1:17.267	Prost	1:17.967
Piquet	1:18.017	Berger	1:18.142
Prost	1:18.200	Piquet	1:18.176
Senna	1:18.508	Senna	1:18.488
Alboreto	1:18.578	Boutsen	1:18.523
Boutsen	1:18.943	Patrese	1:18.813
Fabi	1:19.461	Johansson	1:18.826
Patrese	1:19.507	De Cesaris	1:19.590
Johansson	1:19.761	Alboreto	1:19.612
De Cesaris	1:19.768	Fabi	1:20.301
Cheever	1:20.183	Warwick	1:20.837
Warwick	1:20.701	Nakajima	1:20.891
Nakajima	1:21.708	Modena	1:21.014
Modena	1:21.887	Brundle	1:21.483
Alliot	1:21.888	Nannini	1:21.523
Streiff	1:21.971	Cheever	1:21.592
Brundle	1:22.224	Palmer	1:22.087
Palmer	1:22.315	Arnoux	1:22.303
Ghinzani	1:22.689	Streiff	1:22.434
Capelli	1:22.698	Dalmas	1:22.650
Danner	1:23.046	Capelli	1:22.704
Moreno	1:23.659	Danner	1:22.736
Arnoux	1:24.833	Alliot	1:22.846
Dalmas	1:25.021	Campos	1:24.121
Campos	1:25.760	Moreno	1:24.149
Caffi	1:25.872	Ghinzani	1:24.652
		Caffi	1:27.331

STARTING GRID

No	Driver	Time
28	Berger	1:17.267
1	Prost	1:17.967
6	Piquet	1:18.017
12	Senna	1:18.488
20	Boutsen	1:18.523
27	Alboreto	1:18.578
5	Patrese	1:18.813
2	Johansson	1:18.826
19	Fabi	1:19.461
8	De Cesaris	1:19.590
18	Cheever	1:20.187
17	Warwick	1:20.638
24	Nannini	1:20.701
11	Nakajima	1:20.891
7	Modena	1:21.014
9	Brundle	1:21.483
30	Alliot	1:21.888
4	Streiff	1:21.971
3	Palmer	1:22.087
25	Arnoux	1:22.303
29	Dalmas	1:22.650
26	Ghinzani	1:22.689
16	Capelli	1:22.698
10	Danner	1:22.736
14	Moreno	1:23.659
23	Campos	1:24.121

RESULTS

Pos	No	Driver	Car	Laps	Time/Retirement
1	28	Berger	Ferrari	82	1-52:56.144
DQ	12	Senna	Lotus-Honda	82	—
2	27	Alboreto	Ferrari	82	1-54:04.028
3	20	Boutsen	Benetton-Ford	81	
4	3	Palmer	Tyrrell-Cosworth	80	
5	29	Dalmas	Lola-Cosworth	79	
6	14	Moreno	AGS-Cosworth	79	
6	10	Danner	Zakspeed	79	
8	8	De Cesaris	Brabham-BMW	78	
R.	5	Patrese	Williams-Honda	76	Engine
R.	6	Piquet	Williams-Honda	58	Brakes
R.	16	Capelli	March-Cosworth	58	Spun off
R.	1	Prost	McLaren-TAG	53	Brakes
R.	18	Cheever	Arrows-Megatron	53	Engine
R.	2	Johansson	McLaren-TAG	48	Brakes
R.	19	Fabi	Benetton-Ford	46	Brakes
R.	23	Campos	Minardi-Moderni	46	Gearbox
R.	30	Alliot	Lola-Cosworth	45	Electrics
R.	25	Arnoux	Ligier-Megatron	41	Electrics
R.	7	Modena	Brabham-BMW	31	Driver fatigue
R.	26	Ghinzani	Ligier-Megatron	26	
R.	11	Nakajima	Lotus-Honda	22	Suspension failure
R.	17	Warwick	Arrows-Megatron	19	CWP
R.	9	Brundle	Zakspeed	18	Turbo
R.	4	Streiff	Tyrrell-Cosworth	6	Accident
R.	24	Nannini	Minardi-Moderni	0	Accident

FASTEST LAP

Driver	
Berger	1:20.416
De Cesaris	1:20.917
Alboreto	1:21.124
Prost	1:21.381
Patrese	1:21.491
Piquet	1:21.981
Johansson	1:22.232
Fabi	1:22.246
Boutsen	1:22.769
Palmer	1:23.197
Dalmas	1:23.207
Capelli	1:23.296
Cheever	1:23.390
Arnoux	1:23.999
Danner	1:24.119
Modena	1:24.294
Warwick	1:24.478
Moreno	1:24.488
Alliot	1:24.834
Nakajima	1:24.926
Ghinzani	1:25.196
Brundle	1:25.554
Streiff	1:26.823
Campos	1:27.676

CHAMPIONSHIP POSITIONS

DRIVERS		CONSTRUCTORS	
1 Piquet	73	1 Williams-Honda	137
2 Mansell	61	2 McLaren-TAG	76
3 Senna	57	3 Lotus-Honda	64
4 Prost	46	4 Ferrari	53
5 Berger	36	5 Benetton-Ford	28
6 Johansson	30	6 Arrows-Megatron	11
7 Alboreto	17	Tyrrell-Cosworth	11
8 Boutsen	16	8 Brabham-BMW	10
9 Fabi	12	9 Lola-Cosworth	4
10 Cheever	8	10 Zakspeed	2
11 Nakajima	7	11 AGS-Cosworth	1
Palmer	7	Ligier-Megatron	1
13 Patrese	4	March-Cosworth	1
14 De Cesaris	4		
Streiff	4		
16 Alliot	3		
Warwick	3		
18 Brundle	2		
19 Arnoux	1		
Capelli	1		
Dalmas	1		
Moreno	1		

JIM CLARK CUP		COLIN CHAPMAN CUP	
1 Palmer	95	1 Tyrrell-Cosworth	169
2 Streiff	74	2 Lola-Cosworth	56
3 Alliot	43	3 March-Cosworth	38
4 Capelli	38	AGS-Cosworth	38
5 Fabre	35		
6 Dalmas	13		
7 Moreno	4		

FINAL RESULTS — 1987

CAR No.	DRIVER	R1 Brazil, April 12	R2 San Marino, May 3	R3 Belgium, May 17	R4 Monaco, May 31	R5 Detroit, June 21	R6 France, July 5	R7 Britain, July 12	R8 Germany, July 26	R9 Hungary, August 9	R10 Austria, August 16	R11 Italy, September 6	R12 Portugal, September 20	R13 Spain, September 27	R14 Mexico, October 18	R15 Japan, November 1	R16 Australia, November 15	POINTS	CHAMP. POSITION
1	Alain Prost (F)	1	DNF	1	9	3	3	DNF	7	3	6	15	1	2	DNF	7	DNF	46	4
2	Stefan Johansson (S)	3	4	2	DNF	7	8	DNF	2	DNF	7	6	5	3	DNF	3	DNF	30	6
3	Jonathan Palmer (GB)	10	DNF	DNF	5	11	7	8	5	7	14	14	10	DNF	7	8	4	7	11
4	Philippe Streiff (F)	11	8	9	DNF	DNF	6	DNF	4	9	DNS	12	12	7	8	12	DNF	4	14
5	Nigel Mansell (GB)	6	1	DNF	DNF	5	1	1	DNF	DNF	1	3	DNF	1	1	DNS		61	2
5	Riccardo Patrese (I)																DNF		
6	Nelson Piquet (BR)	2	DNS	DNF	2	2	2	2	1	1	2	1	3	4	2	DNF	DNF	73	1
7	Riccardo Patrese (I)	DNF	9	DNF	DNF	9	DNF	DNF	DNF	5	DNF	DNF	DNF	13	3	11		6	13
7	Stefano Modena (I)																DNF		
8	Andrea de Cesaris (I)	DNF	DNF	3	DNF	DNF	DNF	DNF	DNF	DNF	DNF	DNF	DNF	DNF	DNF	DNF	8	4	14
9	Martin Brundle (GB)	DNF	5	DNF	7	DNF	DNF	NC	8	DNF	DQ	DNF	DNF	11	DNF	DNF	DNF	2	18
10	Christian Danner (D)	9	7	DNF	DNQ	8	DNF	DNF	DNF	9	9	DNS	NC	DNF	DNF	6			
11	Satoru Nakajima (J)	7	6	5	10	DNF	NC	4	DNF	DNF	13	11	8	9	DNF	6	DNF	7	11
12	Ayrton Senna (BR)	DNF	2	DNF	1	1	4	3	3	2	5	2	7	5	DNF	2	DQ	57	3
14	Pascal Fabre (F)	12	DNF	10	13	12	9	9	DNF	13	NC	DNS	DNS	DNF	DNS				
14	Roberto Moreno (BR)															DNF	6	1	19
16	Ivan Capelli (I)		DNF	DNF	6	DNF	DNF	DNF	DNF	10	11	13	9	12	DNF	DNF	DNF	1	19
17	Derek Warwick (GB)	DNF	DNF	DNF	DNF	DNF	DNF	5	DNF	6	DNF	DNF	13	10	DNF	10	DNF	3	16
18	Eddie Cheever (USA)	DNF	DNF	4	DNF	6	DNF	DNF	DNF	8	DNF	DNF	6	8	4	DNF	DNF	8	10
19	Teo Fabi (I)	DNF	DNF	DNF	8	DNF	5	6	DNF	DNF	3	7	4	DNF	5	DNF	DNF	12	9
20	Thierry Boutsen (B)	5	DNF	DNF	DNF	DNF	DNF	7	DNF	4	4	5	14	DNF	DNF	5	3	16	8
21	Alex Caffi (I)	DNF	DNF	DNF	DNF	DNF	DNF	DNF	DNF	DNS	DNF	DNF	DNS	DNF	DNF	DNS			
22	Franco Forini (CH)											DNF	DNF						
22	Gabriele Tarquini (I)		DNF																
23	Adrian Campos (E)	DQ	DNF	DNF	DNQ	DNF	DNF	DNF	DNF	DNF	DNF	DNF	DNF	14	DNF	DNF	DNF		
24	Alessandro Nannini (I)	DNF	DNF	DNE	DNF	DNF	DNF	DNF	DNF	11	DNF	16	11	DNF	DNF	DNF	DNF		
25	Rene Arnoux (F)		DNS	6	11	10	DNF	DNF	DNF	DNF	10	10	DNF	DNF	DNF	DNF	DNF	1	19
26	Piercarlo Ghinzani (I)		DNF	7	12	DNF	DNF		DNF	12	8	8	DNF	DNF	DNF	DNF	DNF		
27	Michele Alboreto (I)	8	3	DNF	3	DNF	DNF	DNF	DNF	DNF	DNF	DNF	DNF	DNF	DNF	4	2	17	7
28	Gerhard Berger (AUT)	4	DNF	DNF	4	4	DNF	DNF	DNF	DNF	DNF	4	2	DNF	DNF	1	1	36	5
29	Yannick Dalmas (F)														9	DNF	5	1	19
30	Philippe Alliot (F)		10	8	DNF	DNF	DNF	DNF	6	DNF	12	DNF	DNF	6	6	DNF	DNF	3	16
32	Nicola Larrini (I)														DNF				

FINAL CONSTRUCTORS POINTS

1 Williams-Honda	137	5 Benetton-Ford	28	9 Lola-Cosworth	4
2 McLaren-TAG	76	6 Arrows-Megatron	11	10 Zakspeed	2
3 Lotus-Honda	64	Tyrrell-Cosworth	11		
4 Ferrari	53	8 Brabham-BMW	10		

Legend:

AUT — Austria
F — France
GB — Great Britain
S — Sweden
D — West Germany
I — Italy
BR — Brazil
CH — Switzerland
B — Belgium
J — Japan
E — Spain
USA — USA

DNF — Did Not Finish
DQ — Disqualified
DNQ — Did Not Qualify
DNS — Did Not Start
DNE — Did Not Enter
NC — Not Classified

Points per placing — drivers: 1 (9 points), 2 (6 points), 3 (4 points), 4 (3 points), 5 (2 points), 6 (1 point).
Only best 11 scores count.